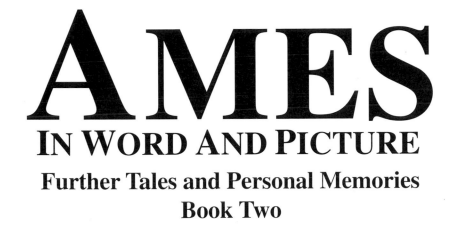

AMES
IN WORD AND PICTURE
Further Tales and Personal Memories
Book Two

By
Farwell T. Brown

© 1999: Farwell T. Brown
Published by: Farwell T. Brown
and Heuss Printing, Inc.
Ames, Iowa 50010 • 515-232-6710
ISBN: 0-9636696-9-9

With a Forward by Janet Klaas

Cover Photo: The French Moto Bloc came through Ames on March 16, 1908. It is shown here as it went west on Boone Street (Lincoln Way after 1914). Photo looks east on hill just west of Beach Avenue. Insert photo at lower right is the American Thomas Flyer. See Chapter 12:
New York To Paris - The Famous Automobile Race in 1908.

Dedicated
to
Ruth Mosher Brown

FOREWORD - By Janet Klaas III

PREFACE IV

ACKNOWLEDGEMENTS V

TABLE OF CONTENTS I

Norwegian History - 1855 - 1945 — Oley Nelson's History of The First Norwegian Settlement in Story County. Written in Norwegian in 1905, and translated into English by Oley Nelson in 1930. Corrected and added to by Anfin Apland in 1945. With a special **dedication by Anfin Apland**, the first mayor of Huxley following incorporation in 1902.

"In The News" - An index of interesting and sometimes significant news items that appeared in newspapers published usually in Ames.

Introduction

List of obituaries included in the Index.

Foreword

This present volume continues the "connecting stories" collected in Farwell Brown's first volume, *Ames the Early Years in Words and Pictures: from Marsh to Modern City,* published in 1993. As the author explained in his preface to that first volume, these articles are not meant to be a definitive history of the community that came to be known as Ames, Iowa. Rather, they give readers the flavor of life from the perspective of a man whose family roots extend to the very beginnings of the town.

Book Two focuses on some of the people whose lives affected not only Ames but also the wider arena of national, and even international, issues. Mr. Brown was especially generous in documenting the lives of Ames women who have furthered the rights or enhanced the career prospects of others. Among these women are: Carrie Chapman Catt, one of the leaders in the women's suffrage movement and the founder of the League of Women Voters; Ada Hayden, the botanist who was the first of her gender to receive a Ph.D. from Iowa State College, stayed on to create that institution's herbarium, and gave her name to a piece of native prairie in northern Iowa; Margaret Sloss, the first woman to graduate from the Iowa State College of Veterinary Medicine; Winifred Tilden, who founded the women's physical education program at Iowa State; Jennie Ghrist, a physician who began her medical practice in Ames before 1900; Mary B. Welch, who founded the first home economics program at a land grant college.

Included are the stories of Jack Trice, the first African American to play on the Iowa State College football team; Tom MacDonald, who after serving as the director the new Iowa Highway Commission, went on to become the director of the U.S. Bureau of Roads where he designed the system of interstate highways that defined transportation in the nation ever after; and Conde McCullough, master bridge designer. Here, too, is the mysterious Christopher Ney, local handyman and recluse, who, after his death, was discovered to have been a one-time governor in the Philippines.

But, in addition to listing the deeds of the famous, Farwell Brown also provides us with some of the everyday quirky happenings among the folks of his town: how Mrs. Hicks figured out how to transport her groceries without personal effort; how a young man seeking romance got really "stuck" in a fog; how an outhouse became one of a chain of local movie houses. Often Brown himself is the focus of these tales: how he was on the wrong end of a cow in a haymow; how he sold an insurance policy to a man in a grave.

Added to these tales of the ordinary and the extraordinary are accounts of battles over roads and school issues, of the many floods in Ames's history, of concern for the values instilled in the community's children, of natural resources—in other words, the same old stuff! And yet, how these issues were dealt with 30, 40, 80 years ago explains much about our present-day responses to these same issues. You only know where you are when you realize where you have been. These are, indeed, our connecting stories. It always amazes me how the stories of this community define us within the larger context of national and world history. Beyond these philosophical reasons for admiring Farwell Brown's gift of connecting, I must say I also like his stories because they are just plain fun. So, once again, enjoy!

—Janet E. Klaas
Information Services Librarian
Ames Public Library

PREFACE

Six years ago in the preface for a group of stories that I'd written, I stated that "I still have a list for future consideration." It has been my good fortune to still be around to enjoy putting together a few more stories about Ames. I would again make the point that this collection of stories does not constitute an organized history of our town, but a thread that unites these stories is woven into the historical fabric of our community.

As in the first collection of stories about Ames, the motivation for the telling of an event from the past has often been a present day experience. Examples are the stories about the "Great Wheel Ride of 1893" or about how "Floods Hit Ames Again and Again." RAGBRAI and the flood of 1993 aren't all that new!

This collection of stories includes a number of biographical sketches of men and women of past Ames generations. Consider these people as representative; there are other personalities of similar interest who might well have been included.

Included are a few of my personal memories that might be described as more entertaining than enlightening! Perhaps, with a little effort the reader can find in them examples of life as it was in an earlier time.

A few years ago a former resident of Huxley gave me an interesting history of the "First Norwegian Settlement of Story and Polk Counties" that had been compiled by Oley Nelson of Slater, Iowa, in 1905. This history is included as "Appendix A" in this collection. As a first hand witness account of early area history it may interest a number of people; including it in this manner is intended to preserve it.

The index of my notes gleaned largely from the early Ames newspapers or other public records is included as "Appendix B." A brief introduction will be found with that lengthy index to explain its uses and limitations. It is alphabetically arranged, and by browsing through it, the reader will find many interesting and significant events of the past.

Under many of the photographs in this book will be found an **identification** number. This number will locate that particular photograph in the photo file at the Ames Public Library in case the reader may wish to obtain further information about the respective photo.

Farwell T. Brown
August 21, 1998

ACKNOWLEDGMENTS

Putting these stories together in book form would not have been possible without the direct assistance of several people to whom I wish to express my appreciation. Throughout my association with the Ames Public Library, Janet Klaas, information librarian, has been the one who has cataloged my photograph collection and has tried to keep me going in the right direction in recording their identification. She has been the official editor of this project. She proofread the entire manuscript with the exception of the Appendices. She also indexed the main stories in the book. Her suggestions have been excellent and appreciated.

Lynette Spicer, communications specialist with Iowa State University Extension, proofread the stories and the cutlines with the pictures; her assistance has been very helpful in getting the material prepared for the printer.

Hank Zaletel, Department of Transportation librarian, has been a continual resource for me. The people in Special Collections / Archives, Iowa State University Library have continued to be of assistance to me in locating necessary information. Kathy Svec, president of the Ames Heritage Association, proofread the "News Index" appendix, eliminating duplications and improving the arrangement of entries.

The people at Beacon Microcenter in Ames have been key players in this effort. Without their continued support I would not have been able to get these stories put together in the first place.

A special thank-you to Dianne Mumm, the artist whose illustrations grace chapters 9, 10, and 40.

My wife Ruth has always been my first proofreader, since I ask her to read the first draft of my stories. She can see missing letters that result from my tendency to fail to communicate correctly with the keyboard of the word processor! She is my primary "encourager" for sure.

Don Heuss and his staff at Heuss Printing must be named among the essential ingredients of this project. It was Don who first suggested putting these stories into print.

Above all, I count all of these folks, and many others as well, as having been my special friends to whom I am indebted as I put the final touches on this collection of stories.

Ames, Iowa
September 7, 1998.   Farwell T. Brown

Chapter 1

Cory Family Cemetery

The Pioneer Cory Family Cemetery is located on what was once Squire Martin Cory's farm. In 1992, a bronze plaque was placed on the site by the Ames Heritage Association to commemorate the birth here in 1862 of Billy Sunday, the noted evangelist and a grandson of Squire Cory. The cemetery is located at the east end of Billy Sunday Drive. It can be seen on the south side of Highway 30, a short distance east of Duff Avenue. The following were my comments on the occasion of the dedication of that plaque on May 30, 1992:

This bronze plaque is dedicated today to the memory of a man, who in his unique way, made an impact upon society at a particular time in history. In this manner we commemorate the memory of Billy Sunday, a native of Ames; we do this because we wish to call attention to the man and to this place.

About this place: We stand on the Cory farm that Squire Martin Cory acquired by U. S. patent under the date of July 10,1852.[1] It was a year later, in 1853, that Nevada was designated the county seat of an independent Story County. This part of Story County was sparsely settled when the Cory family came. It was six years later that the trustees of the Iowa Agricultural College selected a nearby site for their college and model farm.

The Cory family had been here twelve years before the railroad came this way and the town of Ames was laid out. One fact of life for those pioneers was that a high percentage of the deaths in this area in those days were children. Family cemeteries were an immediate necessity. This cemetery represents an important chapter in Iowa's social history.

I like this quotation about cemeteries: " Lives are commemorated; deaths are recorded; families are reunited; memories are made tangible; and love is undisguised. This is a cemetery.

William A. Sunday (1863 - 1935) Ames native and famed Evangelist. ID No.73.375.3

Billy Sunday birthplace and Cory family cemetery plaque dedicated May 30, 1992. Cory Cemetery is in background. Left to right are Everett Ritland, Scot Werkmeister, and Kathy Svec, president of the Ames Heritage Association. Daily Tribune photo. ID No. 163.908.4-5

---

[1] U.S.patent dated October 1, 1851 (160 Acres) and U.S. patent dated July 10, 1852 (160 acres) both to S. M. Cory, all in sec.14-83-24. See Book 3, pages 402 and 403, *Story County records.*

"Communities record respect; families bestow reverence; historians seek information; and our heritage is thereby enriched.

"A cemetery is a history of people, a perpetual record of yesterday, and a sanctuary of peace and quiet today. A cemetery exists because every life is worth loving and remembering always."

I first visited this cemetery when I was about ten years old. Billy Sunday had the habit of sending my father a check each year before Memorial Day to buy flowers, and my father usually brought me down here with him to visit these graves. It looked then as it does now. By that time this farm was owned by Capt. W. M. Greeley and later by his brother, Horace, so it was known as the Greeley farm. This white fence was well cared for in those days. Now that it is cared for by the city cemetery administration, proper care can be anticipated.

---

[2] Warranty Deed dated August 5, 1867 - S. M. Cory to State of Iowa. Contribution to Iowa Agricultural College.

[3] Earlier that same year (1882) Squire Cory had placed his farm in trust for his grandsons, naming J. A. Fitchpatrick, Trustee. W. M. Greeley purchased the farm from Fitchpatrick on March 18, 1883.

From these stones we learn that Squire Cory was seventy years old when he died in 1882. He came from Ohio to this new country. I think he received title to this land because his father, Abijah Cory, served in the earlier Indian wars when Pennsylvania and Ohio were considered the frontier.

Billy Sunday was born here on his grandfather's farm in 1862. His own father had been a Civil War casualty when he died in Missouri before Billy was born. Billy's mother, Mary Jane, brought her three sons back here, and we are familiar with her life raising her family with Squire Cory doing his best to be of help.

Squire Cory was known as an outstanding citizen. In August 1867, after the Iowa Agricultural College was established nearby, he donated twenty acres to the state of Iowa specifically for the benefit of the college's future.[2] (The state's subsequent deed referred to the twenty acres as a donation.)

By examining these stones, we see that Squire Cory's first wife was Mary A. Cory, who was Billy Sunday's grandmother. She died in 1868. By looking at Squire M. Cory's stone, we see that he died in 1882[3] and that he had remarried, and his surviving wife's name was Charlotte. Charlotte later married

The Cory family cemetery located on Billy Sunday Drive east of South Duff Avenue and on south side of U.S. Highway 30 in Ames. Billy Sunday's Cory grandparents, his mother, a brother and a nephew are among those buried here. Sunday and his wife were buried in Chicago. ID No.1.3.1

William Gossard, another early Ames-area pioneer.

One of the more modern stones here is that of Mary Jane Stowell, daughter of the Corys, and Billy's mother, who died in 1916. After Billy's father's death, his mother had married a man named Heiser, who essentially abandoned the family. She later married an itinerate carpenter named Stowell who seems to have been absent much of the time. She spent her last days in Billy Sunday's home in Winona Lake, Indiana, where she died.

Billy Sunday's brother, Albert, is buried here. His older brother, Ed, became a very successful rancher in North Dakota; and, I believe, he is buried there. You will find Ed's son Howard's name on one of these stones.

It is Billy Sunday's fame that draws much of our attention to this spot, although I think that the background and experience of the Cory and Sunday families provide real historical interest.

Billy Sunday inherited natural drives and unique abilities that derived from his beginnings here: his success in Nevada working for Col. John Scott, Lieutenant Governor of Iowa, then his more intense interest in baseball that developed in Marshalltown and on to Chicago. He credited his mother's training for his move out of baseball to the Chicago Y.M.C.A. and then into the work as an evangelist.

I never heard Sunday speak. His popularity with a wide range of people was exceptional. He spoke to packed auditoriums wherever he went. He filled the State Gymnasium at Iowa State in 1914 and packed the First Methodist Church in Ames that same evening. He drew a crowd of 4,000 at the Ames Chautauqua in 1911, the largest Chautauqua crowd ever in Ames. While he never conducted one of his week-long evangelism programs in Ames, he was well-liked in his home town.

When John R. Mott, national Y.M.C.A. secretary and Nobel Prize winner, heard Sunday speak to capacity crowds of students on the University of Pennsylvania campus in Pittsburg in 1914, he said, "You can not fool a great body of students. They get a man's measure. If he is genuine, they know it, and if he is not, they quickly find it out. Their devotion to Mr. Sunday is very significant."

Billy Sunday's one-liners were famous: "Going to church doesn't make one a Christian any more than rolling a wheelbarrow into a garage makes it an automobile," was one. Another was, "Some folks say that a revival is only temporary. So is a bath, but every body needs one." There were many one-liners like that, we are told.

In dedicating this plaque, we are calling attention to Billy Sunday, to this pioneer family and to this place; all three played a role in the community of Ames and of the nation as well.

May 30, 1992

Chapter 2

The War of the Road

The Story of Sixth Street

The merging,[1] in 1984, of Sixth Street with Elwood Drive recalled the tug of wars and controversies that were a part of the early-day discussions and planning when a second road to campus was a local hot issue in the 1920s.

An alleged rabble-rousing speech by an Ames mayor, a near riot on campus and a pistol shot that shattered a window at the Knoll[2] not to mention public statements by local candidates for public office. All played a part in determining which road would be extended to the campus and when.

Boone Road, renamed "Lincoln Way" in 1914, was the only road to the campus for the first 50 years of the town's history. Iowa State College President William Beardshear advocated a second road to the campus from downtown Ames. "You can make it a memorial to me," he had said to a friend. Beardshear died in 1902 and it was about 25 years before a second road linking campus to downtown Ames would be built.

The Sixth Street "extension" seems to have been a popular choice in the minds of townspeople. With Dean Charles Curtiss protecting his sheep pasture and others disliking traffic near the cattle barns, there were problems and delays.

After the Squaw Creek bridge went down in the flood of 1918, the pressure for another road increased. It took over a year to get a new Lincoln Way bridge underway. In those days Story County was the main authority involved. The still young Iowa Highway Commission and the Ames constituency seemed to have problems getting everyone together. Meeting in Vinton on March 4, 1920, the State Board of Education issued an ultimatum: "Ames must build Squaw Creek bridge and pave Lincoln Way to the campus before asking for land to extend Sixth Street."[3]

On March 10, 1920, Ames voted a $15,000 bond issue to cover its share of the new Lincoln Way bridge costs. The vote was 2-1 in favor, with the Fourth Ward reporting the heaviest favorable vote. That the bridge was vital to the relationship between downtown Ames and the college area was the theme of public statements and editorials at the time.

But the construction of a Sixth Street extension, said to have often been on the Ames City Council's agenda, went nowhere. At one point, the Ames city attorney secured a restraining order against the state Board of Education to keep them from interfering in any way with the proposed Sixth Street extension. Apparent conciliatory developments led J. Y. Luke, city attorney, on March 4, 1922, to secure a dissolution of that order.

On March 7, 1922, the Tribune reported that "the Sixth Street problem seems near solution." Representatives of the Ames City Council and the state Board of Education, along with ISC's Dean Anson Marston, and Highway Commission engineers and other personnel, visited possible routes for a second much needed town-to-campus road.

On March 15, 1922, the Tribune announced that a compromise plan to extend Ninth Street along a route following the north side of Squaw Creek to the

Sixth Street's extension to the campus made good use of this railroad structure that was built in 1900 when the C .& N.W. Line became a two track system. Until Sixth Street was extended in 1948 this bridge opening's primary function was that of a drainage structure. ID No. 169.942.1-4

---

[1] Announcement of the opening of Elwood Drive and Sixth Street on Monday, August 29, 1984.
[2] *Des Moines Register,* May 28, 1923, p.1, "Ames Students Defy Pearson"
[3] *Ames Tribune,* March 4 , 1920, p.1, "Squaw Creek and the Board of Control."

north-south drive now known as Stange Road "would make a beautiful drive if extended through campus."

Every indication of agreement finally seemed present. On March 23, the state Board of Education gave tentative approval. ISC President Raymond Pearson announced that, "the Engineering Department will start at once on plans." On July 5, 1923, the president of the Board of Education was in Ames. "The Ninth Street outlet will go through," he gave as his belief in an interview to the Tribune. At its July 1923 meeting, the state Board of Education was expected to give its final approval.

Then a curious series of events produced an equally curious relationship. On July 18, 1923, Ames Mayor Tom Rice, City Attorney J. Y. Luke, and City Councilman J. G. Tilden drove to Iowa City to attend the State Board meeting. Upon arrival there, they were informed that Mayor Rice would not be permitted to attend the meeting. The other two men were invited to attend, however. Several board members gave as their reason for excluding Rice a speech he had given in the early hours of May 28 on the Iowa State College campus. The speech had roused some 1,500 students meeting on campus to a point of near riot such as to cause them to gather in mass at President Pearson's home at the Knoll, on which occasion a shot was fired, breaking a window.

The Ames men stated that the alleged disturbance had nothing to do with the agreement on the town-to-campus road. They would attend no meeting without Mayor Rice, the official representative of Ames.

Upon their return to Ames, the delegation learned that a report had been telephoned back in time for the news release that the State Board had disregarded the plans for the Ninth Street extension and had approved, instead, a plan to extend Thirteenth Street along a route north of Squaw Creek, joning what is now Stange Road north of the Squaw Creek bridge. The Tribune headlines stated that the "Council May Halt New Road" and "City Dads Hostile." The City Council promptly rejected the State Board's action.[4]

What had happened on May 28 when Mayor Rice was alleged to have incited some students to a near riot? The ISC athletic director at the time was Charles W. Mayser who had had a very sucessful ten years as Iowa State's football coach before he became athletic director. Controversies had developed between various college administrators. The Athletic Council and President Pearson had requested Mayser's

resignation. A majority of students, Ames towns-people, and especially Mayor Tom Rice, had come to Mayser's defense.

On the evening of May 27, an ISC men's athletic organization known as the AA club, invited Rice to speak at a mass meeting on campus. The May 28 Des Moines Register carried a front page story under the headline "Ames Students Defy Pearson." The story quoted Rice as telling the crowd of students that, "If your forces stick together you can win your fight - the students have been cowed and should go ahead with their demonstration. Furthermore, no college president nor any college or university on earth can expel an entire student body." Prominent front-page coverage was given the story by the Des Moines newspaper. "1500 protest firing Mayser...hold two hour demonstration with blazing torches at midnight," the article stated.

That is how a controversy on a coaching situation at Iowa State played a part in Thirteenth Street being the first to be extended to the campus. It would be 1949 before Sixth Street was extended.

In April, 1924, Frank Schleiter was elected mayor of Ames, defeating Rice by only 127 votes. The access road continued to be an issue. Rice never fogot that the State Board had "broken an agreement" with the Ames City Council. But all agreed on the need for the road and on June 20, 1925, Mayor Schleiter and several council members drove again to Iowa City and met with the state Board of Education. At that meeting a final agreement was reached. Thirteenth Street would be extended, but this time the plan would include a bridge over Squaw Creek. The road would extend west to the north road at a point just south of the existing bridge north of the campus. The Tribune reported that it was hoped that it would eventually be extended on west to connect with Lincoln Way (now Ontario Road).

On Feb. 23, 1926, M. L. Hutton, Institutional Road Engineer with the Highway Commision announced the completion of the Thirteenth Street bridge but stated that the road would not be open to the public until frost was out of the roadbed. It was not until 23 years later, in 1949, that Thirteenth Street was paved — a few weeks after Sixth Street was paved and opened to the public.

That first Thirteenth Street bridge, an untreated wood structure only 17 1/2 feet wide, had been knocked out by an ice jam on February 5, 1946. That route to the campus remained closed until December, 1947, resulting in excessively heavy traffic on Lincoln Way, which was still a three lane thoroughfare.

4 *Ames Tribune*, July 24, 1923.p.1, "Proposed College Road Rejected at Council Meeting"

A pedestrian death in late October, 1946, at the Lincoln Way and Beach Avenue intersection increased public pressure for more and better access routes between campus and downtown Ames. Two days after that fatality, an Ames service club placed a display ad in the Tribune captioned "In the interests of public safety."[5] The subject of extending Sixth Street, possibly South Fourth Street, as well as widening Lincoln Way and improving Thirteenth Street were back on the agenda. Population growth was adding urgency.

Finally, in the spring, 1948, the Ames City Council, the Story County Supervisors, the State Board of Education, the Highway Commision and the Chicago & North Western Railroad, concluded agreements to extend and pave Sixth Street to the campus. On Saturday, September 24, 1949, a ceremony was held on the Sixth Street bridge, officially opening the Sixth Street route to the campus. Representatives of most of the political entities involved were on hand to assist former Ames mayor Clint Adams, in that ribbon cutting event.

8/18/1984

[5] *Ames Tribune,* November 2, 1946, p.3, Display Advertisement placed by the Ames Kwanis Club.

Chapter 3

The Great Wheel Ride of 1893

The *Register's* Annual Great Bike Ride Across Iowa (RAGBRAI), is a modern-day phenomenon. Good roads and high speed bicycles have made it possible for riders to demonstrate their ability to bike across the state of Iowa.

Wrong on both counts!

If you think that the RAGBRAI idea is really all that new, and if you believe that the accomplishments of today's bike riders are all that remarkable, then consider this:

On July 4, 1893, five young men from Ames — Gates Brown, Russell Reed, Stuart Hutchison, George Tilden, and Roy Gilbert ranging in age from 17 to 20, left Ames on their bicycles, headed for Minneapolis. Their bikes were called "safety" bicycles because they had rear-wheel brakes and because the front and rear wheels were the same size.

The bikes (they spoke of their bicycles as "wheels" then) of that day were a big improvement over the former high-wheel affairs that had been around before 1890. They were powered by a single-speed chain and gear.[1]

Now listen to the description of that 1893 departure from Ames that appeared in that week's issue of the *Ames Intelligencer:* "Gates Brown, Stuart Hutchison, and George Tilden started on their bicycles for Minneapolis Tuesday morning via the C.&N.W.Railroad track, the carriage road being too muddy."[2]

The other two riders (wheelmen) had departed earlier that day; and are mentioned later on in the trip reports.

Most country roads in 1893 were referred to as carriage or wagon roads. Some consisted of mere wagon-wheel paths with grass growing between the worn trails.

Not every small stream was bridged in those days.

Rural roads were dirt, developed first by following pioneer wagon trails between farms and between towns. Road ditches had become somewhat common, and road crowning had been accomplished by frequent dragging with horse-drawn plank drags.

Stuart Hutchison, left and Gates Brown with their new wheels ready to start their ride to Minneapolis. They made it - and then headed back to Ames by way of Chicago. ID No. 18.85.2-3

It was eleven years later that the Iowa legislature created the state's Highway Commission.

Note that the young men left Ames on the railroad tracks. Rock ballast was not in general use, and riding on railroad ties that were stabilized with clay fill could have been quite comfortable.[3]

Leaving Ames, the boys rode on the Chicago & North Western Railroad tracks to a point about three miles east of Nevada. There the roads appeared to be dry enough that they decided to ride on them.

---

[1] Advertisement in *Ames Intelligencer* of July 6, 1893, shows both high wheel and safety bicycles.
[2] *Ames Intelligencer,* July 6,1893, p. 3
[3] C.&N.W. advertised some rock ballast on its mainline in 1890. See: *Ames Times,* June 1, 1911, p.1, "Work on New Road Bed progressing nicely."

However, the wagon road soon became too rough, and they were compelled to push their bikes.

Feeling hungry, the boys stopped at a farmhouse and asked to purchase some milk. The farm wife brought out an eight quart pail of milk. When they asked how much they owed for the milk, she told them to "give five cents to her little boy who was playing in the yard."

After pushing their wheels about five miles northward toward McCallsburg, Reed and Tilden went on ahead because Gates Brown had punctured a tire.

Soon it was dark and Brown and Hutchison spent the first night sleeping in a hammock in a farmyard.

Up early the next morning, Brown and Hutchison fixed the punctured tire and proceeded northward to McCallsburg and then east to Zearing where Gilbert, Tilden, and Reed had spent their first night in the Zearing Hotel.

This 1890s advertisement for the latest in the way of safety bicycles appeared in the Ames Intelligencer of June 30, 1892. ID No.184.1041.2-3

---

[4] Diary of Gates Brown in *Ames Times*, July 13, 1893, p. 2, is source for these details.

By mid-morning the second day, Reed, Brown, and Hutchison had reached Hubbard.

Our Ames wheelmen were not overlooked as they rode northward. At Hubbard two local wheelmen gave them a tour of their town and then accompanied them for two miles as they rode on northward.

From Hubbard to Iowa Falls the roads were in fine shape probably the best that they had yet encountered in the trip, They made that run of 18 miles in one hour and forty-five minutes.

At about 5 p.m. they reached Main Street in Hampton where they were greeted by a group of boys who had attended college in Ames.

Heading north from Hampton, the boys were met by a group of wheelmen from Rockwell who invited them to make a stop at their town. Rain again hampered their progress and they spent the night at the Rockwell House. From here they were compelled to take to the Illinois Central roadbed. Stopping for breakfast at a farm house that morning they were asked to "pay in advance."[4]

Because the ballast on that line was very rough they had to push their bikes most of the distance to Mason City. It took the boys seven hours to travel that twelve-mile stretch.

At Mason City, the Ames boys had lunch and were joined by a group of local wheelmen who accompanied them for a swim in Lime Creek.

From Mason City, they rode on the Chicago, Milwaukee & St. Paul Railway's roadbed making an eight mile run to Plymouth Junction in forty-five minutes — considered good time riding on the ties.

From Plymouth Junction they took the Chicago, Rock Island & Pacific Railroad through Manly and Kenset to Northwood. More heavy rain slowed their progress again, so they had supper and spent the night in a local hotel.

Zearing, Iowa hotel known then as the Zearing House. Some of the Ames wheelmen stayed here their first night enroute to Minneapolis. This photo was taken in 1914 when every town in Story County had a hotel. ID No.183.1032.1-5

The next morning they crossed the state line and passed through Gordonsville.[5] At Glenville they had a lunch of dried beef, peaches, and crackers. Encountering rain again, they reached Albert Lea where they waited for the weather to clear. It was here that Gilbert and Reed, who had originally intended to accompany the group only to the Minnesota stateline, boarded the train for home.

The Grant Hotel, Waseca, Minnesota. Ames wheelmen spent a night here comparing their experience with that of local wheelmen. ID No.184.1039.1-3

The remaining three Ames wheelmen (Brown, Hutchison, and Tilden), experienced good riding on the Minneapolis & St. Louis Railroad tracks most of the way to Waseca where they spent the night at the Grant Hotel. The Ames wheelmen were visited that evening by Dr. A.S.Cummings, captain of the Waseca Wheelmen,[6] and Mr. E. F. White who spent the evening talking "wheel lore" with them.

Continuing on the M.& St. L. Railroad's road-bed, they left Waseca going north through Waterville to Warsaw, finding it hard riding because of rough ballast. After back tracking through Morristown, where they had lunch, they reached Fairbault which they described as a most beautiful town situated on two high bluffs.

They had supper in Farmington, continuing that evening for a forty-mile ride to Rosemont and St. Paul, arriving there at 9 p.m.

The *Minneapolis Tribune* of July 11, 1893, reported the arrival on their bicycles of "Gates M. Brown, Stuart C. Hutchnison, and George H. Tilden, the three students of the Iowa Agricultural College at Ames, Iowa."[7]

---

[5] *Ames Intelligencer,* July 13, 1893, p.7.
[6] League of American Wheelmen, organized in 1880, became the League of American Bicyclists in 1994.
[7] *Minneapolis Tribune,* July 11, 1893, P. 4, "A Party From Iowa."

THE ROUTE

MINNEAPOLIS

ROSEMONT
FARMINGTON

FAIRBAULT
WARSAW
MORRISTOWN
WATERVILLE
WASECA

RICHLAND
HARTLAND

MANCHESTER
ALBERT LEA
GLENVILLE
GORDONSVILLE

NORTHWOOD
KENSETT
MANLY
PLYMOUTH JCT.

MASON CITY

ROCKWELL

HAMPTON

IOWA FALLS

HUBBARD

ZEARING
McCALLSBURG

AMES

The July 13 issue of the *Ames Intelligencer* carried an account of the boys' arrival in St. Paul on the previous Saturday. They had been on the road five days, and the account stated that "On Monday they expected to see Minnehaha Falls and Lake Minnetonka. Tuesday they intended to start out again and are contemplating a return home by way of Chicago. Just when they will be here is not known."

George Tilden, the youngest of the Ames bike riders, appears to have returned home from Minneapolis, probably by train.

In his trip diary published in the *Ames Times,* July 13, 1893, Gates Brown stated that their trip to St. Paul had covered 308 miles in four days and eleven hours. He further stated that "it having rained every day but one and so we had to make 150 miles on the track. Our shortest day was Tuesday, thirty miles, and our longest day was Saturday, ninety seven miles."

Of the original five young men who had left Ames on July 4, only Gates Brown and Stuart Hutchison decided to extend the trip by returning to Ames by way of Chicago.

What route the boys took from Minneapolis is not known, but the July 27 *Ames Times* confirmed that two of the boys had reached Chicago and were arriving back in Ames. "Gates Brown returned this morning from his long bicycle trip. He broke his wheel at Cedar Rapids and leaving Hutchison there came in on the train. Hutchison will ride in and will probably arrive tomorrow."

The *Intelligencer* of August 3, 1893 reported that "The Boys rode twelve days and covered a distance

McKelvey at 3:40 and Ashworth at 3:50.

St. Cloud, Minn., July 10.—[Special.]— Doble registered here on return at 9:25. The total time to Minneapolis and return, including rests, was 16 hours 25 minutes. White was second, at 9:28. Adley ran with Doble until the tire of his wheel broke, seven miles out. A crowd of 2,000 witnessed the finish. Both men were fresh and in excellent condition, coming in with a spurt.

A Party From Iowa.

Gates M. Brown, Stuart C. Hutchinson and George H. Tilden, the three students of the agricultural college at Ames, Iowa, who left that place at 10 a. m. on the morning of the Fourth for a trip on their bicycles to Chicago by way of Minneapolis, arrived in this city Saturday evening at 9:30 o'clock. The distance covered was 303 miles, and the time occupied was 4 days, 10 hours and 30 minutes. On Wednesday and Saturday they covered 100 miles each, and 150 miles of the journey was made over railroad ties. The young men enjoyed the trip and they arrived here in good form. Tilden is the lightest of the trio, weighing only 93 pounds. They will leave for Chicago today and expect to arrive in that city on Saturday.

Handball Challenge.

Duncan, Fitzgibbons and Shaugnessy, of St. Paul, challenge any three members of the handball clubs of Minneapolis to a contest at the St. Paul Handball Court, 519 St. Peter street, to take place next Sunday. the

The Minneapolis Tribune of Tuesday July 11, 1893 p. 4 carried this news item about our Ames wheelmen. ID No. 210.1190.3-4-5

---

8 *Ames Intelligencer,* Aug. 3, 1893, p..7.

of 1024 miles, going to Minneapolis and from there to Chicago."

The story concluded by stating, "No pun intended when we say both of the young gentlemen are 'done brown' from the effects of long exposure to air, wind and sun."[8]

Today's RAGBRAI may be "great," but compare the riding conditions of the 1990s with those of the 1890s. Think I'll take the paved roads of 1996 over the wagon trails and railroad rights-of-ways of 1893.

Consider the fifteen-speed light-weight bike of today as it compares with the single-speed heavy-weight low-pressure-tired bicycle of the 1890s!

Those Ames wheelmen of 1893 were a century ahead of their time. Today's bikers follow their example and are riding on many former mainline railroad right-of-ways where the trains no longer run. Some of the railroad tracks that our Ames wheelmen traveled over in 1893 may be bike trails today! "What goes around, comes around."

June 3, 1996

Chapter 4

Floods Visit Ames

Again and Again

"I do not see the wisdom of spilling water over the country at the rate it has deluged over this section of late. It seems to be a perfect waste!" The year was 1870 and LaVerne Noyes was writing to his father of his reaction to the widespread flooding of the Squaw Creek bottom lands all along the east side of the campus. Noyes was an undergraduate at the Iowa Agricultural College at the time and a member of the first class to graduate in 1872.[1]

LaVerne Noyes, Iowa State Class of 1872. Noyes wrote to his father in the 1870s about the flooding problems that were so frequent on the Squaw Creek bottoms. Photo courtesy Iowa State University Archives, Parks Library. ID No. 174.973.3

LaVerne Noyes became a successful manufacturer of farm equipment, especially the famous Aermotor windmills that later dotted the midwest landscape. Lake LaVerne, on Iowa State's campus, bears Noyes' name.

Would Noyes have had some advice for us today? Probably not, because all that Noyes was concerned about was flood waters surging over and through the timber pasture and open flat hay and corn

---

[1] *Ames Evening Times,* July 21, 1915, p.1, "Had Great Waste of Rain In 1870." Quote from Noyes' letter of October 8, 1870.

land east of the campus. There were three plank bridges that connected the village wagon trails with the college grounds and the open country across the Squaw Creek and the Skunk River to the south and east. In 1870 no buildings of any kind stood where the flood waters moved so menacingly.

Noyes account to his father reminds us that the flooding of river and creek bottom lands "came first," and people came later.

1993 WAS OUR YEAR OF THE FLOOD

Fourteen feet of water stood on Iowa State University's basketball floor in Hilton Coliseum in July, 1993. The waters of Squaw Creek ran over Thirteenth Street, Lincoln Way, Elwood, and South Duff, damaging major buildings and many homes adjacent to the creek west and south of Lincoln Way. The Skunk River, on a rampage, was, in turn, a part of the Squaw Creek's back-up waters that confounded the downstream surge from Squaw Creek's high waters.

The 1993 disaster appears to have been the all-time flood stage for this area.

RECORDS OF OTHER YEARS

Perhaps so, but a review of the history of flooding on the Squaw and Skunk dating from the earliest days of Ames may be revealing. Note must be taken of demographic changes that have taken place over the years. Flooding is not just a matter of the amount and rate of rainfall.

In 1869, the year that Iowa State opened for its first student class, George Tilden arrived from his native home back east and was making plans to locate in this small village where one of the primary indications for a bright future for the community was that "there is to be a college here."

On May 28,1869, Tilden wrote to his wife back in Vermont about their plans to move to central Iowa: "The Skunk River is the highest it has been in four years. Considerable damage has been done to roads."

Three days later Tilden wrote further about local river flooding, "the roads are most impassable, much damage has been done, and it is estimated that it will cost more than a thousand dollars to repair the roads and bridges in this town." That was a lot of money in 1869.

The first newspaper in Ames was the *Intelligencer,* established in 1868. No copies of that publication are available until the issues of 1877. Stories of heavy rains were frequent but few statistics were given in the pages of those earliest remaining issues.

With 1993 flooding vivid in our minds, we examine the rainfall record for earlier years available from the Iowa Weather Bureau now located near the Des Moines River north of Des Moines.

1881 A YEAR OF RECORD RAINFALL

1881 appears to have been the year when Ames, and most of the state as well, experienced an all-time high yearly total rainfall. Beginning that year rainfall statistics for the Ames area are available. Rainfall in 1881 exceeded fifty inches for the calendar year. From the published official Iowa weather report for that year, we find that Ames had 17.40 inches of rain in July with the greatest amount in one day being 5.60 inches. On July 9th the report indicated that over 5 inches fell in Story County. The same report states that during the three day period beginning on July 9th the "total rainfall in Story County exceeded 10 inches." [2]

That 1881 report did not specify the location for rainfall readings. However, from records provided by Iowa State University climatologists, we find that a total of 16.31 inches of rainfall for the month of July, 1881, was recorded adjacent to the Iowa State campus. Such records confirm the state report.

HIGHEST RAINFALL SINCE 1881

Keep in mind that in 1993, the year of "our flood," a recorded total of 16.39 inches of rain fell in Ames during the month of July. That appears to be the highest for the month of July since 1881, based

upon rainfall records established at Ames. The final estimate for the total rainfall in the Ames area for the 1993 calendar year was 56.35 inches as measured at an Ames weather station.[3] That compares with a calendar year total for Ames of 51.9 inches for the year 1881, with the exact location for those readings not specified. A review of long-range yearly rainfall records suggests that 1993 was, in fact, a record year for the past 112 years.

May and June, 1993, rainfall total of 14.94 inches in the Ames area, however significantly exceeded that of the the same two months in 1881, with a total 9.02 inches. This strengthens the idea that 1993 was a record-breaking year for flooding at the confluence of the Skunk River and Squaw Creek.

Flood studies suggest that rainfall alone is only one factor in flooding. Heavy rains preceded by sustained wet weather results in a high level of ground saturation, such that subsequent rainfall produces more runoff which then floods the surrounding plains.

Other factors can be considerd as well. 1881 has still more to reveal to us about the history of flooding creeks and rivers in central Iowa.

Ames was hit hard by that flood of 1881. The July 23 issue of the *Iowa Register*[4] published in Des Moines, reported its correspondent's findings with a dateline of July 21, after he had traveled through the flood stricken Story and Boone counties area. "The storm at Ames and vicinity did lots of damage; the first train just passed through as we arrived in Ames since the storm. Great sheets of water yet covered the bottoms around Ames."

Keep in mind that the *Register's* dateline for that story was almost a week after the main rains had fallen on the Ames area.

The *Register's* writer continued, "We left Des Moines Tuesday morning going north. Everywhere signs of the great flood were visable.....many of the towns had no mail for five or six days."

From Ames, the *Iowa Register's* correspondent moved on to Boone: "In the town of Boone every bridge is gone. Boone County is suffering worse, perhaps, in this direction than any other." He then visited Moingona, and describes the scene of the heroism of Kate Shelley, whose heroic crossing of the railroad bridge over the Des Moines River on the night of July 6, has been long acclaimed.

1892

The May 19, 1892, issue of the *Ames Times* stated that the "excessive rains of last week ... succeeded in stopping the Ames & College Railroad Company's

2   *Iowa Weather Service,* 1881 Dr. Gustavus Hinrich, Des Moines, Iowa, pp 118 and 276.
3   56.35 inches were reported at the agronomy station southwest of the campus. 58.06 inches were reported at the water treatment plant located southeast of Ames.
4   Later the *Register and Leader*; it is now the *Des Moines Register.*

Dinkey trains. Travel became impossible early Wednesday morning. One of the bridges is badly damaged, and the grade on Squaw Creek is washed away." Ames' rainfall during the month of May that year was the fourth highest for the area in over a hundred years.

1900

In 1900, the Chicago & North Western Railroad had changed its original single track mainline to a two-track system. At that time the elevation of the tracks across the river and creek bottoms adjacent to Ames were raised. Also, at that time a bridge span of some sixty-feet length was placed in the railroad's right of way several hundred feet west of the Squaw Creek bridge. For over forty years it provided flood waters coming down the Squaw Creek valley with an "escape valve" thereby taking pressure off of the main railroad bridge over Squaw Creek and also reducing the likelihood of roadbed washouts.

DRAINAGE STRUCTURE BECAME ALSO AN UNDERPASS

A news account in 1908,[5] suggests there had been an understanding in 1900, when the line was converted to a two-track system, that the college would later develop an access road to the campus that would utilize that sixty -foot bridge span a short distance west of Squaw Creek. When Sixth Street was extended to the Iowa State campus in the late 1940s, the city did enter into an agreement with the railroad to make dual use of that apparent drainage structure by also making it an underpass for Sixth Street.

1902

In 1902, Ames experienced a total rainfall for the year of 45.79 inches which was about 50% above normal. In June, a total of 10.01 inches fell locally. July followed with 8.06 inches and August with 7.12 inches bringing the total ninety day rainfall in Ames to 25.19 inches, over 50% of that year's total. At the time, local papers carried frequent references to continuous wet weather. On June 12, 1902, a news item reported local damage to the C.& N.W. tracks. "It has been a long time since the railroads had to be reported in this respect, but the heavy rains of the

The little steam Dinkey engine, without its passenegr car,"tests" the Squaw Creek bridge. Picture may have been as early as 1902. The line was electrified in 1907. Photo from the Edward Myers collection. ID No. 25.123.1

past week or ten days have made all kinds of trouble for the railroads."

1909

Bottom lands around Ames were reported under water again in 1909. A year earlier a new bridge had been built over Squaw Creek on Lincoln Way, then known as Boone Street. The *Ames Intelligencer* July 1, 1909 lead story headline proclaimed, "Heavens Unloaded - Injures the Road." The entire Squaw Creek bottoms were under water almost to the power plant. A portion of a dike that had been built between the railroad embankment south to Boone Street had been washed out. "All day Sunday....a force of men hauled dirt to build this up and by sundown the gap was fairly closed."[6]

Lincoln Way bridge over Squaw Creek in 1908, the year it was built with Luten patented plans selected by Story County Supervisors. It collapsed in late June of 1918 from effects of flood waters that year. Photo Courtesy of the Iowa Department of Transportation. ID No. 203.1148.5

---

[5] *The Ames Intelligencer,* October 29, 1908. p.1 "To Protect Lives Of Ames Students." Mentions access road that had never been built.

[6] The earth levee would have been about where Elwood Drive is located today between Lincoln Way and Sixth Street.

This October 4, 1909 photo of the Squaw Creek bridge shows how it was severely tested within a year of its construction. Should there have been four rather than three spans was a question added to those previously raised by bridge engineers. ID No.77.398.3

That 1909 account gives us a clear picture of problems that the flooded Squaw Creek had created. The bottoms were under water "except for a small island on which many of the hogs and sheep were herded Sunday and until the flood had receded sufficiently so that they could be taken off. A large flock of sheep south of the tracks would have drowned had not a force from the College and the neighborhood gone into the water, finally landing them on the interurban tracks."

Squaw Creek bottom land in 1908. You could reach the campus during flood stage on the street car or on foot by way of the street car tracks. Photo courtesy Iowa Department of Transportation. ID No. 3.13.1-2

---

7 The "Melan" bridge was a patented design obtained for a fee by the county supervisors. Guaranteed for a five year period, the bridge was one the *Ames Intelligencer* of July 1, 1909, had stated "ought to last for all ages." On January 3, 1918, Federal Judge Martin J. Wade for the Southern District of Iowa rendered his opinion invalidating the patents on these bridges. Six months later the Ames bridge collapsed.

8 *Ames Evening Times*, December 31, 1908, "Fine Structure Now Completed." This item contains reference to the "west bridge over the bayou " being abandoned since the new bridge was large enough to "allow all the water that comes down the Squaw Creek to pass under."

9 *Ames Evening Times*, September 29, 1915, p. 1, "Much Loss From Recent Rains."

The 1909 news story referred to the new Melan bridge down on Boone Street (Lincon Way), stating that when it had been built the year before, it had been thought that the three-arched span would be adequate to take any potential flood waters. Just one year later the flood waters had practically filled the arches and severely threatend the new bridge. The article continued, "It was the opinion of experts who viewed the bridge Sunday that at least one more arch would be necessary." It was following the Squaw Creek flood of June, 1918, - just nine years later - that the bridge collapsed.[7]

It should also be noted that prior to 1908 the county supervisors had maintained a dry land plank-span in the Boone Road (Lincoln Way) roadbed midway across the Squaw Creek bottoms as a potential escape valve for anticipated flood waters.[8]

1915

The September 29, 1915, issue of the *Ames Times* carried a front page report of excessive rain damage to roads and bridges adjacent to Ames. "The wooden bridge across the Skunk River east of Thirteenth Street went out early in the week and others were seriously threatened."[9]

A comparison of the years when Ames experienced flood damage reveals that, while in some instances, there was a correlation with widespread high rainfall totals, that has not always been the case. The rainfall may have been excessive only locally for a particular short-time period. Flooding at any given location can be damaging either way.

You are looking at the south abutment of the old red bridge over the Skunk River about two miles north of Ames. Photo taken in 1918 following the complete destruction of the bridge in the heavy flood that year. This bridge ran north- south at a point about a half mile around the river bend to the north of the present bridge on W. Riverside Road. Photo Courtesy Iowa Department Of Transportation. ID No. 203.1148.4

East Thirteenth Street bridge the day after it sustained flood damage in 1915 Note the sagging section at the far end of the bridge. Damage had been extensive, although this bridge was one of the least damaged of the Skunk River bridges in the Ames area that year. Photo courtesy Iowa Department Of Transportation. ID No.122.669.1

The wash out section of Lincoln Way west of Squaw Creek in 1918. Not only was the bridge soon to collapse, but the road bed and utility lines had to be reestablished. I recall that this section was temporarily bridged. Note the Iowa State College heating plant in the distant background. Photo Courtesy Iowa Department of Transportation. ID No.171.956.3

DAMAGING FLOOD OF 1918

The June 4, 1918 *Ames Evening Times* reported heavy damage from "the most serious rain storm that has visited this section in years. Rain coming down in torrents fed rivers and small streams which already were swollen as the result of the precipitations of last week, causing them to overflow and flooding hundreds of acres of bottom land. Squaw Creek going on a rampage has made a great lake between Ames and the campus, the high waters taking out the foot bridge leading from the cinder path, and great stretches of the Lincoln Highway grade were washed out. Street car traffic was abandoned."[10]

South Duff was under water as the Skunk and Squaw formed a vast lake in the area.

Prof. F. S. Wilkins, weather observer for the College Farm Crops (Agronomy) Department, reported that 2.93 inches had fallen Monday night bringing the total rainfall since 7 p.m. Sunday (June 2nd) to 5.1 inches. The June 7, 1918, issue of the *Times* reported that 7.96 inches had fallen on Ames during the first five days of June. Precipitation in Ames for the month of May had been 6.45 inches with most of that falling after May 15. The total rainfall for the 20 days through June 6 was locally registered at 14.41 inches. All of this indicates that the ground all around Ames had become saturated by the arrival of the heavy rains of June.

Looking south across the sixty foot break in Lincoln Way that resulted from the Squaw Creek flood of 1918. Note the utility pipe line exposed by the washout. Photo courtesy Iowa Department Of Transportation. ID No.203.1148.1-3

---

[10] *Ames Evening Times*, of June 4 ,5,6,7, 1918, all major front page stories.

The Squaw Creek bridge on Lincoln Way after it collapsed in late June 1918. The bridge had been seriously threatened by high water the year earlier and its collapse was not a real surprise to Dean Marston since he had pointed out the weaknesses in the bridge plans selected in 1908. At that earlier date, the State Highway Commissioin did not have a final say in the selection of bridge plans. Photo courtesy Iowa Department Of Transportation. ID No. 134.739.3

Typical scene during flood stage. Looking northwesterly from point near Squaw Creek Lincoln Way bridge. Elwood Drive is today located just beyond the trees in the foreground. Photo courtesy Iowa Department of Transportation. ID No. 170.952.2

Local damage was reported to be high with basements full of water. The lead on the *Times* story of June 4 was that "Shortly after 3 o'clock this afternoon, the Lincoln Way bridge east of Ames gave away under the pressure of the rising stream." The Lincoln Way bridge over Squaw Creek, that had been new just ten years earlier, fortunately withstood the actual flood stage but collapsed on the last day of June having been seriously weakened by the flood waters. The Goddard family of Ames was driving over the bridge just as it collapsed late in the day. They were rescued, but their car was left stranded on the remaining water and sewer mains that were located below the traveled roadway of the bridge.[11]

The street car bridge over Squaw Creek withstood all of the floods, but this 1918 picture shows what happened to the footbridge located nearby. ID No. 13.57.1

[11] *Ames Tribune,* July 1, 1918, p. 1 story about the bridge collapse.
[12] Divided responsibility for replacing the bridge caused delays. See: *Ames Tribune,* March 11, 1920, -Ames voters approve bond issue to cover Ames's share of bridge cost.

Lincoln Way was not yet paved in 1918. A sixty-foot segment of Lincoln Way west of the bridge had been washed out and was temporarily spanned with a plank bridge until the fill could be replaced. A temporary detour bridge was built around the washed-out Squaw Creek bridge; it was not replaced with a new permanent bridge until late 1921.[12] As of that time the only buildings that were in the path of the Squaw Creek flood waters were a small number of portable hog shelters that were along the north side of Lincoln Way near the Beach Avenue corner.

After the Squaw Creek bridge on Lincoln Way collapsed in 1918, this detour bridge was built. Because of divided jurisdictions in replacing the bridge, this wood bridge remained in use until 1921 when a new bridge was completed. Photo courtesy Iowa Department of Transportation. ID No.112.615.1

There was no significant development in the lowland areas, other than the gas plant located just east of Ames. A few minor farm buildings existed in 1918 east of town on Lincoln Way, on South Duff Avenue, and Thirteenth Street east of the cemetery. Except for the concrete bridge over Squaw Creek, the bridges south and east of Ames were of the old narrow "red bridge" design. All were damaged seriously in that 1918 flood.

South Duff Avenue sometime in the 1930s. Looking north on Highway 69 from point north of Squaw Creek bridge.. Note that the only commercial developement then was the sales barn on the east side. Eschbach Music House had a sign board on the west side. Surrounding land appears much as it did when classed as swampland sixty years earlier. Land-filling and road widening projects were yet to come. ID No.166.925.4-5

The gas plant at the foot of the hill just east of town was flooded and out of operation for some days as a result of that flood.

The total rainfall for 1918 was normal. However the sixty day total for the months of May and June placed them near the top for a fifty-year period. The significance of the 1918 flood to Ames was its damage to local businesses, and the destruction of roads, bridges, and crops.

As the population of Ames grew, the flood stages were increasingly impacting our city. More notice and more concerns were involved.

THE WORST FLOOD IN HISTORY

In 1944, the flood waters again visited the plains of Squaw Creek and the Skunk River with a vengence.[13] Again the flooding was acclaimed to have been extreme in its effects. This time it was the "worst" in the history of local flooding, to quote the local headlines that day. 4.53 inches fell on Ames the night of May 18, 1944, followed the next evening with 3.68 inches. That totaled 8.21 inches most of which was said to have fallen within a twenty-four hour period.

Looking southwesterly from Stange Road toward the Squaw Creek and the campus beyond. This could have been any of the flood years. Veenker golf course is now where all that water is. ID No. 136.752.2

Much of the Skunk River bottom lands east of Ames looked like this the day following the 1944 flood. ID No. 174.975.3

The 1944 downpour of May 19 fell within such a short period of time that water was running in the streets to depths of several feet. Water fell so fast that homes located on relatively high ground experienced torrents of water pushing in grade windows and filling their basements. Street gutters could not move the water fast enough. A number of Main Street buildings were filled with water that had entered by basement windows or exterior stairwells. The Sheldon Munn Hotel's basement was full of water.

The Grand Avenue underpass was "devastated" by the 1944 flooding. It was several days before traffic could again use the underpass. Mud slides had cluttered the street. Photo courtesy Iowa D .O.T. ID No. 91A.487.1

Thousands of dollars of merchandise was destroyed by flood waters. Montgomery Ward, J. C. Penney, Carr Hardware, Younkers Store, and the Ames Mattress Company were among those reporting heavy inventory losses. The *Tribune* had 14 inches of water on its floor at one time that night and only one of four linotype machines was dry enough to use the next day.

The Grand Avenue underpass was completely flooded. Two motorists who had attempted to drive through it had to abandon their cars and swim to safety. The next day the underpass looked like a war zone with tons of soil washed down into the roadway.

College Creek had overwhelmed many Campustown business places because the drainage structures that carried the stream under the store buildings were not adequate to carry such a volume of water in so short a time. Much grocery and general merchandise was destroyed. A characteristic of the 1944 storm was that the flood damages were spread generally over a large number of businesses and individuals.

FLOODING SINCE 1944

Those who have lived in Ames very long are familiar with the more recent times when the floodwaters have covered the low lying areas in Ames adja-

1993 flood stage on Squaw Creek. Looking westerly across Lincoln Way west of the Lincoln Way bridge. The highway, Elwood Drive and all of the parking lots were under water. The water was swirling over the intersection of Elwood and Lincoln Way. ID No. 155.860.5

cent to the Squaw Creek and Skunk River. The flooding that occurred on June 27, 1975, resulted in damage to the new Iowa State Center buildings, and was described as being the "worst flood since 1918." Again in 1990, flooding in Ames rated the record books. In both these years, damage to both private residential and commercial property was significant. In a sense, those occasions were just more proof of a flooding pattern that had long ago been established.[14]

When preliminary studies and reports had been prepared during the planning stage for the Iowa State Center, the emphasis was directed toward "flood proofing" of the proposed structures.[15]

"Flood-proofing" appears to have become a new term, but it was not a new thought. In 1937, when plans for a new Ames High School building were on the local agenda, there were persistent suggestions that the land west of Squaw Creek and north of Lincoln Way would be a suitable school site. An educational consultant from Iowa City concluded that such a site "eliminated itself since the cost of protecting it from floodwaters might well exceed the cost of the building." He was promptly criticized by proponents of the site for dismissing the location "out of hand' without first determining the cost of possible flood protection.[16]

WHAT IT MEANS TO US NOW

One hundred and twenty-five years have passed since LaVerne Noyes expressed his opinion of the waters that overflowed the Squaw Creek bottom lands. The 1881 flood that was so well recorded in

history was a hundred and fourteen years ago. We are told that there were a number of factors that may have contributed to the times and extent of past floods in this (or any geographic area). Such possible factors have included the construction of drainage ditches upstream to hasten the water away from cultivated fields and into the natural streams. Farming methods have increased erosion.

The most significant change that has occurred over the years has been the increase in the number of structures that have been placed in the very spaces that repeatedly have been the flooded plains. In 1881 the damage was limited to fences, crops, plank bridges and minor farm buildings. Each recorded flood experienced by us has had some increase in the quantity of man-made structures in the floodplains. Bridges became larger and of more permanent construction. There are more roadways. Land that had been classified as swampland at the time Ames was founded, and that lays within what is now our city limits, was filled to permit commercial development. Sometime before 1918, an earth dike was constructed west of Squaw Creek in the hopes of diverting flood waters away from crops.

By 1993, Ames had raised and widened the roadbeds adjacent to the Squaw and Skunk. Elwood Drive was a major improvement; it closely parallels Squaw Creek and functions as a dike as well as a roadway. All roadways are now paved. Paved parking lots and large buildings are there to be dealt with by the occasional rampaging waters that the local streams try to handle in the manner dictated by the laws of nature. The results have been clear and obvious to many observers.

Referring to the flooding along the Mississippi in 1993, Bruce Hannon, professor of geography at the University of Illinois wrote, "The flood damage

The flat area east of the stadium looked like this the day following the high water of 1996. Flooding was not nearly as bad as in 1993. The car is headed south on Elwood. The softball fields beyond are all under water. ID No,183.1035.3

---

13 *Ames Daily Tribune,* May 20, 1944, p.1, Headline story.
14 *Ames Daily Tribune,* June 27, 1975, and June 18, 1990.
15 *Iowa Natural Resources Council's Report,* August 15, 1966.

and the resulting human anguish now taking place on the Mississippi River is not caused by Mother Nature...it is the result of the work of man. Flood sounds negative to most people, but to nature it is an expected event, historically bringing a rich supply of nutrients, followed by a burst of growth."[17]

In 1993, televised commentaries called attention to the fact that when a dike broke on one side of the Mississippi, the waters flooded hundreds of adjacent acres, and as that happened, water flowed off of hundreds of flooded acres on the opposite side of the river. Nature always has had to be reckoned with. Water has the power to find "its place" on the map.

The point is that when you protect one site you, in turn, jeopardize another.

It is a simple principle that when you put rocks in a bucket, it will hold less water. Today, there is more recognition of such realities. A seemingly new concensus is that the floodplains are a "part of the stream bed." The floodplain is literally a part of Mother Nature's *rain barrel* built into her system for both storage and development.

An historical perspective suggests that it is there that the matter rests. The American Indians had the reputation of never locating *their* villages in floodplains; just possibly, they had the right idea.

March 3, 1995

---

[16] The consultant at that time did suggest that the cost of "floodproofing" likely would exceed the cost of building.
[17] Universisty of Illinois, College of Liberal Arts - *News Letter, Winter, 1994,* Article entitled "Don't Blame Mother Nature."

Chapter 5

Trains: Crossing Problem Has Long History In Ames

It's time for an update on an old story - with new twists.

In 1873, few trains made scheduled stops at the Ames depot. The Chicago & North Western Railroad's time table for that year shows two passenger trains arriving in Ames from Chicago each day. By 1885, the C. & N.W.'s time card was showing six eastbound trains per day and five westbound trains. Six of those trains were passenger trains.

VILLAGE LOTS
FOR SALE

The subscriber offers for sale some very desirable residential lots situated in

Black's Addition to Ames

THESE LOTS ARE

Pleasantly Located

Within five minutes walk of the railroad depot in a section of the town that is fast filling up with a good class of citizens, and near the Union Grade School. In Plain view of the Railroad and Business Streets.

TERMS EASY

On long or short time, as may be desired.

Inquire of   ISSAC BLACK
Ames, Dec. 9, 1869 -

The railroad had determined our town's location and had given it a name. The railroad brought us our first residents, the folks who really started our town and those who staffed the Iowa Agricultural College nearby. Building lots located near the railroad were considered choice; they sold the best.

In 1904, soon after the new Ames depot was built, there were six eastbound and nine westbound trains

scheduled through Ames. All of those were passenger trains. The famous "Overland Limited," the "Pacific Express," and the "Colorado & Oregon Express," examples of west coast passenger trains, were included.

The development of the north/south rail branch line in the mid-1870s made Ames a major rail center for both passenger and freight traffic. In 1904, there were eleven north and south trains scheduled through Ames including such trains as the "St. Paul & Sioux City Express" and the "Dakota & Des Moines Express."

In 1911, Ames was claiming twenty-six east and west passenger train arrivals and in addition there were fourteen north and south passenger train departures - all on the Chicago & North Western Line. Including the Fort Dodge, Des Moines & Southern's electric interurban trains, the Ames Intelligencer, in a front page story, suggested that there were more passenger trains out of Ames per day than there were out of Des Moines.[1]

Through the mid-teens, over twenty-four passenger trains a day made scheduled stops at the Ames depot. In addition, many special trains were brought in to accommodate Excursion Day and Field Day programs at Iowa State and college students at vacation breaks. That was before the days of good roads and student-owned cars. At one time the Ames depot reported the largest sales of passenger tickets for the C. & N. W. Line in the state of Iowa.

Our population reached five thousand in 1915; automobiles were becoming the way of local travel, and rail travel was attaining high levels. Getting across the main-line railroad tracks was an occasional problem. Fatal accidents at downtown grade-crossings occurred. In 1917, a foot subway was added to the depot for safety reasons. The job of the crossing-gate operators had become stressful.

PEOPLE PETITION FOR A VIADUCT

On August 21,1916, the Ames City Council was presented with a petition requesting a viaduct and an

---

[1] *Ames Intelligencer*, August 3, 1911, p. 1, "Study in Transportation."

underpass.[2] The matter was referred to the Streets and Alleys Committee. In May of 1918, the committee[3] recommended the construction of a viaduct over the tracks at Carroll Avenue. At that location, the elevation of the tracks was lower than at existing crossings further west in the business district, and a viaduct would fit into the area easily. A formal meeting between that Ames committee and railroad officials was held to discuss the proposal.

A May 7, 1918, front-page story in the Ames Evening Times carried the heading, "RAILROAD DISCOURAGES VIADUCT CONSTRUCTION."[4] World War I railroad operations were in the hands of the federal government at the time. "There is a war on", the railroad officials reminded the Ames committee. The cost of that viaduct, estimated at $30,000, would require the approval of Railroad Director General William G. McAdoo in Washington. If approved, it "would be highly improbable that materials for the construction could be secured," the committee reported. The project had been stalled but the committee would continue to "work on the viaduct

plans so as to be prepared when a better opportunity arrived."

On May 3, 1919, a tragic accident occurred at the Grand Avenue crossing; Raymond Duckworth, aged 17, and J. F. Williams were taking mail from the main post office to the station "A" postal station located on the Iowa State campus. Raymond was driving. As they approached the Grand Avenue crossing, a west bound passenger train was preparing to depart from the depot. Duckworth's attention had been drawn to the soon-to-depart locomotive as he made his decision to proceed across the tracks. As a result, he failed to see the crossing guard frantically rushing into the center of the grade crossing waving his hand-held stop sign. The mail truck was hit by an incoming passenger train, instantly killing Williams and fatally injuring Duckworth.[5]

Six accidents happened at the same crossing that year.

At that time a city ordinance[6] restricted train speed within the Ames city limits to 8 miles-an-hour, and a state law allowed speed up to 15 miles-an-hour when a flagman was present. Those regulations had long been unenforced. Safety at rail crossings in Ames was a growing concern. There were suggestions, then, that there should be an underpass at the Grand Avenue crossing.

This photograph shows a south view of the Grand Avenue grade crossing in 1936 before construction of the underpass began. Note the flagman's shelter at left, the interurban depot at upper right, and the Ames High Field House in distant upper left. Photo courtesy Iowa Department of Transportation. ID No. 130.716.4-5

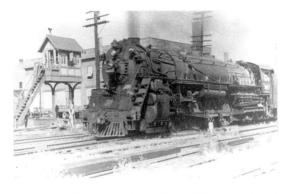

Crossing guard tower once located at the Kellogg crossing when the gates were controlled by on site personnel. ID No.100.544.1-2

CHAMBER ADVOCATES AN UNDERPASS AT BROOKRIDGE

By 1926, the Ames Chamber of Commerce[7] was advocating an underpass between Brookridge and Russell Avenues. By late 1927, the city council and the Ames City Engineer, John Ames, were ready to act. Detailed plans were developed for an underpass that would connect Brookridge Avenue at the Sixth Street intersection with Riverside Drive to the south

[2] *Ames Evening Times,* Auigust 23, 1916, p.1, "Agitate Viaduct and Subway." Called for viaduct at Carroll and a subway at Clark Avenue.

[3] Committee members were E. J. Morevets, fourth ward councilman; John Brindley, councilman at large; Seth Morris, second ward councilman; and J. Q. Wickham, city engineer.

[4] *Ames Evening Times,* May 7, 1918, p.1, "Railroad Discourages Construction of Viaduct."

[5] *Ames Evening Times,* May 3, 1919, p.1, "Speeding Train Crashes Into Automobile Killing One and Seriously Injuring Another."

[6] Ordinances City of Ames, p. 59, Chapter 7, Ordinance No. 209, Section 23, "Speed of Trains." Passed April 26, 1909.

[7] *Ames Tribune,* Dec. 18, 1926, p. 1, "Subway Up To R.R." plan initiated by Chamber.

of the Chicago and North Western's main line and of the Fort Dodge and Des Moines Interurban tracks.

The railroad quickly filed objections with the Iowa Railroad Commission. Their primary objection was that the cost of such a project would require the issuance of securities which could only be done with the consent of the Interstate Commerce Commission. They further pointed out that the proposal would create a new point of crossing the railroad's right-of-way while leaving the existing downtown crossings unchanged.

On March 29, 1928,[8] a formal hearing was held in Ames on the city's proposed Brookridge Avenue underpass. Through the questioning of Ames City Attorney J. Y. Luke, John Ames presented the city's case for the thoroughfare. It would provide a shorter, safer route between downtown Ames and the campus for a substantial number of Ames citizens.[9]

The railroad's attorney, George Hise, of Des Moines, asked John Ames if, after acquiring the proposed underpass, the city might also demand other subways such as at Duff or Clark Avenue. John Ames replied that "perhaps they might," to which Hise said, "Well, that's too much for a town the size of Ames."

That proposal seems to have been shot down as

effectively by the railroad as was the 1918 proposal for the viaduct at Carroll Avenue. It would be twenty years before a similar proposal could be activated with the extension of Sixth Street to the campus involving the conversion of the 61-foot drainage span to use as a roadway under the railroad several hundred feet to the west of Squaw Creek.

In the meantime, in 1928, the Ames City Council adopted an ordinance[10] calling for a grade crossing at Clark Avenue where none had previously existed. The school board requested the crossing because the location, in 1927, of the Ames High School field house on Lincoln Way had resulted in high school students crossing the mainline tracks at an unsupervised point to reach the field house.[11] The rail-

This is a view to the southeast during construction of the Grand Avenue underpass. Train service continued during the entire construction period. Photo courtesy Iowa Department of Transportation. ID No. 127.700.2-4

---

8 *Ames Tribune,* March 29, 1928, p. 1, "Subway Case Aired Today."

9 *City Council Minute Book* No. 6, p. 341-342, Ordinance No. 383 (Reasons and specifications).

10 Actually two ordinances: No. 393 and 394 extending Clark Avenue to Lincoln Way and the railroad crossing, Dec. 17, 1928.

11 *Ames Evening Times,* December 18, 1928, p. 1, "City Demands Crossing." Petitioned by Ames School Board.

Aerial view of downtown Ames in the mid-1940s. The area adjacent to Lincoln Way in the foreground has seen substantial development since that time. Many of the private homes have been removed for commercial development. Note the Ames Grain and Coal buildings that were then located on the west side of Duff near the railroad tracks. Today modern office and business buildings are in that location. Photo by the late Olav Smedal.

road obtained what amounted to a permanent injunction against the city on that matter. Clark Avenue's proximity to the passenger station appears to have been the main factor in the court's decision.[12] Not until 1971 was a grade crossing opened at Clark Avenue, long after passenger service had ceased.

PLANNING BEGINS FOR GRAND AVENUE UNDERPASS

By the mid-1930s, city and highway engineers had begun serious talk of an underpass at the Grand Avenue rail crossing. When early survey work was underway, some highway engineers expressed doubt that a satisfactory underpass could be constructed within the distance between the Fifth Street intersection and the Lincoln Way corner on Grand Avenue. Depth and drainage as well as overall distance were factors. Some time in 1936, plans were proposed that were pronounced workable. Included in the planning was a sixty-foot shift westerly in the center line of the Grand Avenue intersection with Lincoln Way.

In 1935, the city sought a grant of $100,000 under the Federal Railroad Crossing Elimination program. On September 23, 1936, Claude Coykendall, an administrative engineer for the Iowa Highway Commission and also a member of the Ames City Council, announced that the funds originally slated for the Grand Avenue project had been used by other similar projects in Iowa. Coykendall stated that the "local project will likely be included in a similar apppropriation in 1937, and that further action to carry this project through will be taken at that time."

On November 3, 1936, Ames voters approved the transfer of $25,000 from the municipal electric fund to the underpass project as the city's share of the cost. Total estimate of the project cost was $354,000.[13] Since Grand Avenue and Lincoln Way were primary highways, the project was handled by the Iowa Highway Commission with the balance of the cost covered by federal and state funds.[14]

The affirmative vote was 2,312 with 2,005 voting against the proposition. The majority vote of 307 seems small considering the history of the need to improve the rail crossings in Ames. The days leading up to the vote revealed a campaign level equal to that of a national election. Some felt that the railroad should pay the major share of the cost. Residents living close to the underpass objected to anticipated increased traffic. A few felt that the overhead lighting would encroach upon their privacy.[15]

The Grand Avenue underpass was completed in 1938.[16] A validation of the usefulness of that underpass to the citizens of Ames is the inconvenience and frustration that were experienced during 1996 when its driving lanes were repaved and otherwise improved.

PASSENGER SERVICE DISCONTINUED

In 1960, passenger service was discontinued by the C.&N.W. line through Ames. Five years later, the city arranged to have the railroad's switching yards moved two miles east of town to accomodate an increasing need in downtown Ames for off-street parking. Today the railroad no longer serves students and other members of the traveling public as it once did so well.

The railroad no longer has the personal tie to our town that it once had. It is like a stranger in our midst as it speeds through town with its high-volume freight usually with both distant origins and distant destinations. While Amtrak passenger service remains a hope for the future, there is no doubt about the priority of freight now and in the future.

Some have asked why the railroad was permitted to place their right-of-way at grade level in the original town of Ames. The obvious answer is that this was the common practice across the pioneer plains, especially when the railroads had laid out the towns and assigned their very names. The situation in the late 1800s in no way resembles the circumstances of today. In the 1920s and later we had twenty-four passenger trains a day with double-sections of perhaps a dozen fast streamliners per day. Today we have an average of fifty-five fast, diesel-powered freight trains per day,[17] a major percentage of them with a hundred or more cars.[18] Add to that the much higher automobile traffic counts of today.

---

12 *Ames Tribune,* July 17, 1929, p. 1, "Railroad Wins First Skirmish." (Passenger cars often were boarded in proposed crossing area.)
13 *Ames Tribune,* August 31, 1937, p.1, Ben Cole had winning bid at $282.000 which included all but right-of-way cost.
14 Final statement of agreement between city and Highway Commission was dated March 1, 1938. *City Council Minute Book.* No. 8 p.234.
15 *Ames Tribune,* Nov. 2, 1936, p. 5. Full page advertisement in opposition to proposition.
16 Certification of Completion dated August 9, 1938. Project Story County FAGM 72-E.
17 Union Pacific Railroad 1996 central Iowa segment. Line growing by 8+ trains per year.
18 Freight trains made up of returning empty grain or coal cars, reach totals of 200 cars.

Interrupted street travel resulting from the location of a major railroad artery within the Ames business district, causes concerns for the safety of drivers and pedestrians. It involves time loss for drivers caught in lines of cars while long freight trains clear the crossings. Fire protection is no small concern, as well. It is bad economics.

MORE LONG FREIGHT TRAINS ANTICIPATED

With faster, longer trains going through Ames in numbers that are expected to significantly increase in the future, we now find a growing interest in solving the problem of the railroad barrier in downtown Ames. Just what solutions are available? Will there be another underpass or perhaps a viaduct placed at a strategic Ames rail crossing in the somewhat near future?

Stay tuned.

January 9, 1997

Aerial view of central business district of Ames in 1946. You are looking straight down on the railroad yards located in the center of downtown Ames. Photo taken before the railroad depot grounds were sold to the City in 1951 for parking lot development. In 1965 the Ames High Field House in upper left of picture was sold to a shopping center developer. Final arrangements were made in 1967 to move the railroad's switching yards to a site east of town. Commercial development has since been extensive on both sides of the rail line. Increasing numbers of longer freight trains now pass through Ames at higher speeds. Photo by the late Olav Smedal.

Chapter 6

The Misplaced Building

(How the building that is now our city hall was located in downtown Ames.)

When the Ames High School building that had been built in 1938/39 was dedicated on April 28, 1990, as Ames's new city hall, two problems had been solved. A satisfactory use had been found for a fine building that, as a school building, was poorly suited because of its location. Also, Ames's critical need for a suitable city hall had been met. This building, as a city hall, is today ideally situated to serve the people of Ames for a long time to come. The following tells the story of the building whose origins were rooted in controversy.

This account starts in late 1936[1] when the Ames School Board[2] began to seriously deal with the fact that the high school building that had been new in 1912 was now inadequate. Located between Fifth and Sixth streets on the east side of Clark Avenue, the three story building was overcrowded and obsolete in other ways as well. Its site provided no room for expansion. The building would better serve the school system in other ways.

In December, the board was discussing building plans with architects. After exploring the advantages of various locations, the board wanted to determine the availability of options on open land off of Thirteenth Street west of Grand Avenue.

On December 8, the board met with the Ames Planning Commission to discuss available school sites and voted to cooperate with that commission in developing a building plan for the school district.[3]

By February, 1937, the school board had made known their interest in building a new and modern high school on land available on the northwest corner of Grand Avenue and Thirteenth Street. Several options for tracts had been obtained along the north side of Thirteenth Street including a 20 acre tract of land located west of the Grand Avenue corner.

Building a new high school at the Thirteenth Street location became a four-to-one choice of board members. Such a location would permit a campus-type high school plant. Adequate space for physical education and athletic activities, as well as for ex-

This Ames High School building, built in 1881, was the original building on the site between Fifth and Sixth Streets on Clark Avenue. When a new high school building was built in 1912 on the east side of Clark Avenue, this 1881 building became an elementary school. In about 1924 it became Ames' first Junior High School. ID NO. 197.1117.5 (1910ca)

The High School building built on the east side of Clark Avenue in 1912. It served as our High School until 1939, then became a Junior High School It was torn down in 1981. ID No. 124.682.1

---

[1] At the school board meeting on November 23, 1936, four possible sites for a new high school buiding were discussed. D. S. Triplett was asked to obtain information on various site costs. *School Board Minute book No. 5,* page 200.

[2] Board members were: W. H. Root, highway engineer, president; Dave Edwards, coal and ice business; R. D. Feldman, dentist; R. M. Vifquain, Agricultural Education Dept.; Prof. W. H. Meeker, Engineering Dept.; M. G. Davis was then ending his term as superindent. J. L. Larson was superintendent elect.

[3] Ames Planning Commission members were: F. C. Schneider, Highway Commission engineer; H. M. Hamlin, extension specialist; P. H. Elwood, head of Landscape Architecture Dept. at Iowa State College; Mrs.David Edwards, and Mrs H.A.Munn.

This 1938 Aerial photo looks north from Ninth Street with Northwestern Avenue on left and Roosevelt Avenue at right. (Roosevelt School in foreground) In 1937, the school board was obtaining options on the open land seen here above Thirteenth Street that extended to Grand Avenue. The entire area north of Thirteenth was as yet undeveloped, and was the board's choice location for the new High School's location. Photo courtesy of Jim Triplett. ID No. 165.919.1-2

pansion to meet future building needs, would be provided.

Soon, however, an unfavorable reaction materialized to the school board's announced plans. A committee that became known as the "Fourth Ward Committee," composed of folks living in west Ames, was organized. Prof. E. C. McCracken,[4] new on the staff at Iowa State College in 1935, became the chairman. McCracken was the committee's motivator and spokesman; under his direction, publicity and campaigning in opposition to the board's decisions would change the course of plans for a new high school building.

***

[4] In addition to McCracken, Assistant Professor of Physics, the other members, all on the Iowa State College staff, were: Prof. J. V. Atanasoff, Physics Dept. ; Prof.W. M. Vernon, Engineering; Prof. L. J. Murphy, Engineering; Prof. J. E. Evans, Psychology, and Prof. F. C. Dana, Industrial Economics. All of these men were highly qualified in their respective academic fields. In this instance they seemed to present a classic example of hubris when their achievements in the academic sphere caused their failure to respect and accept the well researched recommendations of the local public school administrators.

The Grand Avenue and Thirteenth Street location was practically out in the country, McCracken contended. It was too far for fourth ward high school students to be transported. After school activities would be difficult for most students who did not live north of downtown Ames. McCracken and his committee felt that some other locations would be more satisfactory.

Locations suggested that might be more suitable to McCracken's group included:

(1) The open flat land west of Squaw Creek along the north side of Lincoln Way. Such a location would be central to both the west and east sides of town.

(2) The board already had the Ames High School Field House located on the south side of Lincoln Way and east of Grand Avenue. It was argued that combining a new high school with the existing facilities already there would be more economical than starting over at the north Grand Avenue location proposed by the board.

(3) The open land lying north of the Chicago &

North Western Railroad tracks and between Brookridge and Squaw Creek. The central location made this option commendable.

(4) The existing site of the old Central School on the west side of Clark between Fifth and Sixth Streets. The location in the center of town made it a good location for the high school, the fourth ward committee contended.

FOURTH WARD COMMITTEE'S CHOICE

On February 8, 1937 the Fourth Ward Committee met with the school board. McCracken read, for the information of the board, a petition requesting that a bond issue for $150,000 be authorized, which with the $150,000 now in the sinking fund, would be used:

(a) To construct a new high school building".. on the site of the present Central Junior High School and to purchase additional adjoining ground, the total cost not to exceed $200,000.

(b) To purchase an adequate site in the fourth ward and construct thereon a grade school. Also to construct an addition to the present Welch School for a gymnasium, auditorium, and music room. The total cost of all these grounds, buildings and equipment not to exceed $100,000.

The committee, however, withheld filing that petition, explaining that they intended to file the petition only in case another petition, requesting a bond issue for construction of a senior high building on the Thirteenth Street site, was filed.[5] The Fourth Ward Committee was bargaining for a say in decisions about a new high school.

EDUCATOR'S ADVICE SOUGHT

In view of the number of locations proposed for the new high school, the school board brought Dean C. P. Packer of the University of Iowa's College of Education to Ames to study the matter. Looking back now after fifty years, Dean Packer's recommendations make interesting reading.

Of the low land west of Squaw Creek, Dean Packer warned "The low land belonging to the College located between the downtown and College section eliminates itself because it is subject to overflow. Any adequate protection against this would probably cost more than the school plant itself."

Dean Packer's top choice for the school's site was the board's announced choice. Packer's report included this comment: "The territory on the north side of town in the vicinity of Thirteenth Street and Grand Avenue is, without doubt, the best and only sensible place to locate the school. Forty or fifty acres of land may be secured which permit not only giving the school plant itself adequate setting but will permit development of a play field, tennis courts, parking space, all of the many necessary features of a modern school plant."

As for the "downtown" site at Clark and Fifth, Dean Packer felt that location "automatically eliminates itself as being too limited in area even with possible extensions. If business occupancy about it is further extended, and there is no reason to believe it will not be, it becomes increasingly undesirable as a high school center aside from its very limited area." He further stated that this site perpetuated the problem that *resulted from students having to cross the heavily traveled mainline C.& N.W. tracks between the school and the field house.* That site could offer only a short term solution at best.

About the field house site on Lincoln Way, Dean Packer felt that it had serious drawbacks but would still be a better choice for the high school than the Clark Avenue and Fifth Street site.

In the meantime, the Ames Planning Commission brought Flavil Shurtliff, a nationally recognized city planning engineer from New York, to Ames to advise the city on overall expansion of city facilities. As a part of his study while in Ames, Shurtliff considered various sites for the new high school. His recommendation was that the Thirteenth Street location was, without question, the logical site to choose. In his opinion, the city was about to make substantial growth to the north.[6]

On February 16, 1937, a public meeting, sponsored by the Fourth Ward Committee, was held in the Collegiate Methodist Church. There were 100 in attendance on that occasion. The consensus of that meeting was to ask the board to ask voters to choose between three possible sites for a new high school. A straw vote taken that evening indicated substantial support for the downtown Central School site.[7]

On February 26, 1937, the planning commission advised the school board that they unanimously rec-

---

[5] *School Board Minute Book*, No. 5, p.217.

[6] *Ames Tribune,* March 5, 1937, p.5. See question No.53.

[7] On February 8, 1938, a delegation of fourth ward women called upon Superintendent Larson asking him to convey to the board their suggestion that a site east of Beach Avenue on the south side of Lincoln Way be considered. They suggested that such a location would encourage favorable fourth ward votes and reduce transportation costs. The delegation included Mrs. P. G. Robinson, Mrs. H. H. Knight, Mrs. C. A. Iverson, & Mrs. E. L. Cady. *School Board minutes:* February 8,1938.

This aerial photo shows the railroad depot grounds located one block south of Ames High School as it appeared before the city acquired depot ground for off street parking. Note that there was no crossing at Clark Avenue. High school students crossed the tracks on foot every time they went to physical education classes at the field house on Lincoln Way. Passenger trains stopped at the Ames depot extended well beyond Clark Avenue, the apparent reason for a court injunction that prevented a legal crossing at this location. Photo by the late Olav Smedal.

ommended the Thirteenth Street site. "We can find no reason to continue to build on the present (Central School) site," their report stated, pointing out that their responsibility, as charged by the city ordinance, was to advise all city boards on such building decisions. The Central site should be cleared as soon as a new high school is completed and should be then combined with the old high school building site on the east side of Clark to make an adequate area for a junior high school operation. The Central School site would be best used for school grounds including physical education purposes.

The board decided to ask the voters to choose between the Thirteenth Street location and the old Central School site. The decision to hold that referendum was made in spite of the fact that the board members had the authority to make the site selection themselves. Pressure on the board regarding site selection had them concerned for the passage of the important bond issue involved.

The referendum was set for March 8, 1937. Some school board members were confident that the Thirteenth Street site would be selected.

That vote was to settle the question of a location for a new high school. The election of board members also was a part of that referendum. The Fourth Ward Committee sponsored their own candidate[8] for one of the openings on the board, and they distributed handbills across the town asking for folks to vote for the downtown Central School site.

QUERIES PRESENTED TO BOARD

The school board, when they set the date for the referendum, asked the public to submit questions which the board would collectively answer before the day of the voting. A public meeting was then set for March 3 at which time the questions would be presented together with the board's answers. There were 118 questions submitted; 57 of the questions were submitted by McCracken. On March 4, the *Tribune* published 40 of those questions together with answers. On March 5 and 6, the *Tribune* published the remaining 78 questions with the board's responses. Those questions dealt with such matters as transportation of students, bonding levels, how large Ames would have to be before there could be two high schools (one for each side of town), and what would be done with the field house.[9]

Questions also had to do with why the board had not considered such sites as the one adjacent to Brookridge Avenue and on the east side of Squaw Creek. Wasn't the board overlooking the flat land west of Squaw Creek as a site that would "unite the town" because of its location?

A map showing the senior high school student

---

[8] Their candidate was P. G. Robinson, professor of mathematics at Iowa State. His statement made on March 5 on the front page of the *Tribune* reflected the attitude of the Fourth Ward Committee. In advocating a site "near the population center" he stated, with reference to the state owned land located west of Squaw Creek, "I rather object to its being cast aside with the simple statement that it overflows." He further stated that we need and want a senior high building, but the people must face the fact that if 40 percent ...oppose a chosen site (board's choice of Thirteenth Street), it will be next to impossible to get a favorable vote on a bond issue." (See note No.10)

[9] One question (submitted by the board itself) was: "What is the school census for the fourth ward for the past ten years and what is the school census for the three downtown wards for the past ten years?" The answer was that the current census showed that there were 753 school students in the fourth ward and 2,126 students in the downtown wards. The ten year growth was 19% for the fourth ward and slightly more in the downtown wards. See question No. 95 *Ames Tribune,* March 8,1937, p.8.

population distribution appeared in the *Tribune* of March 6, 1937. On it was a dot for each senior high student as they were related to the two locations in question. It explained that 34 fourth ward students lived beyond the two mile line as measured from the Thirteenth street location, while 62 students lived beyond the two mile line as measured from the Clark and Fifth Street location.

The board was also explaining that putting the high school near Squaw Creek would not decrease transportation costs as compared with the Thirteenth Street location. It had been shown that 75% of the student body lived in downtown Ames and that the percentage of the high school enrollment living within one mile of the Thirteenth Street site was well within the criteria for a high school location.

Also on March 6, 1937, a rebuttal to the board's answers to the 118 questions was printed in the *Tribune*. Written by McCracken, he stated that his committee disagreed with much of the board's information. One of the questions had asked if Ames Superintendent M. G. Davis had carried on academic work under Dr. Packer in Iowa City. The board's answer was, "Yes. In any event, however, this should not discredit either Superintendent Davis or Dean Packer." In his rebuttal at this point, McCracken charged that "Dean Packer's trip to Ames was merely a matter of form and only a verification of Superintendent Davis's conclusions on the matter."

CENTRAL SITE WINS OUT

On Monday, March 8, 1937, 2,009 Ames voters went to the polls. The downtown, or "Central site" won approval by a margin of 299 votes: 1,154 for Central - 855 (42.44%) for 13th & Grand. P.G.Robinson, the Fourth Ward Committee's candidate for the school board, unseated W. H. Root, who had been serving the board as its president, by a margin of 17 votes (1,011 to 994). A center of town location for the high school had been the decisive issue.[10]

The referendum on the bond issue and the related debate on the plans for both a high school building and improvements in the fourth ward were to follow.

On April 2, 1937, since the board was not proposing to include a new elementary school in the fourth ward in the forthcoming bond referendum, the Fourth Ward Committee submitted their counter petition calling for the inclusion of a new elementary school as well as a gymnasium addition to Welch School with the same bond issue for the new high school. It was understood that two referendums would be required.

The board's own petition, which was for bonds to build a high school and the addition of a gymnasium onto Welch School, came to a vote on May 5, 1937 with 1,854 citizens voting. 1,673 voted favorably and 170 voted against the petition.

A few days later the board publicized their opposition to the fourth ward's counter petition which was to be voted upon a few days later.[11]

On May 12, 1937, the fourth ward's petition drew a vote of 1,136 with only 56 favorable votes and 1,075 voting no. The board had lost on the deci-

Ames High School (1939 - 1961) that replaced the 1881 building. It was built on this site as the result of the referendum held in 1937 that had gone against the board's recommendation to build on land at the Thirteenth Street and Grand Avenue location. ID No.118.648.1

The Ames High School (now Ames City Hall) as it appeared in an aerial photo in 1950s. Across Clark Avenue to the east of the high school was the 1912 high school building that became a junior high school in 1939. The 1912 building was torn down in 1981. Note that the new high school building was bound by streets and developed properties. Photo by the late Olav Smedal. ID No. 164.910.3-4-5

[10]Remembering the Fourth Ward Committee candidate's statement about 40 percent opposing a chosen site, it can be pointed out that in that referendum of March 8,1937, slightly over 42 percent of the voters opposed that downtown central site. (See Note No.8)

[11]*Ames Tribune* of May 11,1937, p.1. School board issued statement opposing the bond issue to be voted upon the following day.

Aerial photo taken after 1951 and the conversion of a main portion of the depot grounds into city parking lots. This picture shows the south side of Ames High School at the right. At left on south side of Lincoln Way is the Ames High field house. Students still crossed those railroad tracks enroute to the field house every school day. Photo by the late Olav Smedal.

sion as to where to build and had won on the less important matter of building an elementary school in the fourth ward at the same time.

It would be twenty-eight years before the school board could arrange to purchase the eight residential properties located immediately west of the high school.[12] In the meantime with Public Works Administration funds that had been awarded, it had been possible to include an auditorium and gymnasium with the new Ames High School.

By 1958, high school enrollments had approached the maximum capacity of 800 for that building on Clark Avenue downtown. With enrollments growing, the board was having to discuss plans for a new high school in a location that would permit expansion.

The result was our present-day high school located on an adequate tract of land between 16th and 20th streets on Ridgewood Avenue. Soon after the present high school was opened in 1961, the student enrollment passed the 1,000 count. After 1961, the downtown high school building was converted to use as a junior high.

With younger-aged students using the downtown building, open areas for physical training and a playground had, in some ways, become even more criti-

cal. The field house was sold. In 1967 the City of Ames vacated the one block of Wilson Avenue that bordered the west side of the school building. This block plus the lots acquired in the block to the west provided some much needed school ground area. Until that time the building had literally been a sidewalk bound building.[13]

Ground had been purchased in 1964 on the south side of Sixth Street about six blocks west of the school and located west of the railroad viaduct for athletic practice and physical education classes for junior high students. In the meantime, the students who used that building since 1939, of necessity, had adapted to the rather serious limitations that every expert consultant had predicted when the site was selected in the first place.

In November of 1958, Ames voters overwhelmingly approved the bond issue for the new and better located Ames High School that we still have today. This time the west Ames vote was 626 to 165 in support of the proposal. The town was unified on that one. This time the board had wisely selected the new site making the bond issue the only matter to go to a referendum.

E. C. McCracken, the man who had so actively coached and spearheaded the movement in 1937 to persuade Ames voters to build a high school on the one block-square downtown location, moved away from Ames in 1938, apparently some months before the new building opened. As we drive past the building today we might well realize that time has worked out a correction in the matter. The new high school

---

12 Deed records indicate that the board had paid about $168,000 for eight residential properties. The houses were all sold for $1 each with the stipulation that the purchasers remove them within a specified time. Deeds were dated in late 1966 and in 1967.

13 "Street-bound" might be a better description. Stepping outside of that building found you literally "on the street."

that opened in the fall of 1939 was, in fact, a fine structure. As a school building, however, it was in the wrong environment to function for very long in meeting Ames's educational needs.[14]

Certainly that building had served up its last ounce of utility as a school building and has blossomed into a fuller life as a "well located" City Hall.

Sept.1994

---

[14]On January 3, 1938, the Ames City Planning Commission passed a resolution, which they passed along to the school board, expressing their continued disapproval of building a new high school on the old Central School site between Fifth and Sixth Streets on Clark Avenue. They advised the purchase of additional land nearby to make the site "reasoanably satisfactory" and that an effort be made to rezone the area to slow down further business development.

Chapter 7

From Excursion Days To VEISHEA

The idea of bringing Iowa people to Ames to see Iowa State College in action was not new with the founding of VEISHEA in 1922. Iowa State's President William M. Beardshear, back in 1898, had invited the people of Iowa to visit the college campus, and see what was being done for them at Ames.

In his History of Iowa State College, Professor Earl D. Ross, wrote that Dean Charles F. Curtiss had observed a similar program at the Guelph Agricultural College, and suggested the idea to President Beardshear. Beardshear became president of Iowa State in 1891 and named Curtiss to his post as Dean of Agriculture in 1897, replacing Tama Jim Wilson when Wilson became the nation's Secretary of Agriculture, and a member of President McKinley's cabinet.

The Iowa Agricultural College was established under the provisions of the Morrill Act of 1862.[1] It was to be the "People's College," and Agriculture

---

[1]Created by the Iowa legislature in 1858 it was designated as Iowa's land grant college in 1864.

Excursion Day in 1898. These folks were at the depot to welcome visitors arriving on the trains. Left to right are Mary Tilden, Abbie Drake, in long dark dress, Beulah Bingham, with parasol, Bess Reed, and Harry Brown, a senior that year at I.S.C. ID No. 5.21B.1-3

was the major industry in Iowa. During the regime of President Chamberlain, Beardshear's predecessor, there had been some controversy about the curriculum at the College. Agricultural interests in the state had expressed opposition to the teaching of courses at Ames that some believed did not bear directly upon farm operations. Beardshear, with his broad understanding of the educational needs of Iowa people, came to be spoken of as a man of the people. Beardshear was quick to find ways to bond the people of Iowa to their College at Ames.

THE FIRST EXCURSION DAYS

At President Beardshear's request, the Chicago & North Western Railroad provided special excursion rates for visitors to the campus on August 17, 1898.

Examples of round-trip rail fares to Ames from various points were:[2]

Clinton.	$2.50
Belle Plaine	1.50
Cedar Rapids	1.75
Boone.	.45
Marshalltown.	1.00
Jefferson.	1.50
Nevada.	.25
DesMoines..	1.00
Webster City.	1.00

Station agents on the C. & N. W. Main Line and north-south branches all across Iowa were sent ample supplies of printed invitations to be supplied to local citizens at their respective ticket offices.

This was Beardshear's invitation to the people of Iowa:

To our college neighbors of all classes: Greeting.

There will be a grand autumn jubilee of the farmers, mechanics, and laboring people of Iowa, together with their friends at the Iowa State College October 4. You, your family and special friends are most cordially invited to be present.

All the friends of the three H's - Head, Heart and Hand and of the man with his coat off in the blaze of this nineteenth century are thrice welcome.

An excellent program consisting of the exhibition of all the departments of the college, bands of music, and addresses by eminent speakers including State School Superintendent Barret and Governor Shaw will be provided. There will be cheap excursion on a number of railways that day. Everybody invited in behalf of the College Authorities.

Wm. M. Beardshear, President

Twenty-five hundred excursion tickets were sold by the railroad. That was in addition to regular rate passengers that came to Ames that day. Hundreds flocked from all around central Iowa. The *Ames Intelligencer* stated that the crowd visiting the campus that day exceeded expectations. "Six thousand is a conservative estimate of crowds that day," the paper stated. Secretary Fowler, of the state fair, was here that day and estimated the crowd on campus to have been ten thousand.

"President Beardshear has purchased a large tent for use on the campus during Excursion Day celebrations. It has a seating capacity of three thousand." -Ames Intelligencer - August 11, 1898. ID No.145.798.5

A local news account stated that the people who came to Ames "were pleased with what they saw," and the remark that was common was, "I had no idea of the size and magnitude of the college. The benefit that will come to the college from these people who will tell in their home neighborhoods of the things they saw at this magnificent property of the state will be incalculable and (will) greatly increase attendance."[3]

The *Intelligencer* of August 11, 1898 announced that, "the Ladies Aid Societies of the Baptist and Methodist Churches are arranging to serve lunches on the College grounds to the Wednesday Excursionists." Ames residents met the trains that day to guide visitors to the campus, usually by way of the Ames & College Railroad (Dinkey) that departed from its downtown terminal north across the tracks from the C. & N.W. depot. That same issue reported that President Beardshear had arranged the purchase of a large tent with the seating capacity of 3,000 for use on the campus during the Excursion Day programs.

[2]*Ames Evening Times,* Sept. 29, 1898.
[3]*Ames Intelligencer,* August 18, 1898.

In addition to inspecting the campus, the Excursion Day crowds were guided on tours of the various college buildings by students and faculty who also explained the activities being carried on in them. Inspecting the College's collection of farm machinery and livestock was also the order of the day.

The local paper reported that "there was a literary program in the great tent that enthralled the people."

Dr. Beardshear presided and made a welcoming address; then Gov. Shaw and John Cownie of the state board of control[4] spoke. Dr. Bearshear said, in substance, "I like this enthusiasm. Any cause good enough for the hearts and heads of the people is worthy of their enthusiasm, and I certainly see it here today. I never felt so much like a boy in my life as I did last night when I lay awake for hours, afraid that it would rain, and afraid that you would not come! But you are all here. In the face of great gatherings, in the face of the magnitude of statistics that make Iowa better than the gold fields, there is no product of earth or heaven that in the scales will weight more than these *boys and girls*, for whose education this institution was founded, and in whose interests you are here today."

---

[4]Predecessor of the present Iowa Board of Regents.
[5]The 4 H symbol was adopted in about 1911.

The legislature had established the College as a coeducational school. Beardshear did not miss an opportunity to point that fact out when he said "the one grand purpose of this work is the building up of an all-around man and woman. I would not give a cent for a man without a good steady, all-around woman at his side, and we are here to make them both."

The governor included in his remarks the advice that "farmers should send their sons to college that they may be made thinking men; thinkers are needed in this day of close competition." John Cownie advised the visitors to "learn more about the institutions of the state so that they would favor more liberal appropriations." His words were loudly applauded.

Dr. Beardshear's terminology was significant, as was that of the governor. It was farm folks that they referred to frequently. Over 50% of Iowa's population in the late 1800s lived on Iowa's farms. Beardshear had referred to the students as "boys and girls." In recent years the principle of "parentis locus" has been abandoned on college and university campuses. Note also Beardshear's use of the phrase, the 3 Hs, "Head, Heart, and Hand" in his 1898 invitation. Jesse Field (Shambaugh), of Shenandoah, founder of the 4-H movement, may have been present that day. (The 4-H program originally used the 3 H symbol).[5]

Excursion Day participants, in 1904, are watching a parade as it passes Agricultural Hall. This building has been renovated and is today named Carrie Chapman Catt Hall. ID No.29.146A.2

On September 29, 1898 the *Ames Intelligencer* announced, that "the Second Grand Excursion to the Iowa Agricultural College will be run to Ames on October 4th. The unprecedented success of the first Excursion led the college people to commence at once to the end that a second excursion be run this fall. The people of Ames having learned a great deal with the last excursion will be in better shape to handle people than they were before. The college campus and the college grounds, in general, will be at their best at this particular time.and the people of Iowa should not fail to take advantage to see the grandest of Iowa's educational institutions. Secretary (Tama Jim) Wilson will be here, and an excellent program will be prepared."

1901

"Seven thousand people visited the state's big institution last Thursday, taking advantage of the low rates" stated the September 16, 1901 issue of the *Ames Intelligencer*. The first train arrived at 8 o'clock and they kept arriving until noon. The C. & N.W. ran five regular and seven special trains into Ames from Clinton, Elmore, Moville, Toledo, Jewell, Audubon, Onawa, Paulina, Missouri Valley, Harlan and Des Moines. The motor line and hacks transported the crowd to the college grounds.

The Ames depot grounds had been cleared of most of the boxcars usually there for switching so that the special trains could remain on siding during the day.

At 2:45 the exercises were begun in the big tent on the central campus. President Beardshear addressed the large audience speaking of the growth of the college and the special needs occasioned by the fire of the previous winter that had destroyed the main building. P. A. Smith, veteran newspaper man and a member of the house of representatives, spoke along the line of a legislative campaign for appropriations. Music was provided by the college Glee Club, and State Superintendent Barret concluded the program with an address.

The *Intelligencer* described the occasion: "A large majority of the visitors were farmers from all over the state interested in their agricultural college, in its fine stock, its barns and its dairy. To most, the occasion was very similar to a county fair. Over in the shops, in Agricultural Hall and in other buildings of the school, great crowds stood and watched the handiwork of the students."

"There was no school in the classrooms during that day. Students worked in the shops with promises of double time, and freshmen walked around in their cadet uniforms going through their music drill for the benefit of the spectators."

YOU ARE ALWAYS WELCOME AT THE PEOPLE'S COLLEGE

1902

President Beardshear's death occurred on August 5, 1902, and Dean Edgar Stanton became acting president of Iowa State. "You are always welcome at the people's college" was emphasized in Stanton's statement of welcome to excursion visitors that year. That year Excursioin Day took place on October 10. Excursion Days sometimes involved two days of programming for the visitors.

By that time, it had become the custom to invite school bands from Iowa high schools. That year music by the Liscombe Band, the College Cadet Band and Peshak's Band was featured. That custom continues today with many school bands coming to Ames for VEISHEA parades. In 1902, Iowa State had 1,400 students enrolled. 1,100 students were reported to have remained on campus to participate in carrying on the programs for the excursionists. There were addresses, picnics, tours and special "get acquainted" conferences that involved invited legislators.

1903

The fourth annual Excursion Day in Ames was held on September 26, 1903. "Ames entertained fully fifteen thousand people, about eight thousand of which came on trains alone," stated the *Ames Intelligencer* of October 1, 1903. The account continued, "These Excursions prove very satisfactory to the President of the College, as to the entire faculty, to note the fact that so many people are interested enough in this great institution to come and see as well as learn from it."

1904

Excursion Day had become a regular annual event on the Iowa State campus. In 1904 the occasion referred to the special day as "An Old Fashioned Basket Picnic and Harvest Home Festival." The printed program for September 30, 1904 was captioned, "Excursion Day - and Harvest Home Festival."

The C. & N. W. Railroad was still granting special rates from a variety of points on their line to Ames for the people of Iowa. There were eleven excursion special trains that pulled into the Ames depot on that October day. One train from the west pulled fourteen coaches and was said to contain over 1,200 people. A total of twenty-thousand visitors were reported to have been on campus that day.

At 12:45 a livestock parade formed at the barns on the east side of the campus and with visiting bands, and farm machinery made what the local Intelligencer called a "very interesting and instructive parade" around the central campus.

A highlight of the 1904 celebration was the laying of the cornerstone for the new "Central building" that stood on the site of the former "Main" building. Twelve thousand people witnessed that event as it was conducted by President Storms and Governor Cummins.[6]

1906

The *Ames Evening Times* of October 11, 1906, referred to Excursion Day of October 5 as having been a "Hummer" estimating that 8,000 visitors had

[6]In 1938, Central Building was renamed "Beardshear Hall" in memory of former President William M. Beardshear.

[7]There were a few years when the C.& N.W. did not offer excursion rates because they offered such special rates for the Iowa State Fair instead.

come from out of town to see the campus for the day.

1907 - 1908

Two years lapsed in the customary Excursion Day celebrations due to the lack of agreements with the railroads. However, because of many reports of disappointment on the part of Iowa people, the authorities succeeded in again making satisfactory arrangements with the C. &. N. W. line to run the excursions to Ames.

THEY CALLED IT A RIOT IN 1909

Following the 1909, Excursion Day[7] the October 7th issue of the *Intelligencer* reported a "Student Riot." It seems that about 300 students came downtown on Friday night..."took in the North Western station.".. then "invaded" the business section. They hauled a wagon from Morris Livery, placing it across the streetcar tracks. Parley Sheldon generously offered them free rides to the campus on the streetcar, which they turned down.

They next visited the Olympia Candy Kitchen and helped themselves to about $3 worth of candy. Moving then to the Scenic theater they marched

Another view of the 1904 Excursion Day celebration. The Dinkey railroad tracks can be seen in the foreground. The campanile on central campus and the large meeting tent can be seen through the trees at left. ID No. 29.146A.1

through the house... "with much gusto" with sensible people "tapping their heads knowingly." Back to the pop corn wagon at the Douglas corner the crowd demanded free pop corn and peanuts. Because Frank Smith refused that request, someone threw a cabbage at his wagon breaking out one of the plate glass windows. The town marshall finally arrested three of the boys releasing them on $10 bonds.

On Saturday morning President Storms and Mayor Tilden held a consultation deciding to drop charges after the boys agreed to pay the $16 in damages they had caused. The editor commented that "it is far from our intentions to say that the boys shouldn't be permitted to have their fun, but rioting goes beyond the borderline of fun. We believe that a word of caution is unnecessary, because the boys have probably already come to the realization that they carried their Friday night romp a bit too far."

That writer for the Ames newspaper back in 1909 seemed undecided whether to refer to that post celebration as a "riot" or as a "romp."

A tradition had begun that later involved program days on the local campus for Iowa people that were known variously as "Harvest Home Excursions," "College Days," "Farm and Home Weeks," and a wide range of short courses for Iowa citizens.

College Day in 1910. The crowd is waiting in front of Central Building (renamed Bearshear in 1938) for the big parade. Note the three leaf clover emblems representing heart, head and hand. In about 1911 a fourth leaf was added to represent "health" in the mission of the 4H program. ID No.158.873.3-4-5

The Ag Carnival in May 1915. Exhibits and carnival attractions are seen here south of State Gymnasium. A baseball game is in progress in background. ID No. 152.840.3-5

Daisy dance performed by Iowa State senior women as part of May Day celebration in 1910. Six women in center wore yellow cheese cloth dresses representing the center of the daisy. Others wore white to portray daisy petals. May Day celebration became part of VEISHEA in 1922. Photo courtesy Iowa State University Library / University Archives. ID No.145.798.1-2-3

St. Patrick's Day parade brought the engineers downtown, shown here in March 1907. ID No.133.730.1

The word "Excursion" seems to have given way to more accurate descriptive words as the result of the development of the automobile and good Iowa roads. Railroad special rates were a factor in getting people to Ames until about 1910.

Later, there were special days for respective college divisions. (Ag Carnival, St. Patrick's Day, Home Economics Festival and May Day celebrations on campus.) Finally, in 1922, VEISHEA was organized

Civil Engineers march on campus on St Patrick's Day in 1911. ID No.150.826.3

and continues to this day. The Excursion Day celebrations of earlier years were most often in October to relate to the farm harvest season. Today, VEISHEA is held in the spring of the year. But the purpose is still to bring the citizens of Iowa to Ames to see for themselves what is being done for them on the Iowa State campus.

In 1922, VEISHEA brought all of the division celebrations into one all-college exposition. The first VEISHEA parade went downtown by way of Lincoln Way. A prize winning float was this Home Economics float entitled "Household Arts." Original photo courtesy of Dave Burlingmair.   ID No. 203.1153.5

April 18, 1995

The 1916 St Patrick's Day parade came downtown following ceremonies held that morning on the steps of Central Building (Beardshear Hall).   ID No. 88.467.1-2

Chapter 8

Where Did Those Boys Go!

Three boys were lost. Last seen at about five p.m. on Sunday, they had disappeared into thin air.[1]

The Ames fire whistle blew at an early hour on Monday, April 8, 1918. Repeated at short intervals, it signified a public emergency more urgent than the usual house fire. Word quickly circulated that the Kaiser had been captured.

Some were reporting that President Wilson had been assassinated!

The telephone company's switchboard lit up. All operators were called back to handle the emergency. The Kaiser had not been captured nor had President Wilson been assassinated. Three boys (two were age six and the other was eight) had disappeared. Glenn and Gale Clem, twin sons of Mr. and Mrs. R. R. Clem, and Harley Grover, son of Mr. and Mrs. W. H. Grover, had last been seen playing in their backyards on Twelfth Street late Sunday afternoon.

The boys' parents were near panic with anxiety.

Ames Police Chief Fred Willey, policeman John Kelso, Mayor Ed Graves and Street Commissioner Art McCoy had conducted a search throughout the entire night without success. Ames Boy Scouts had joined the search. School officials excused high school students to help find the boys. Central School's janitor organized a search party made up of 65 boys. Iowa State College offered student volunteers. Squaw Creek and Skunk River beds were combed, ravines checked, and alleyways double-checked by volunteers.

Foul play, including abduction, was feared. Still no clues.

More rumors surfaced to add to the concerns. Boys had been seen in the sand pit over on the Skunk River. Someone reported seeing some boys climbing into a box car that had since been moved out with a freight train.

Gale, Glenn, and Harley in the meantime were literally "in the dark." They were unaware of the efforts that were being exerted to find them.

At about five o'clock on Sunday afternoon, they had become curious about a vacant house located on

Gale Clem, at age six. Today, he is still an Ames resident. He remembers well the events that occurred in 1918, just three days after his sixth birthday, when he and his twin brother Glen created a wave of anxiety across our town when they seemed to drop off the "face of the earth." ID No. 176.988.2-4

Glen Clem, at age six when he and his brother, Gale, were the object of a city wide search when they found a unique way to "disappear into thin air." ID No. 176.988.2-4

---

[1] *Weekly Tribune,* April 8, 1918, p.1, and *The Ames Evening Times,* April 8, 1918, p.1.

the northeast corner of Grand Avenue and Twelfth Street. The house was locked up tight; but a coal chute located on the far side of the house offered a very attractive solution to that problem.

After checking all of the rooms, they decided to see how dark it might be inside a large walk-in closet on the second floor. All three entered the closet and closed the door; they found themselves in total darkness.

To their dismay, they discovered that they were locked in; there was a slip lock on the outside of the closet door. They panicked; kicking and screaming they tried over and over again to get that door open. They huddled on the floor exhausted. They slept some. It got cold as the night became, it seemed to them, an eternity.

During the night, Mrs. Clem and a neighbor entered the house, but the boys were so frightened that they kept very still. The Grover boy, older than the Clem boys, had insisted that there might be man-eaters lurking in a vacant house.[2] Harley's older sister had recently filled him in on tales of goblins and the likes of "man eaters."

During the night the boys thought they heard Mr. Clem going slowly up Grand Avenue on his motorcycle. They yelled at the top of their voices, but to no avail.

The fire whistle was blown routinely every hour, indicating that the boys had not been found. Finally, the boys saw a sliver of light under the closet door, indicating that day had dawned.

Bob Thompson was Ames High School's coach and physical training teacher. At about eight o'clock, he decided to again check that vacant house. He found that locked closet. Opening the door, he discovered the frightened boys huddled there.

---

[2] Is as recalled by Gale Clem, 1996 interview.

First reports described the boys as being asleep when Thompson found them. Later the boys said that they had heard Thompson and had attempted to call out, but their voices had been so weakened by their ordeal and by the closeness of the air in the closet, that Thompson had not heard them.

Gale Clem, an Ames resident today, recalls that as they walked into their backyard that morning there was a large crowd on hand. The fire whistle at the light plant was blown for a long ten minutes to let the town know that they had been found!

Gale tells how it took time to "live down" that experience in 1918, with everyone asking them why they went into that house in the first place. At first they were reluctant to talk much about it. They were not too sure about how much to say regarding the way they got into that vacant house.

There was immediate thanksgiving. The two families felt great relief. Everyone in Ames that day rejoiced with them over the happy outcome.

As for the boys, they recovered fast. The Clem boys happily greeted their dog that had been with them the day before, and they had a good breakfast. By mid-morning they were off to school and back to "near normal." In time they would realize that they had experienced more adventure than they had bargained for.

The *Ames Tribune* writer, in the issue of April 8, 1918, admonished readers not to blame the boys too much. "It was just a case of boys being boys. Some of you older duffers have caused just as much anxiety to your parents in days gone by...place yourself in the place of the three boys and there you are."

It had been a day in the life of our town. A very big day, *and night,* in the life of those three boys!

May 31, 1996

Chapter 9

Coal Mining History Near Ames

Coal, Coal:

"We have made arrangements to deliver Squaw Creek coal to parties in the city. You can save from 25 to 50 c. per ton by leaving your order with us." Best grade now $4.25 H.T. & B. Co. *Ames Intelligencer* of December 2, 1882

Zenorsville miners occupied small shanties located on the hillsides adjacent to the mines. Mining families engaged in the raising of livestock, poultry and gardening on a self sufficiency basis. Photo probably from the late 1880s. Photo courtesy of J. Howard Clemens ID No.19.89.2

Coal made the United States the leading industrialized nation in the world. It also heated our homes and cooked our food. If you are much over sixty, you

Sometime after 1905 the Zenorsville Church was moved from the Zenorsville village less than a mile to the southwest corner of the county road intersection one mile west of the Boone County line. It continued to operate for many years. Photo courtesy of Mamie Eisenhower birthplace. ID No.193.1094.1-3

---

[1] In 1851 in Sec.12 of Jackson township in Boone County. See *Boone County Historical Soc. Trail Tales,* No. 52 - p. 16
[2] *Boone County History* (1914) Vol. I , p.222

grew up in a home with a coal furnace and a coal room in the basement. You did your share of shoveling coal into that furnace and also took out the ashes. Soot on winter snow and burned out chimneys may be remembered.

The town of Zenorsville on December 16, 1885. Unincorporated, the town had a U.S. Post Office for years. It was located west of Gilbert a half mile into Boone County. At one time Zenorsville had three active coal mines. Photo courtesy J. Howard Clemens. ID No.19.89.3

Before changes in the distribution of heating fuels made Iowa coal obsolete, local coal was a valuable commodity.

Ames once had coal mines nearby. The first such mine was opened in the fall of 1871 by Will Parker and his brother in Section 1 of Jackson Township in Boone County. By the 1880s, there were three operating mines in the area located about three miles west of Gilbert. In 1872 the Hutchison brothers (John and James), who came from a Pennsylvania coal mining background, had acquired the original mine and its operation.

The village of Zenorsville[1] developed near the mine site. By the 1880s, the Hutchison mine was producing 7,000 tons annually. It operated to a depth of 100 feet under a 40-acre area with a coal vein three feet, nine inches thick. In 1882, Hutchison Brothers employed 40 men in their mine.[2] The coal was said to be of a high quality.

In 1880, the inspector of mines reported that the J. Clemons mine employed 50 men, the Hutchison Brothers mine, 35, and the Joseph York mine, 8, making a total of 93 miners employed. That same report indicated that the coal vein at each of those mines was four feet, two inches thick. Zenorsville was reported to have 400 residents. There was a general store, a post office, a meat market, a few other business shops, a church, and a schoolhouse.

The Zenorsville mine operations in the late days of its existance, probably around 1905. The view is believed to be the entrance to one of the slant shafts that opened onto bottom lands at the foot of the hill bordering the Squaw Creek west bank. The location is about a quarter mile south of the county road that runs west from Gilbert. On a marginal commercial basis, coal was being removed from several such slant shafts as late as the depression years of the 1930s. Photo courtesy J.Howard Clemens ID No.193.1093.3-5

Zenorsville store operated by Jim Hutchison. Zenorsville existed as a village community from the 1870s until about 1915. In addition to his store, Hutchison also operated one of the mines in Zenorsville. Photo courtesy Boone County Historical Society ID No. 19.89.1

Zenorsville was never incorporated; however it had a United States Post Office from June 29, 1876 through Dec. 5, 1900. For a time in the 1890s the

Zenorsville mines were the primary source of coal for the Iowa Agricultural College at Ames.[3] By 1900, the coal mines were worked out to the point that operations were no longer were profitable. Miners and their families then moved elsewhere for employment. Some of the houses and stores were moved to other locations. Some were said to have been moved over to the town of Gilbert.[4]

Today, the former site of the mining village of Zenorsville is beautiful rolling timbered pasture and farm land. Walking through the area, you see slag piles that have eroded for a century. A few old foun-

Slag pile that remains from the Zenorville mine operations. 1976 Photo - Farwell Brown. ID No.25.124.1

Indications of one of the vertical mine shafts found on the hillside west of Gilbert in about 1976. Surrounded by fencing, it was full of water that appeared to be quite deep. ID No.25.124.2

dations remain on the hillsides. Years ago, I strolled the area and came upon the remains of a mine shaft. Brush had been piled over its top to prevent anyone from stumbling into what appeared to be a deep water-filled pit.[5]

THE FIRST SUMMIT MINE

In April 1893, a few years before the Zenorsville mines ceased operations, a five foot vein of coal was struck at the W. S. Johnson farm, three miles north of

---

[3] College buildings were heated by individual coal-burning stoves or funaces until a central-heating plant was built in 1908.
[4] The State Mine Inspector's report for 1901 shows that the J. York Mine was operating for local distribution only, in 1901.
[5] Coal was being removed on a small scale from one or more slant shafts near Squaw Creek by local people as recently as the 1930s.

The scene at the first Summit Mine on October 12, 1895 following the tragic fire that broke out in the mine shaft late the day before. Four men lost their lives when the fire severed the cable that might have brought them to the surface. Photo courtesy of Eugene Eness. ID No.139.765.1-2

Gilbert and four miles southwest of Story City.[6] A mine company was organized with F. H. Greenwalt, Nevada; Harry Wilcox, Story City; A. H. Sprague, Berwick; W. L. Doolittle, Ames; O. J. and G. A. Benjamin, Nevada. Greenwalt was elected president. Capitalization was reported to be $259,000.

A number of coal mining companies sought to purchase the rights to the mine field, but Greenwalt announced that such offers would be declined. In September 1894, the *Story City Herald* reported that the Summit Mine had more orders than it could deliver.

On Oct. 11, 1895, the Summit was the site of a tragic accident when four men on the night shift were suffocated in the mine after they ignited a fire to create a draft for ventilation. An explosion spread the fire into the shaft. The wire cable that operated the

elevator cage was so overheated that it severed on the first attempt to bring the men to the surface. Rescue became impossible.[7]

Smoke was discovered early that evening coming from the lower mine shaft; it was 11 o'clock that night before the fire could be extinguished and the mine cooled sufficiently for a rescue crew to enter. Because of the dense smoke, it was not until 6 o'clock the following morning that the bodies of the four victims were discovered together in a room off of the shaft at the 100-foot level.

Repairs were made and a Story *City Herald* news item on August 14, 1896 reported that the mine was preparing to employ 100 men that fall and winter.

That first Summit Mine continued operating through 1922 when the state mine inspector reported its production limited to local consumption.

A SECOND SUMMIT MINE

In 1923, a second mine opening was announced by a newly organized Summit Coal Company at a location about a quarter mile east of that original 1893 mine.[8] The mine's production of eight million tons was predicted by an appraisal firm. An investment

---

[6] Located in the southeast quarter of section 21 of Lafayette township. Vanderwerker to W. S. Johnson Bk.27, p.214, Story County Land Records.

[7] *The Iowa Register,* October 15, 1895, morning edition, p.1, story: "Miners Meet A Living Death." *Ames Intelligencer,* October 17, 1895, p.1, story: "Death In a Mine."

[8] Located in the northwest quarter of section 27 of LaFayette township. Adjacent to the Chicago & North Western tracks.

The second Summit Mine on the Chicago & Northwestern rail line three miles northeast of Gilbert was forced to close by excessive underground flooding in 1928. Sketch by Dianne Mumm from June 6, 1924 Ames Tribune newsprint photo. ID No. 203.1150.1

of $90,000 in the venture was reported by the *Ames Tribune* on June 13, 1924.[9]

The second Summit Mine was extensively promoted in Story County. Samples of Summit coal were displayed in Ames store windows. News stories and advertisements stimulated interest. William C. Anderson, an experienced mine operator from Des Moines, was the mine's superintendent. J Q. Wickham, former Ames city engineer,[10] was the consulting engineer in charge of the mine's construction and equipment. Directors included O. J. and G. A. Benjamin, owners of the *Nevada Journal;* F. H. Greenwalt, coal operator of Nevada; E. M. Ogden, farmer of Nevada; E. L. McConkie, banker of Nevada; E. B. Hall, Ames coal dealer; Dr. D. W. Harman, M.D. of Ames; and Peter Holt, merchant of Ellsworth. Neal Clemmer was president of the new company.

News reports on the Summit Mine were optimistic. New machinery was expected to be capable of extracting 2,000 tons of fuel a day. "According to computations by state inspectors, the two strata, one 90 feet below the surface of the ground, and the other 30 feet below that, contain from 8,000,000 to 10,000,000 tons of coal within reach of the shaft," stated the *Ames Tribune* story of May 16, 1923. Leases were signed with farmers in the mine's vicinity on 900 acres of land, promising royalties on coal removed from below their respective properties.

By June, 1924 the Summit Mine was reported to be in full production with 50 men employed full time, and an expectation that the number of employees would soon reach 400.[11]

The new mine was being described as (potentially) the county's "second largest employer," with the mine bringing new residents to the Gilbert and Ames communities. Twenty - five residents of Ames became stockholders.

But it was not to work out as planned. That second Summit Mine had operated for about four years when it was forced to cease operations because of

[9] *Ames Tribune,* June 6, 1924, p. 8, Advertisement of the Summit Coal Company, stating that the Summit Mine could produce coal for $1.00 less per ton than more distant sources.
[10] Wickham was Ames City Engineer, 1910 - 1920.
[11] *Ames Tribune,* June 6, 1924, p. 1, "Story County's Coal Mine In Full Operation."

the equipment's inability to pump water from the shafts fast enough. The artesian water flow that exists in that area[12] — the underground water forces that fed numerous flowing wells in the vicinity-was a problem too costly to deal with. In the words of one who was close to the project, it had gone "belly-up."

Coal mining in the Gilbert area had come to a close by 1928.

We have diminishing slag piles, some old foundations in an open pasture, and a few recorded memories to remind us of early-day coal mining successes, of a tragedy and of plans that failed to materialize, all of which once played some part in the economy of our community. In the meantime, other fuels have replaced coal in much of our everyday lives.[13] Today, it is the low sulphur coal that is mined in states like Wyomimg, Kentucky, or Arizona that fuels our local power and central-heating plants. Few private homes or business buildings are now heated with coal.

Slag pile remaining today at the site of the second Summit Mine located near the C.& N.W. tracks northeast of Gilbert. ID No.195.1110.1-2.

THE ZENORSVILLE REUNIONS

Twenty years after most of its inhabitants had moved elsewhere, a few of the former residents of Zenorsville who still lived in the area decided to have a reunion. It began in September, 1918, when between three and four hundred old settlers, neighbors, and friends gathered near the old mines for an old-fashioned picnic and entertainment. The decision was made to make the Zenorsville reunion an annual event.[14] R. B. Hutchison was elected the first reunion president. Those early reunions were held at Hutchison's Pond, located on the Squaw Creek bottom west of Gilbert.[15]

The third reunion was held on August 26, 1920 at Hutchison's Grove (Pond).[16] A picnic dinner was followed by music by a family orchestra from Madrid. Fletcher Clemons was elected president for the following year. Solos included a whistling solo by a woman from Boone and an address by Rev. Hill of Boone. Talks, including an historical sketch of Zenorsville,[17] were given by former residents of Zenorsville.

Those Zenorsville reunions continued through 1930, when the last one to be publicised drew 300 people to the Lester Martin Woods, located a mile north of the Zenorsville Church. Grant Baker, of Boone, presided. A male quartet composed of Van Ess, Leonard Nelson, Clarence Kelly, and Kenneth Goodrich, of Boone sang several songs and talks were given by Grant Baker, Judge Whittaker, Anton Nelson, Representative Hollingsworth, Will Criswell, and Robert Craig. Those from away included residents from Ames, Gilbert, Boone, Jefferson, Story City, Des Moines, and Mason City. "Old residents (of Zenorsville) and their descendants to the third generation, were present."[18]

17 March 1997

---

12 Several artesian wells flow in the immediate area. The mine appears to be in a line with them.

13 Today, oil and gas heat our homes. The Ames Municipal light plant burns Arizona coal; Iowa State University's heating plant burns Kentucky coal.

14 *Ames Tribune,* July 31, 1919, p. 6, "Old Settlers To Picnic Near Old Mine Site."

15 Tradition has it that John L. Lewis, the famous mine labor leader attended one of the Zenorsville reunions.

16 *Ames Tribune,* August 27, 1920, p.4 "Zenorsville Has Pleasant Picnic."

17 Historical sketch of Zenorsville was written by Bruce Hutchison.

18 *Ames Tribune,* September 10, 1928, p.4, "Zenorsville Folk Meet in Reunion." It was held in the Lester Martin woods. The latest publicized reunion was held in September, 1930. See *Ames Tribune,* September 9, 1930, p.2, "Zenorsville Old Settlers Picnic Draws 300 Sunday."

Chapter 10

Meet Me at the Fair!

Following the Chautauqua program days of late summer was the local fair to look forward to in the fall every year. Chautauqua was held in August and the fair came in September or early October.

There was an explanation for the timing of the fair. The Fair Board, organized in 1913, had entered into a cooperative arrangement with the Ames Chautauqua Board to make joint use of the Chautauqua grounds. Because it was a celebration of the harvest season, the fair followed Chautauqua, a very workable arrangement. The Fair Board built and maintained the livestock buildings and track located below the hill on that part of the property owned, but not used, by the Chautauqua Board. The Chautauqua auditorium and the concession buildings used intensively by Chautauqua were also essential to much of the fair's programming.

That fair, held in Ames, was known as the "Central Iowa Fair." An attractive feature of the fair was that they always let school out one full day during its usual three-to-four-day run.

That a fair might be held in Ames was first publicly suggested in 1910. It had been discussed among Ames business leaders before that. There had been a county fair held annually since 1869[1] in Nevada, and there was a feeling that Ames should not duplicate or compete with Nevada's fair. The fair held in Nevada customarily had one day designated as "Ames Day" when "half of the town" of Ames migrated to Nevada. The fair held in Nevada was abandoned in 1910.

The County Fair in Nevada had been held on a fourteen-acre fairgrounds located in the northeast corner of town where a grandstand, race track and exhibition buildings had been built.[2] Sponsored by the Agricultural Society of Story County, the grounds were reincorporated in 1904 with the stated mission the "promotion of agriculture, horticulture, forestry, animal industry, manufactures, domestic arts, amusements, *the holding of fairs,* and for entertainment purposes."[3]

The County Fair had been popular with farm folks and townspeople alike. Every conceivable class of livestock competition was held. The domestic arts competitions usually filled an entire page in the *Nevada Representative* with the names of winners.[4] In October, 1879, Col. John Scott of Nevada, well known stock breeder and one time Lt. Governor of Iowa, described the Nevada fair: "Story County is central in the state; it grows grain and grasses - it has no city. It feeds grain and grasses to horses, cattle and swine. Its fair women and brave men seek to discharge known duties. Out of these elements, year by year, it constructs a fair. Its exhibitions are always reasonably good, and the attendance and receipts are such that the managers have always paid dollar for dollar, and had something left to make re-

---

1   Mortgage Record Book D, p.140, May 7, 1869, County Recorder's Office. Story County Agricultural Society. Original Articles of Incorporation, David Child, President. Purpose: The "improvment of agriculture, horticulture, mechanical arts, and rural domestic economy." "Its principal place of business shall be at Nevada, Story County, Iowa." Members named in articles included: T. C. McCall, I. A. Ringham, T. E. Alderman, David Child, W. G. Murphy, L. W. King, Tobias Kindlespine, James Hawthorn. etc.

2   *Land Record Book P,* p. 356, Warranty Deed dated May 7, 1869, John Goodin to Story County Agricultural Society. Land in w1/2 Sec. 5 -83-22, Story County, Iowa.

3   Articles of Incorporation Record Book No. 1, p.228. February 19, 1904. Story County Recorder's Office. Incorporators: E. C. Button, E. H. Dewel, Jay A. King, R. A. Frazier, and D. M. Grove.

4   *Nevada Representative,* September 22, 1870, "Story County Fair - A Grand Success." Winners in every livestock class listed.

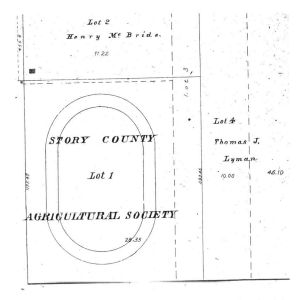

Plat of the Story County fairgrounds in 1903, located on land that cornered on what is today Eleventh Street and "T" Avenue in the northeast corner of Nevada.

Grandstand at the Story County fairgrounds in Nevada in 1909.   The fairgrounds, situated on fourteen acres at the northeast corner of Nevada, were abandoned in 1910.   Drawn by Dianne Mumm from a newsprint photo.   ID No. 190.1127.1

pairs and improvements."[5]   Scott had glowing words about the imported horses from France that had improved those used for "farm purposes while a few horses of good trotting capacity had *stimulated breeding for speed.*"

The County Fair in Nevada, by most reports, was considered successful.   But there was a persistent problem when it came to covering the mortgage interest on the fairgrounds.   The association board felt that the solution would be for the county to own the property.   A proposed $6,000 county appropriation proved to be unpopular among farm folks.   Nevada and Ames voted favorably on the matter, but most farm townships rejected the proposition.[6]   The *Nevada Representative* reported on November 11, 1910, that the voters had rejected that idea by a vote of 2,296 to 1,373.

With the closing of the County Fair in 1910, a group of enterprising Ames men proceeded to plan for a fair to be conducted in Ames.   The first fair to be held in Ames was a one-day affair held at the Chautauqua grounds.   Speeches by all four candidates for the Iowa governorship were featured.   Five

thousand people, mostly farmers, crowded into the auditorium to hear the Republican, Democratic, Progressive, and Prohibition party candidates.   "A unique political feast," the *Ames Intelligencer* called it. "AMES DISTRICT FAIR A MAGNIFICENT AFFAIR" was their headline of October 4, 1912.

By May 30, 1913, the Central Iowa Fair had been incorporated, and all arrangements made for a full scale fair that year.[7]   Incorporators were C. L. Siverly, C. C. Alm, Ed H. Graves, S. S. Kooser, C. A Stewart, George H. Maxwell, W. T. Barr, Charles F. Curtiss, Carl Rosenfeld, J. J. Grove, and Parley Sheldon.   The names of well-known area farmers, Ames businessmen, Ames's perennial mayor (Sheldon) and the dean of Iowa State College's Agricultural Division (Curtiss) will be recognized.

The fair was a crowd pleaser according to the *Ames Times* of October 3, 1913.   "The sensational nature of the three day fair just closed proved that there is a place for the agricultural fair and that such a place is Ames in the heart of the richest agricultural section of the state."   Judging in all agricultural categories were completed on the second day.   Prizewinning livestock had been paraded around the track that afternoon.   Afternoon classes at the college had been dismissed so that students might attend.   Entertainment at the auditorium included tightwire walking, vaudeville, aerial sharp shooting and novelty acts. Again, a capacity crowd of was reported on the fair's second day.

[5]   *Ames Intelligencer,* October 3, 1879, p.3, "Our County Fair" by Col. John Scott of Nevada.

[6]   *Ames Intelligencer,* November 3, 1910, p.2 "Fair Grounds Are A Good Investment." Editorial favoring tax support of fair grounds in Nevada,

[7]   *Articles of Incorporation, Book No. 2,* p. 2, May 30, 1913, Nevada, IA. Story County Recorder's Office. Iowa Fair Association incorporators as named in body of article.

Each succeeding year saw the Central Iowa Fair grow in attendance and interest. Following the October, 1914, fair the Ames *Times* carried a front page story quoting "out of town" exhibitors, who appeared at many Iowa county fairs, as saying that the one at Ames was "the cleanest fair" that had been seen. The president of the Farmer's Alliance of Allerton, Iowa, had been so impressed with the fair in Ames that he asked the fair secretary, Ed Graves, to come to Allerton to advise them in planning for their next years fair.

Advertisement for the Central Iowa Fair in the Ames Evening Times of September 25, 1914.

That 1914 fair featured Blanch McKenney-Hunter with her twelve trained high-jumping and trick-riding horses and high-diving dogs that appeared each afternoon and evening of the three-day fair. Another special attraction at that 1914 fair was the presence of Frank Gotch, world's champion professional wrestler of Humbolt, Iowa. Gotch served as a livestock judge as well as referee of a wrestling match scheduled for the closing night of the fair.

Additioinal live stock buildings were added to the fairgrounds in 1915 and 1916 to accomodate in-

creasing numbers of entries. Rural schools in the county, as well as Ames and some college classes, were excused so that students could attend the exhibits at the fair in Ames.

The hillside that extends north to Thirteenth Street provided a natural grandstand facility for the race track that had been developed on the low ground to the east. Crowds estimated frequently at several thousand sat on the hillside for the afternoon and

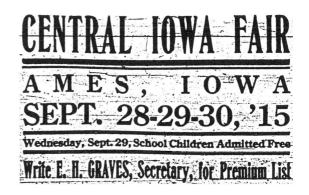

evening entertainment. I recall sulky races, livestock parades that were conducted following the judging schedules, pony shows, and bareback trick riders.

Barbecued buffalo was served fair-goers on a clear but cool September 27, 1916. But the big attraction at the track that afternoon was the mule-cart race. Only bankers were invited to enter. The T*imes* of September 29, 1916, reported that "H. W. Stafford,

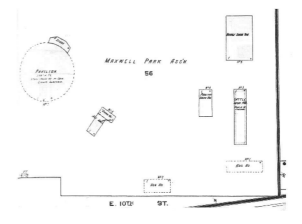

Plat of the Maxwell Park fairgrounds in 1920 in Ames. The grounds located between Tenth and Thirteenth Streets and east of Maxwell Avneue are now a part of the Ames Cemetery. The pavilion shown, was located among the oak trees that still stand in the cemetery. A race track was located to the north of the horse barn shown at right which was at the bottom of the hill to the east side of the grounds.

president of the Ames National Bank, yesterday afternoon emerged as the winner of the famous mule race. After a vigorous effort in making the two laps around the dirt track, his mule breasted the tape carrying his driver to victory." The nearest to Mr. Stafford was John Donohue, cashier of the Story City National Bank. C. L. Siverly, cashier of the Union National Bank, and W. D. Meltzer, vice president of the Commercial Savings Bank admitted their failures as mule drivers. The news account stated that Stafford's mule had been disqualified because a whip had been used; however, no other winner was named so he appears to have remained the winner of "record."[8]

With the end of World War I, the 1919 fair had made special provision to entertain our war veterans.

Farm implement dealers set up exhibits at the Central Iowa Fair in about 1915. This display was located in the main park area near the auditorium. This entire area is today a part of the Ames Municipal Cemetery. ID No. 7.26A.3

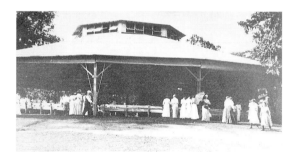

Chautauqua Auditorium dedicated in honor of Capt. Wallace M. Greeley in the fall of 1912. It was used for major Central Iowa Fair programs and presentations starting in October 1912. ID No. 23.114.1-3

[8] *Ames Evening Times,* September 29, 1916, p.1, "Bankers Drive Mules As Feature Of Fair Program."
[9] *Ames Evening Times,* September 21, 1920, p.1 "County Schools Have Sent Fine Display To Fair." "Needle Work Exhibits Excel. Tempting Fruit Exhibits Too."
[10] *Ames Evening Times,* October 3, 1925, p.2, "Big Year For Horse Pulling Contests."

Free admission to the park and a special barbecue were provided veterans on September 25. Chicken-fanciers seemed to have been plentiful that same year. Poultry exhibits were arranged in the main auditorium, and were reported to have been the "biggest" poultry exhibit ever held in Story County. Livestock and grain exhibitors represented all corners of the county.

By 1920, local automobile dealers placed new cars on display at the Central Iowa Fair; farmers were becoming as much interested in cars as in farm machinery.

The 1920 Central Iowa Fair ran four days beginning September 21. Attendance records and records in numbers of exhibits were set. "County Schools have sent fine displays" stated the Ames *Tribune.*[9] Most area schools dismissed classes so that students could attend the fair in Ames. That year the evening entertainment headlined as the "Mardi Gras Girls" and a program described as "Jewell Fantasy," were held in the Chautauqua auditorium drawing capacity crowds. Our local fair was booking talent shows that were appearing at state and county fairs throughout the Midwest.

By the mid 1920s, Iowa State College's "dynamometer" was a big attraction in the afternoon schedules at county fairs. Farmers entered their draft horses in pulling contests. Hitched to the dynamometer, and timed with a stop watch, the machine recorded the strength or pulling-power of a team. Farmers were fascinated as they watched their teams demonstrate their determination and strength.[10] That demonstration was combined with the sulky race and bareback riding events down on the track at the east side of the grounds.

Iowa State College's dynamometer was popular at midwest state and county fairs, and horse shows to determine the pulling power of a draft horse team. Developed by Prof. E.V. Collins of Iowa State, it was also built for a number of colleges and universities in adjoining states. Shown here in 1923, it was a major attraction at the Central Iowa Fair in Ames. Courtesy of Iowa State University Library / University Archives.

Addresses by the Story County Farm Bureau president, the governor of Iowa as well as horseshoe pitching contests, community singing, basket picnics, and special afternoon and evening attractions were all there to enjoy.

The Ames fair was a major social as well as an economic event of the year. Throughout the early 1920s, the Central Iowa Fair was a booming success. The Central Iowa Fair had become a four-day event for the entire county. Exhibitors who exhibited at the state fair also were entered at the Ames fair. A Chester White hog shown by W. T. Barr, vice president of our Central Iowa Fair, had won first prize at the Iowa, Minnesota and Wisconsin fairs that same year. A prominent stockbreeder was quoted in the *Ames Times* in 1921 as stating that he considered the local fair of primary importance because it was there that he was able to make sales of breeding stock and

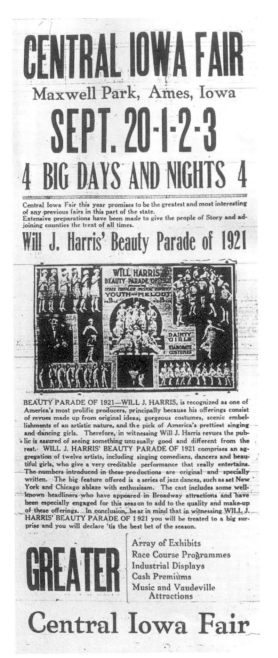

Advertisement for the Central Iowa Fair in the Ames Times of July 26, 1921. Maxwell Park was the site of the Chautauqua auditorium and concession buildings that were shared with the fair association. Located south of Thirteenth Street and east of Maxwell Avenue, the seventeen acre park is part of the Ames Municipal Cemetery today. ID No. 199.1126.3

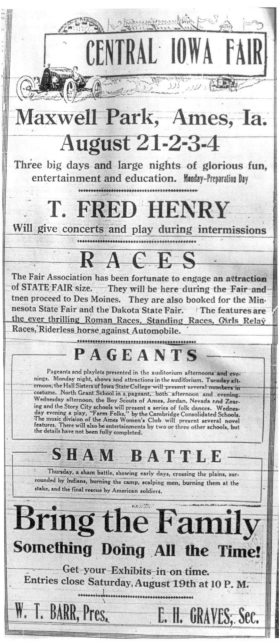

Advertisement for the Central Iowa Fair in the Ames Times of August 5, 1922. IDNo. 199.1126.2

50

otherwise establish contacts with neighbors with common interests.[11,12]

I recall a large crowd sitting on the hill to witness a sham battle between Indians and soldiers in an afternoon pageantry of pioneer days. (Although I believe that particular history must have taken place at some place in Iowa other than in Story County).

A pageant was presented on the final night of the 1923 fair. Representing the settlement of Story County, hundreds of folks from around the county took part in that dramatic event that included choral numbers and band accompaniment. I recall the final number in that presentation when a Mrs. Zumwalt sang the "Indian Love Song" with a spotlight on her as she stood center stage in the open amphitheater. The hillside was "standing room only" that night.

That 1923 Central Iowa Fair proved to have been the last of the fairs in Ames.

Although the Central Iowa Fair had been well-patronized and there had been little discouraging publicity about the financial results, 1924 found a diminished enthusiasm on the part of fair board members. The *Ames Tribune* of August 8, 1924, reported that A. M. Norris, an Ames businessman, had been appointed chairman of a committee to determine the fate of the enterprise.

The August 14, 1924, *Tribune* carried a front page headline that announced that the "Central Iowa Fair Will Be Discontinued This Year." Norris's committee reported a lack of sufficient support on the part of area breeders and exhibitors. Also, Ames merchants were showing little interest in the continuance of the fair. There was little explanation as to why interest in the fair had waned; however, several reasons were apparent. The road to Des Moines was now gravelled. That, combined with better cars, made getting to the Iowa State Fair, nearby in Des Moines, easier for Ames-area exhibitors and spectators alike.[13]

In addition, the same men always had to plan and carry out the fair program every year. That point

was alluded to in a news item stating that those who had been assuming the resposibilties felt "that it was time for others than themselves to continue the institution."

Ames was not to be "denied." Fall is the time for a fair—if not a fair, something *like* a fair. So, "Achievement Day" was created under the joint auspices of the Story County Farm Bureau, A. H. Pickford, county agent, Paul Taff, state leader of boys and girls 4H Club work, and the Ames Chamber of Commerce. Story County winners at the state fair would have their entries on exhibit on Main Street in Ames. Special boys and girls club exhibits and also special youth programs were scheduled. A large tent was put up on the Ames Grain and Coal Company's grounds on South Duff. Iowa Secretary of Agriculture, Mark Thornburg, was to be the featured speaker for the "big day" on October 16, 1925.

The *Tribune* of October 16 described Achievement Day with glowing words. "With specimens of the crop that made Iowa famous displayed in Ames business houses and the impressive exhibits of Story County Boys and Girls clubs lining Main Street, not a doubt remained today of the exceptional progressive spirit of Story County citizens." With more that 100 entrants in the corn show, there was the judging of corn, sheep, pigs, poultry, and clothing that began at 1 p.m. Announcements of winners and awards were made at the big tent that evening. The spirit of the fair lived on.[14]

Some people nearby still wanted a fair that was called a *fair*. In 1928, the folks at Story City, with P. C. Donhowe, E. E. Mayhew, and P. A. Olson acting as the official organizers, developed the "Tri-County Fair" to be held in Story City.[15] With the first fair held October 10-12, the Tri-County Fair soon became a complete fair with all of the usual agricultural departments. Exhibits, talks, and judging took place in various church basements, the high school gymnasium and auditorium with special evening entertainments at the local opera house on Main Street. Ball games between Story County schools were held at the high school ball park. Opening day of the Tri-County Fair was usually an all-communiuty day with a parade headed by a visiting band and dignitaries.

Eligibility for agricuiltural entries in the Tri-County Fair was residency in Story, Boone, or Hamilton counties. By 1936, the Tri-County Fair in Story City was referred to as a combined 4H Achievement Show and Tri-County Fair, held August 24 - 26.[16] The next year, 1937, the Tri-County Fair was without horse, cattle, or swine participants. Main attention was centered on judging women's depart-

---

[11] *Ames Evening Times,* September 13, 1921, p.1, "Gates Open September 20th; Fiddlers will run rapant."

[12] *Ames Tribune,* September 17, 1921, p.1, "Livestock Exhibited At Fair Will Include Many Champions of State."

[13] Note also that the once popular Chautauqua program that shared the grounds with the Central Iowa Fair was also winding down at this time. Chautauqua was last held in Ames in 1926.

[14] *Ames Tribune,* October 16, 1925, p.1, "Thousands Visit Ames Today."

[15] *Story City Herald,* September 6, 1928, p.1, "Tri-County Fair Is Coming."

[16] *Story City Herald,* August 20, 1936, - p.1, "Tri-County Fair and 4H Achievement Show." Article includes premium list and rules.

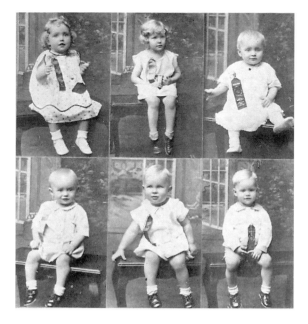

Baby Health Contest winners, Tri-County Fair in Story City, 1930. Top row, left to right, Wilma Ruth Halleland, Randall; Betty Delores Olson, Roland; Betty Joan Peterson, Gilbert. Bottom Row, left to right, Charles Leonard Johnson, Story City; Howard Clark Brattebo, Story City; Clifford Hans Hanson, Story City. Photo from Story City Golden Jubilee Book, p. 152, Paul A. Olson, publisher, 1931. ID No.213.1212.2-3

The Story City Herald advertisement in October 1930 for the Tri-County Fair held in Story City. ID No.202.1145.4-5

Heifer Show at the Tri-County Fair, 1930. Photo from Story City Golden Jubilee Book, p. 153, Paul A. Olson, publisher, 1931. ID No.213.1212.4

ment activities, poultry, small grain, corn, vegetable, and fruit exhibits. Entertainment that year was a football game between State Center and Story City, and a band concert on Main Street.[17]

That 1937 Tri-County Fair was the last to be held, and was the last of the broad-based county fairs in Story County.[18] Very much alive today, however, is the 4H Fair held in Nevada each year. One of the first 4H Achievement Shows in the county was held in 1931 in Ames at the Ames High School Field House and in the Highway Commission sheds nearby. On June 28, 1939, the Story County 4H Fair Association was incorporated with Nevada becoming the location of their permanently-established fairgrounds.[19] Incorporators were D. A. Jay, Ames; C. S. Toot, Nevada; T. Z. Henryson, Story City; C. A. Coggshall, Cambridge; Glenn Randau,[20] Ames; L. P. Larson, Ames; L. H. Wengert, Colo; Clarence Hilburn, Nevada; and Lee Riddlesbarger, Nevada.

The 4H Fair was rooted in the boys corn and the girls sewing clubs of post World War I days and of the 4H achievement days that began in the 1930s as "traveling" exhibits that found it in Ames, Nevada (and in Story City as part of the Tri County Fair in 1936).

---

[17] *Story City Herald,* September 7, 1937, - p.1, "Dates Set For Tri-County Fair." No showing of horses, cattle, sheep or swine.
[18] *Story City Herald,* October 13,1938, "Husking Contest Here Next Thursday." Replaced the Tri-County Fair.
[19] *Articles of Incorporation,* Filed July 11, 1939. Incorporators were as stated above.
[20] Glenn Randau served as secretary/treasurer for the 4 H Fair for twenty-five years.

The 4 H fairgrounds in Nevada in 1945 looking northeasterly. Today the Story County Extension office is located on the corner at right center beyond the livestock barns. Photo courtesy of the Story County Extension.

Today the 4H Fairgrounds, located in the southwest corner of Nevada have been improved with adequate buildings for the exhibits and demonstration work by the 4H members and patrons of Story County. The true spirit of the "old time fair idea"— that is, the advancement of education and industry, combined with an element of accomplishment and celebration can be said to still exist in Story County.

16 Sept. 1997

Chapter 11

Boy Scouts Had Vital Pioneering Days In Ames

The first leadership training program conducted in behalf of the Boy Scout and Campfire organizations this side of New York City was conducted on the Iowa State College campus in 1914. Ernest Thompson Seton, nationally recognized naturalist and the designated "scout" of the Boy Scouts of America, and Dr. Luther R. Gulick and his daughter Frances Gulick, founders of Campfire, presented lectures and youth leadership training demonstrations. Their participation was a major feature of Iowa State's week-long Rural Life Conference that began June 22, 1914.[1]

Over 200 attended the first day's session. Seton and the Gulicks explained the purpose, emphasizing the place of nature and camping in the scouting and camp fire programs. Ames scouts and camp fire girls were camped during the day on the campus and became participants in their demonstrations.

On the second night of the conference, Seton and the Gulicks, aided by Prof. E. C. Bishop, conducted an Indian council near the campanile. Seton called upon others who gave talks around a council fire to explain Indian customs as they related to scouting and campfire programs. A large crowd that evening was inspired by the presentations. It was on that occasion that William Gaessler and his wife, Myrtle, became deeply impressed. Their life-long support of the campfire program in Ames began that evening.

Boy scouting in the United States was organized in 1910, patterned after the boy scout program that had begun in England two years earlier under the direction of Lord Baden-Powell. Ernest Thompson Seton had lectured during the Ames 1910 Chautauqua platform and had, on that occasion, met with a group of Ames boys and men at a picnic held on the Chautauqua grounds.[2] After hearing Seton tell stories of nature lore and of the new scouting, the boys were enthusiastic and ready to get into the program. Walter Fiss, then the director of the Ames Boys Y.M.C.A., recognized the need for the scout program and adopted the camping and nature study ideas outlined by Seton. Boy scouting had begun to take root in Ames.

By January 1912, E. C. Bishop, extension specialist at Iowa State, organized a scoutcraft school for those who wished to know more of the work of the Boy Scouts and the Girl Pioneers of America. Invited to the class were adult leaders, including teachers in public and Sunday schools especially interested in working with boys and girls between the ages of 12 and 18. The class was held once a week for eight weeks in the First Methodist Church.[3]

AMES COUNCIL BOY SCOUTS OF AMERICA

On March 11, 1914, Herman Knapp, treasurer of Iowa State College, Prof. E. C. Potter, Rev. L. C. Harris, Prof. J. C. Pomroy, Prof. H. A. Scullen, Prof. J. C. Cunningham, Rev. J. P. Clyde, and L. W. Forman met at Alumni Hall on the campus and formally established the Ames Council of the Boy Scouts of America. Herman Knapp was elected President and J. C. Cunningham, vice president of that first council. E. C. Potter was named treasurer and L. W. Forman was elected secretary.

That first council appointed a committee to correlate the work of the Boy Scouts with that of the college Y.M.C.A. and with the work of the Inter-Church Council and Sunday School League. Subsequent to that first meeting, the executive committee of the council invited Prof. G. B. MacDonald, Prof. M. F. P. Castellae, Harry Brown and G. E. Linden to become members of the council.

H. A. Scullen became the first Ames scout commissioner. By October, he reported ten active boy scouts. In July and August, 1914, Ames scouts carried out their first camp operations. Tents were set up on the north side of the Skunk River opposite the old Soper's Mill about eight miles north of Ames. The

---

[1] *Ames Evening Times,* June 24, 1914, p.1, "Indian Council Near Campanile Last Evening."
[2] *Ames Intelligencer,* August 18, 1910, p.1, "Boys To Organize American Scouts."
[3] *Ames Daily Tribune,* January 25, 1912, p.1, "Boy Scouts and Girl Pioneers."

The first Ames Boy Scout Council was organized on March 11, 1914. Ames Boy Scouts held their first camp sessions on the Skunk River north of Ames near the site of the historic Soper's Mill. H.A.Scullen, Iowa State Extension, was in charge in 1914 and again in 1915 with the aid of Warren Pollard, Ames school music director. Photo shows camp set up in 1915 on north bank of Skunk River. Photo provided by Preston Niles, one of the campers in 1915. Others believed included: Paul Potter, Victor Beach, Barclay Noble, and Alford Carleton. ID No. 45.222.4

Preston Niles, one of Ames's first boy scouts, provided this picture taken when the Ames scouts camped on the Skunk River at Soper's Mill in 1915. Ames boys swam in the Skunk River and in Squaw Creek in those days. It was more than ten years later that Dad Carr built Carr's pool at Ames. ID No. 45.222.3

first group of scouts to set camp were accompanied by Mr. Scullen. The *Tribune* of July 24, 1914 reported that the "boys enjoyed the fishing, hunting, and swimming that the river affords and are making large plans for the next such trip." Preston Niles, one of the boys on that camping trip, has provided us with a picture of their camp site. Other boys included on that first Ames scout camp experience were Chevelier Adams, Gedes Niles, Paul Potter, Hiram Munn, Ronald Kooser, Ted Nowlin, and Lyman Olson.

Fourteen Ames boy scouts returned for the week of June 7 - 14, 1915 to the same camp site on the river eight miles north of Ames. H. A. Scullen and Warren Pollard, music director for Ames schools, were in charge of a well planned, week-long camp experience. Camp routines were established in advance. The boys had duties to perform each day. Swimming, fishing, and hiking occupied their afternoons. Each evening they had a campfire with "lights out" at nine o'clock. Visiting hours at the camp were announced for Wednesday and Friday afternoons 3 to 4:30 and 7 to 8 the same evenings. An enjoyable event of the week was an invitation to visit the camp of the Gilbert campfire girls located nearby. The boys later returned the courtesy and entertained the girls.[4]

In addition to the scouts who camped the year before, campers in 1915 are believed to have included

Victor Beach, Barclay Noble, Richard Beckman and Alford Carleton.

During this period the Ames scouts conducted frequent camp events, often setting up at locations north of Ames on the Skunk River. It was not long after those early camping events became popular with the scouts that Dr. A. B. Niles, a prominent Ames veterinarian, turned over the historic Craig log cabin, located on his farm about a mile northeast of Ames, to the Ames Boy Scout Council for the use by Ames scouts. It remained the popular overnight campsite for Ames scouts for many years. In 1938, Preston Niles, son of Dr. Niles, moved the log cabin to his orchard along Highway 30 north of Missouri Valley, Iowa, where today it is operated as a museum by the Harrison County Conservation Commission.[5]

The historic Craig log home located on Dr.A.B.Niles' farm northeast of Ames. (Shown here before the protective siding had been removed to make the logs visable.) Dr. Niles made this log cabin available to the Ames Boy Scouts for their camping activities. The scouts maintained the log home until 1938 when Dr. Niles son, Preston Niles, moved it to Missouri Valley, Iowa to become a major part of his historical museum. Since the death of Preston Niles, the museum, including the log home, is ownd by the Harrison County Conservation Board. ID No. 45.223.1-2

---

[4] The scouts were: Manning Howell, E. Scovel, M. Hunter, Earl Shull, Arthur Holdredge, Ronald Kooser, Robert Potter, Paul Potter, Ted Nowlin, Clinton Adams, Victor Beach, Tom Gibbs, Eugene Watkins, and Elmer Mathre.

[5] *Ames Daily Tribune,* January 22,1938, p.1, "Old Scout Cabin Near Ames Is Torn Down" by Arthur Johnson.

By 1917, H. A. Scullen reported to the council that Ames had three active scout troops with a total membership of fifty boys. G. B. MacDonald, forestry professor, H. S. Thurston, and H. G. Singer, industrial arts teacher at Ames High School, were scoutmasters. They were aided by five assistant scoutmasters.

The Craig log home after the protective siding was removed. (Preservationists today prefer that siding be left on these historic structues so they may last longer. The logs should be exposed on the interior only.) **Camp Machacammac** *or "House on The Hill" was the name the scouts gave their cabin camp site. Photo shows the east end of the log home. Note the exterior of the original stone fireplace. ID No.68.349.1*

A June 23, 1918 gathering of Troop 3 of the Boy Scouts of America, sponsored by the Ames Congregational Church. From left in front are: Robert Irwin, Parker Meltzer, Clinton Adams, Clarence Goddard, Loren Bower, and Eber Sherman. Back row, from left: A.S Thurston, Scoutmaster; W.A.Bower, Scoutmaster; Floyd Scarborough; Gordon Glidden, Leslie Crabbs; Will Sherman; Lyle Miller; A.S.Miller, Assistant Scoutmaster. ID No. 22.110.13A

In 1920, the Ames Boy Scout Council took as one of their goals the hiring of a scout executive. Fred C. Eggers was selected to fill that position in early June.[6] Eggers had been a student at Iowa State before the war when he had left for training at Camp Dodge. Following the war, he returned to Marshalltown where he successfully served as their scout executive until being hired by the Ames council. By returning to Ames, Eggers was able to spend part time continuing his education at Iowa State.[7]

In July, 1920, Ames scouts camped on Pine Lake near Eldora for a week.[8][9] Camp Scullen provided the Ames boys with experience in campcraft, nature study, swimming and boating. Bevier Spinney, one of the older campers and an Ames High student at the time, served as cook. A *Tribune* account quoted the boys as unanimously stating that Spinney "sure makes a good cook and fills the bill." A special event of the camp week was having Eldora townspeople provide transportation for the entire group to an Eldora band concert. A second week at Camp Scullen was held from August 7 -14 for Ames scouts who had been unable to enroll for the earlier session.

The number of troops in Ames had increased and the court of honor had been advancing local scouters through the first class level. By 1923, Ames had three Eagle Scouts.

In 1921, under Fred Eggers' leadership, the first of several summer camps was conducted on the east bank of the Des Moines River on a knoll located about a mile north of the old Lincoln Highway bridge west of Boone. The camp later became known as "Camp Kooroq." The campsite had its own spring for drinking water, and the river provided campers with opportunities for swimming and water sports. Hikes to points of interest were included in a busy camp schedule. A rustic mess hall was well-screened to keep out flies. Six or seven pyramid-type tents provided sleeping quarters for close to forty scouts. Sleeping bunks were rustic with rope "springs." B. E. Hynds was the camp chef that first year at Kooroq, making a big hit with the boys.[10] Ames men visited the camp several evenings during each camp session to give talks to the scouts as they gathered around the campfire.

During the time Eggers was scout executive, the Boy Scouts headquarters was located in City Hall.

---

[6] Council Meeting, May 20, 1920. Approved the employment of Fred C. Eggers of Victor, Iowa, to be full-time executive from June 1, 1920, to Sept. 15, 1920, at salary of $175.00 per month with privilege of taking up to nine hours of college credit, at the rate of $100 per month. See minute book, pp. 91-92.

[7] Ames Boy Scout Council minutes on pages 104 -23 provide references to arrangement. Eggers' work proved to be very satisfactory in improving the organization and growth of scout work in Ames.

[8] *Ames Tribune,* July 17, 1920, p.1, "Boy Scouts Will Have Great Times."

[9] In 1919, a number of Ames scouts had attended the Des Moines scout camp held in the Ledges State Park. *Ames Tribune,* Aug.11, 1919, p.1, "Ames Scouts Start Ten Day Camp Monday." Ames scout leaders were Charles Miller and Richard Beckman.

[10] I believe he was camp chef in 1923 and may have been in several other years as well.

TIMBER HITCH LODGE

In 1922, the Ames Lions Club financed the building of Timber Hitch Lodge and arranged the lease of the site for it on the north side of Fifth Street north and west of the Masonic Building to serve as the Boy Scout headquarters.[11] Prof. A. H. Kimball, a Lion member and head of Iowa State's Architectural Engineering Department, designed the 16' x 34' cabin.

Timberhitch Lodge was built by the Ames Lions Club to be the Boy Scouts headquarters. It was located on the north side of Fifth Street immediately west of the present Ames Public Library. Scout headquarters remained there until 1928, when the lease on the lot expired and a permanent building was erected on that site. It served the boys well for many Boy Scout functions. It later became a part of a house located on South Riverside Drive where it finally was the victim of the 1993 Squaw Creek flood. ID No.15.71.2

Bob Williams was our bugler at scout camp Kooroq over on the Des Moine River in 1922. He also was bugler for winter camp held in the Ledges State Park. A 1925 Ames High graduate, Williams operated his shoe repair business on Main Street until retiring in 1964. The Durlam & Durlam store is today located where Williams operated his business for many years. ID No. 168.938.1-5

At first it was on the main floor, but later was moved into the large basement room located on the south side of the building where there was an outside grade entrance. In 1922, the scouts were provided office space in the basement of the First Methodist Church where the scout executive's desk was partitioned off by a canvas curtain in the northwest coner. It was in that location when I joined the Boy Scouts in late 1922.

Lions Club members volunteered most of the construction labor involved, and it was put into use in late 1922. It provided office space for the scout executive, and also was the meeting place for court of honor events and council meetings. It remained the scout headquarters until 1928, when the lease expired and the property was sold to become the site of the commercial building that remains there today.[12]

Fred Eggers resigned as scout executive at the end of 1921, and E. G. Stowell of Des Moines became his successor in January, 1922. In late December of 1922, the first of several winter camp expeditions was carried out by Ames boy scouts. A three day camp, known as "Camp White Eagle," was set up in the Ledges State Park. The pyramidal tents each had its own heating stove. Thirteen scouts were on hand with several adult leaders.[13] E. G. Stowell, Samuel Battell, Art Francis, A. R. Janson, Allan Rosenberg, Russell Daubert, and Verne Adamson were the older leaders bringing the total number of winter campers to twenty. The park ranger, Carl Fritz Henning, directed the boys' activities a part of each day, demonstrating outdoor woodcraft, how to lay trails, and other aspects of scoutcraft.

---

[11] *Ames Tribune*, July 6, 1922, p.1, "Boy Scouts Will Have Log Cabin Here For Their Headquarters."

[12] The log-slab exterior cabin was then moved to Brookside Park. Later it was moved to South Russell Avenue where it was converted into a residence. It became a casualty of the 1993 flood.

[13] The scouts were: Frank Adams, Robert Speers, William Battell, Kenneth Burnett, Weston Jones, Chester Ide, Rees Paine, George Thurber, John Hawley, Donald Fish, Floyd Williams, Robert Williams, and Dwight Clark.

The Intertior of Timberhitch Lodge on Fifth Street. Headquarters were moved to the basement of the Library after 1928. ID No. 197.1121.1-2-3

STORY COUNTY COUNCIL BOY SCOUTS OF AMERICA

In their November 22, 1922 meeting, the Ames Boy Scout Council decided to extend the council's territory to include all of Story County. It was during Stowell's leadership years of 1922, 1923, and 1924 that the council became known as the Story County Council of the Boy Scouts.

E. G. Stowell had coined the name "Kooroq" (camp in the valley) in 1922 for the scout camp west of Boone.[14] There were four one-week camp sessions that year. Two rowboats (one with an outboard motor) and a canoe were brought up to camp from Des Moines that year. Boating excursions were made

The Ames's Boy Scout camp Kooroq was located on the Des Moines river west of Boone in the 1920s. From left are Cliff Smith, chef; Verne Adamson, assistant camp director, and E.G.Stowell, scout executive for the Story County Boy Scout Council. In the background is the outline of the rustic mess tent. Nearly "fly proof," it was well protected from weather; we never missed a meal. ID No.15.72.2

to the high-bridge upstream from camp. The tom-tom beat called scouts to evening campfires. Songs that were sung, such as "By A Western Water Tank" or "Kooroq Will Shine Tonight," were long remembered. Adult scout leaders and Ames business and professional men presented inspirational character building talks at those campfires. "Taps" sent the scouts to their bunks, and a bugle call woke them in the morning.

Jess Cole remembers how he, Don Stevens and several other scouts were given the privilege of returning the boats to Des Moines at the end of the camp season in 1923. It was a twelve-hour scenic boat ride down the river for the boys. Hiram Munn was waiting for them at the boat dock in Des Moines to bring them back to Ames.

Fred Battell's official Boy Scout diary that he carried in 1923. Today as a resident of St. Paul, Minnesota, he still maintains an interest in scouting. ID No.202.1145.1-2-3.

---

[14] *Ames Tribune,* July 10, 1922, "Boy Scouts," special column. Lists campers and describes program details.

My first experience at camp came in 1924. The 1924 Camp Kooroq sessions were full. I recall the day we hiked down to the Ledges State Park, crossing the river at the original site of the Kate Shelley Bridge near Moingona. That hike saw all of us passing the fourteeen mile hike test. Cliff Smith was chef all four sessions. It was at camp in 1924 that I completed my first class qualifications and acquired my first merit badge. I also recall the evening of fun when a "snipe hunt" was staged. The occupants of the six big tents were organized into Indian tribes that year, the Delawares, Ioways, Blackfeet, Seminoles, Fox, and Sioux. Russell Daubert, the son of Iowa State's swim coach, was in charge of swimming. Russell Daubert later was swim coach at Michigan State and taught camping and nature lore there as well.

Winter camps continued to be popular with Ames scouts.[15] With Stowell, Russell Daubert, and R. R. Griffith as leaders, a group of scouts spent three days, starting December 22, 1923 camping at "Camp Machacammac" (house on the hill) northeast of Ames. On one of those days, the scouts hiked up to Lake Comar for a skating party, visiting Soper's Mill on the way. The scouts learned to identify trees in wintertime; built a bridge over the stream that passed near the cabin at the foot of a ravine; and constructed several rustic lean-to shelters for future campers.

Winter camp was a part of the Ames scout program through 1924 when twenty-five Ames scouts under leadership of E. G. Stowell and Russell

Daubert, his assistant, and the scoutmaster, Sam Battell, returned to the Ledges State Park December 29, 30, and 31. They were accompanied by Ray Murray of Hackensack, Minnesota, an experienced northern Minnesota woodsman who served as a special instructor to teach the scouts about living in the woodlands in wintertime. The scouts were housed in two cabins in the lower Ledges where they slept on straw matresses.[16]

It was during 1924 that Ames organized a Sea Scout Troop, including Iowa State students in its membership. R. S .Griffith, an Ames scout, was assistant skipper. Troop 9 was the Sea Scout "ship." In weekend jaunts to Clear Lake, sea scouts learned to handle various-sized boats and made the "long cruise" required for advancement.[17] This was the first of the Ames Sea Scout troops. A second such troop was organized in the 1940s as the SSS Sea Hawk with Lynn Richardson as its skipper and Leland Benz the ships mate.[18]

These scouts are lined up in front of their tent for inspection. This was during one of the 1923 Camp Kooroq sessions west of Boone. Russell Kintzley, an Ames High graduate of 1927, is the scout in the middle. ID No. 187.1061.1-3

At Camp Kooroq we swam in the Des Moines River. In thoses days it seemed quite satisfactory. I think this picture caught me out in the 'deep'. ID No. 15.71.1

---

[15] *Ames Tribune,* December 28, 1923, p.6, "Scouts are Enjoying Winter Camp Sports."
[16] *Ames Tribune,* December 29, 1924, -p.1, "Ames Scouts Leave For Winter Outing."
[17] *Ames Tribune,* May 21, 1925, p.6, "Boy Scouts."
[18] Cecil Monnohan, John Erickson, Bob Mulcahy, Wayne Reed, Harold Hopkins, Dow Mitchell, Milton Soma, Robert Phillips, Robert Books, Paul Mitchell, Dick Pride and Ed Collins were members of the SSS Sea Hawk Troop.

Carl Fritz Henning, early custodian of the Ledges State Park, shown in the 1920s sitting in front of his headquarters cabin in the lower Ledges. Henning, a true naturalist, was always available to assist the Ames Scouts during their camping experiences. ID No.184.1041.4

Early in 1925, E. G. Stowell resigned as Scout Executive in Ames and accepted the position as executive at Iowa City.[19] Russell Daubert served for a few months as an interim executive until Art Francis, who had assisted Stowell the previous year, was hired to serve as scout executive. Francis served until the end of December, 1926 when he resigned to accept a position with Iowa State College. During 1925 and 1926, the Ames Boy Scouts experienced a great deal of camping activity at Camp Machacammac.

In 1926 the Lions Club sponsored a bird house contest. That big martin house in the second row, second from the right, won me a prize in the "large bird" category. ID No.55.272.4

Twenty-one scouts spent the week ending July 7, 1925 at Camp Kooroq west of Boone. Camp routine that year was more rustic than previous Kooroq sessions with the boys doing more of the camp preparation themselves. Day hikes in the area and a boat trip down the Des Moines River to the Ledges were included in the program. Jack Mayo was a popular camp cook and Don Caswell, a 1925 Ames High graduate, was in charge of swimming.

The Scoutmasters Association held a number of training sessions during the period. An overnight camp session for scoutmasters was held at Machacammac with Professor G. B. MacDonald, and Professor J. E. Smith of Iowa State's forestry and geology departments, respectively, providing useful training in recognizing trees and rock formations in the area.[20] Such meetings were held to "provide the

boyhood of Ames all that is good and possible for them."[21]

In August 1927, C. R. (Clyde) Hesse became the full time scout executive for Story County.[22] Growth in scouting activity in Ames and in other Story County communities was evident under his leadership. The number of scouts in Story County had increased by 129% by mid-1928, with 18 active troops and 337 scouts.

In 1928, Ames scouts placed 29 Lincoln Highway markers as a part of a national Boy Scout project. Fifty Ames scouts met at the corner of Kellogg and Lincoln Way on the morning of September 1, 1928. With the national deputy scout executive, Andrew Janson,[23] in charge of the special ceremony, speeches were made by Dr. L. H. Pammel, head of the Botany Department at Iowa State College, Fred C. Tilden, veteran of the Civil War, and Parley Sheldon, banker and for many years the mayor of Ames. Sheldon lifted the first shovelful of earth as a marker was dropped into its hole. Others present were A. H. Fuller of the Rotary Club, Earl Weaver of the Lions Club, and Joe Robinson of the Kiwanis Club. Harry Brown and E. C. Potter represented the Story County Council of the Boy Scouts.

Concrete markers were placed in Ames at Kellogg Avenue, Grand Avenue, Hazel Avenue, and at West Gate. Steel markers were placed on the Squaw Creek bridge. That day, Ames boy scouts placed markers along Lincoln Highway from a point two miles east of Ames to a point three miles east of Boone.[24]

TALL CORN AREA COUNCIL ORGANIZED

In September of 1928, representatives from Story, Boone, Greene, and Carroll counties met in Boone and organized the Tall Corn Council of the Boy Scouts of America. Seventeen active scout leaders from the towns of Ames, Boone, Roland, Jefferson, Carroll, and Glidden were present at that meeting. Eighteen scout troops and 510 active boy scouts were included within the new scouting area. Clyde Hesse, scout executive for the council, announced plans to devote time in developing scout leadership in the area outside of Ames. Melvin Tudor would give his full attention to Ames scout activities.[25]

In June 1929, thirty area scouts attended Camp Mitigwa, the Des Moines scout camp located southwest of Ledges State Park on the west bank of the Des Moines River. Four Ames troops were repre-

[19] *Ames Tribune,* Feb. 11, 1925, "300 Attend Boy Scouts' Annual Banquet In Ames." announced Stowell's move to Iowa City.
[20] *Ames Tribune,* Jan. 13, 1925, p.2, "Scouting In Ames."
[21] *Ames Tribune,* May 21, 1925, p.6, "Boy Scouts." (scouting news.)
[22] *Ames Tribune,* August 18, 1927, p.1, "New Boy Scout Executive here."
[23] *Ames Tribune,* August 9, 1928, p.5, "Boy Scout Manual Illustrator Doing work at Iowa State"
[24] *Ames Tribune,* Sept. 1, 1928, p.1, "Boy Scouts Place 29 Hiway Markers."
[25] *Ames Tribune,* Sept.14, 1929, p.1, "Tall Corn Scout Council Formed."

sented; two from Nevada; and one from Maxwell. Gerald Vance, William Bittenbender, and Norman Harvey were named honor campers at Mitigwa that year. Many merit badges were earned by the Ames boys, including the life-scout award to Gerald Vance. This was the first year that Ames scouts attended Mitigwa, I believe.[26]

Twenty three Boone scouts camped at Spring Lake, near Grand Junction in Greene County, that last week of June in 1929. They were visited there by Clyde Hesse.

In 1930, Ames scouts signed up for four sessions at Camp Rainbow located on the Raccoon River near Lake City. Lewis Amme, well-known Ames chef, was in charge of food preparation, and older Ames eagle scouts staffed the camp with Clyde Hesse of Ames in charge throughout the camp season.[27] Earlier that year, the Tall Corn Council had entered into preliminary plans to purchase the 35-acre Nic-O-Let Park, on the Des Moines River west of Boone, with its modern swimming pool, planning to convert it soon to the area's scout camp.[28] Although the location was ideal and the terms favorable, that plan was later abandoned.

In January 1930, a chapter of Alpha Phi Omega, a boy scout honorary, made up locally of eagle scouts was organized on the Iowa State campus. Twelve original members included Fred Battell of Ames. The group provided, and continues to provide, older scout leadership to the scout program.[29]

Some of the boys of Ames Troop 3 cooking their evening meal over an open fire at their "private" cabin north of Ames on the Skunk River in about 1938. This was after the Craig log cabin had been moved to Missouri Valley, Iowa. ID No. 148.814.3-5

In February 1932, the Tall Corn Area Council became the Tall Corn Council within the Des Moines Area Boy Scout Council. The four-county area of Story, Boone, Greene, and Carroll counties thus became a part of the larger eighteen-county area that made certain economies available. The depression of the 1930s did not reduce the need for the scouting program; however, it had become more difficult to equitably raise funds when the economy was in distress. Under the new arrangement, Clyde Hesse remained in charge of the four-county area. Administrative costs were consolidated. For example, Camp Mitigwa, the Des Moines scout camp, by then well established, was made available to the entire Tall Corn area scout program.

Throughout the years, Ames scouts have engaged in many community activities. During World War I, Ames scouts were recognized for their sale of war bonds. In 1918, the scouts made an important contribution to the successful search for three Ames boys who had mysteriously disappeared. In 1924, the Ames Social Service League publicly thanked the scouts for "gathering and repairing more than enough toys to supply the need at the Christmas season." The annual scout banquet in February, celebrating the founding of scouting, had become a tradition. Scouts provided demonstrations of their scoutcraft work on such occasions. By 1930, Ames had a good number of eagle scouts in its ranks.[30]

In 1935, three Ames adult leaders received the "Silver Beaver" award for their service to scouting. G. B. MacDonald, L. W. Forman and Harry Brown had each served on the scout council since its inception.[31] John Hiland's name was added in 1938 to the names of Ames men receiving the award.[32] These were the "pioneers." There have been a number of Silver Beaver awards to Ames adult leaders since that time as well.[33]

[26] *Ames Tribune,* June 29, 1929, p.1, "Three Named Honor Campers."

[27] *Ames Tribune,* May 30, 1930, p.1, "Plans Complete for Summer Camps."

[28] *Ames Tribune,* January 23, 1930, p.1, "Nic-O-Let Bought for Scout Camp."

[29] *Ames Tribune,* January 25, 1930, p.1 "Eagle Scouts Form Organization Here." Also: Letter from Fred Battell to Farwell Brown dated December 6, 1993. Battell indicates that they were later advised by the national scout headquarters that membership should not be limited to eagle scouts.

[30] Included were Fred Battell, Howard Erwin, Gordon Stiles, Chester Ide, Alford Carleton, Floyd Williams, Dwight Clark, Kenneth Wallace, Audrey Erickson, Maxwell Smith, Otto Richardson, Norman Harvey, Sabin Nichols, Holmes Brown, Frank Brown, William Bittenbender, Seaman Knapp, Gerald Griffith and Robert Root. Eagle scouts were those acquiring a specified number of merit badges in addition to having passed all of the first class tests.

[31] *Ames Tribne,* February 15, 1935, p.1, "Harry Brown Awarded Silver Beaver for Distinguished Service to Boys at Court of Honor."

[32] *Ames Tribune,* December 17, 1938, p.1, "Hiland Given Silver Beaver For Scouting."

[33] J. C. Cunningham, Art Francis, H. W. Richey, F. E. Brown, Gerald Malone, A. J. Englehorn, Robert K. Goodwin, Henry M. Black were added during intervening years to Ames' list of Beaver award recipients.

Ely Brewer, Scout Executive, in front of the Richey nature cabin. Following the untimely death of Ames Scout, Robert Richey, his parents gave this cabin to Camp Mitigwa in his memory. Richey was a law student at the University of Iowa at the time of his death.

Hundreds of Ames boy scouts have attended Camp Mitigwa. Following the untimely death of Ames eagle scout Robert Richey, the son of Prof. Harry Richey, the Richey Nature Study Cabin was added to the Mitigwa camp facilities. It was dedicated October 9, 1939.[34]

Harold Hegland was chairman of the Ames district in the 1940s after it became known as the "Broken Arrow District."[35] More Ames boys were attaining the rank of eagle scout.[36] The first of a number of scout expeditions to the Philmont Scout Reservation in New Mexico was led by Don Watts who today remains an active boy scout supporter in Ames.[37]

The Des Moines Area Council has become the Mid-Iowa Council. Today there are 16 boy scout units in Ames involving 626 scouts. Of these present day scouts, 395 are cub scouts, a program that became a part of Ames boy scouting in 1932.[38]. The boy scout program still has as its goal (to paraphrase a quote from Scout Executive Clyde Hesse of many years ago) the "training of good citizens."

Fred Battell, retired and now of St. Paul, Minnesota, in a letter to me recently, commented, "I have

---

34 Robert Richey, Ames High School class of 1934, died October 13, 1938, of cancer.
35 Cliff Grund was district commissioner and Art Francis was chairman for cub scout activites at that time.
36 *Ames Tribune,* 1942, "They Set Eagle Scout Record." Included were: Thomas Maney, Harry Price, Louis Cooper, Frank Ferguson, Paul Vance, David Maney, Irving Pratt, Owen Shadle, and Dean Hausrasth.
37 In 1941, merit awards for adult leadership were presented to Edgar V. Collins, Lee V. McMillan, Don Watts, and Art Risse, all of Ames.
38 *Ames Tribune,* May 10, 1932, p.1, "Ames Will Soon Have Cub Pack in Action."
39 *Des Moines Register,* July 10, 1937, p.2, "Scouting Grows Up." Reprinted from *Time Magazine.*

Broken Arrow District scouters at Ft. Pella (Stockade Fort) at Camp Mitigwa, July 1997. Left to right: Robert "Buck" Melton*, Tom Norton*, Diane Meyer, Max Noack, Peg DeHoet, Jim De Hoet*, Ethan Olberding*; Bob Folkmannn and Steve Pendry, scout leader, Troop 140. Members of Ames Troop 140 are sponsored by Bethesdsa Lutheran Church. (Diane Meyer is with Pack 160.) These scouters were in session the day I visited Camp Matigwa. After taking this photo, I had lunch with them in the Pella Stockade. * Indicates an Eagle Scout.

Scout executive Ely Brewer leads a session with Ames scout leaders at the Pella Stockade (Camp Mitigwa) in July 1997.

fond memories of my scouting days in Ames when I was a young boy. Troop 2 was, I think, the first troop in the Fourth Ward. It was sponsored by the Collegiate Presbyterian Church. G. B. MacDonald was the scoutmaster." Fred's brother Sam was later a scoutmaster and his younger brothers Richard and William were also very active scouts in Ames.

Scouting attracts and serves boys from all economic levels of society. Much might be said about scouting's special ability to serve boys of our middle class society including those less economically advantaged. The scout program long ago became "of age," as pointed out in a feature article in the *Des Moines Register.*[39] Once a boy has qualified as a first-class scout, the entire merit badge program opens up a wide range of interest areas that leads the scout across the threshhold not just to his teenage interests but to possible lifetime interests. Career oriented merit badge units include "animal science", "American cultures," "agribusiness," "art," "environmental science," "journalism," "architecture," and "fish and wildlife management," to mention a very few of the over one hundred subjects offered to scouts today. Because the overall scout program has stayed current with the needs of boys, it continues to serve them well.

Ames Troop No. 196 had produced thirty-five eagle scouts by the time I took this picture of their flag in 1997. The flag was held by two eagle scout candidates (not shown) at the time. ID No.200.1133.3-4-5

Lewis Harris & Associates conducted a research study for the Boy Scouts of America in 1995. Their report includes these conclusions: "Former scouts credit their scouting experience with many positive effects on their lives and on society in general." "Many *leaders* who were not scouts endorse the scouting movement as beneficial to society." and "Former scouts indicate higher ethical and moral standards than non-scouts, particularly among those boys who have tenures of at least five years in scouting."[40]

Since the first days of the Boy Scouts of America, the program has provided men and boys the opportunity to work together to develop the traditions of healthy living. Its place in the scheme of society is as vital today as it was in 1910 when it was first made available to Ames boys by Ernest Thompson Seton. Scouting is today a leading youth program. There is much talk of a more diverse society, and it must be recognized that there must also be diversity among organizations as well. No one organization can best serve all elements of our population as it has come to exist today. The boy scout organization, by remaining true to its objectives, continues to serve a significant part of present-day society.

The boy scout program, as has been demonstrated in the Ames experience, reflects the devotion of a group of Ames men who, as early as 1910, recognized the value of scouting to boys. Its success is also the result of the continued interest, effort, and commitment of several generations of scout leaders who have served since. The final proof of the boy scout experience is found in the hundreds of scouts themselves, many of whom will tell you, of fond memories of their scouting days and of the contribution made by the scouting experience to their adult lives.

July 6, 1997

---

[40] "The Values of Men and Boys in America," a research study conducted by Louis Harris & Associates for the Boy Scouts of America, May 10, 1995, 28 pp. See also: Graduate thesis written by Delores Crum, student at Augsburg College, following the Harris Study. Her thesis evaluated the mid-Iowa program, among her conclusions: "The majority of Iowa respondents indicated they continue to believe in the scouting values of family, community, duty to country, respect, thrift, helping others, and doing one's best."

Chapter 12

New York-To-Paris

The Famous Automobile Race In 1908

New York to Paris by car - and the route called for those cars to pass through Ames, Iowa!

The year was 1908, and six cars lined up near Times Square in New York City for the start of the first international automobile race ever held. Promoted by the fledgling Automobile Club of America, it drew attention across the country that resembled the excitement of the effort to fly the Atlantic nearly twenty years later.

The six cars left New York on the morning of February 12, 1908. There were three French cars, the De Dion, the Moto Bloc, and the Sizaire et Naudinan; an Italian car, the Zust; a German car, the Protos; and an American car, the Thomas Flyer.

The projected route crossed the United States from New York to San Francisco, then by boat to Alaska, across the Berring Sea to Asia and through Siberia to Europe, Germany and ending at Paris. A total of 21,000 miles, or 13,000 miles on land and 8,000 on water. Of the thousands who witnessed

the start of the race that day in New York, "barely a handful expected the cars to reach Paris."[1]

The little one cylinder French car, the Sizaire Naudin, was the first to drop out. Confronted immediately by snow storms, it did not survive the Hudson River Valley. By Erie, Pennsylvania, the American Thomas was in the lead followed by the De Dion and the Zust. They covered 220 miles in one day between Erie and Toledo, Ohio, but blizzards slowed progress to only seven miles on the fourteen-hour day that followed. They were forced to travel along railroad right-of-ways at one point near South Bend, Indiana.

Add snow drifts to the country roads of 1908 and you have the story of the race as it battled its way across the midwest.

On February 20, 1908, Mayor Parley Sheldon of Ames received word that the Des Moines representatives of the American Automobile Association, with the Howard Auto Car Company serving as host, would banquet the "around the world racers" at the Ames Hotel upon their arrival here. The arrival date was expected to be February 20 or 21. The racers had been banqueted in Chicago; Ames would do the same according to Sheldon.[2]

When the racers reached central Iowa the banquet was set for March 2. A special interurban car brought the Des Moines delegation consisting of their Fire Chief Burnett, Chief of Police Jones, and ten

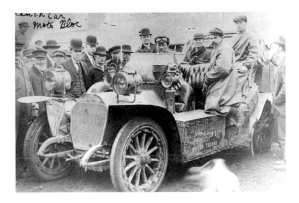

The French Moto Bloc shown here enroute through Story County. This picture was taken in Nevada. on March 16, 1908. Notice the attire of the the French crew of three. Photo courtesy of Carl W. Allen, Nevada, Iowa. ID No. 213.1209.1-4

[1] *New York To Paris 1908,* p.10, by Floyd Clymer, Reprinted 1951.
[2] *Ames Evening Times*, February 20, 1908, p.6, "Auto Racers Will Dine Here."

The Ames Hotel as it appeared in 1908 when the banquet was held there to honor the New York to Paris racers. It was on the north-west corner of Main Street and Duff Avenue. ID No.44.219A.1

Des Moines business men. They were joined by two Boone representatives. Ames Mayor Parley Sheldon; Dr. A. B. Storms, president of Iowa State College; L. M. Bosworth; Lon Hardin, publisher of the Ames *Evening Times*; Rev. William Minchin; and F. E. Colburn the official college photographer, were on hand to assist in hosting the occasion.

The American car, the Thomas Flyer, arrived in Ames moving slowly as it entered town with a locally appointed escort.[3]   A big crowd was on hand as handshakes and greetings were exchanged in front of the hotel at the corner of Main Street and Duff Avenue. The *Times* reported that it was a fine occasion, but somewhat a disappointment because the crew of the American car, after they had said "thank you" had passed up the banquet and immediately continued their drive westward.   "It was without doubt one of the finest banquets that have been spread

---

[3] Warren Beckwith with his White Steamer was the honor escort according to the *Ames Times* report.

[4] *Ames Evening Times,* March 5, 1908, p.2, "Auto Banquet A Nice One."

[5] *The Longest Auto Race,* by George Schuster, 1966, published by the John Day Company, p.45.

[6] *Ames Evening Times,* March 5, 1908, p.1, "Endurance Is The Object."

[7] *The Longest Auto Race,* by George Schuster, 1966, p. 46. Letter: P.D.Sargent to George Schuster.

[8] *Ames Evening Times*, March 5, 1908, p.1 "Spent Night Here." "Italian Car In Endurance Race From New York To Paris Spent Night In Ames."

in this city for a long while," a local news account reported.[4]

The crew of the American car had passed up that banquet held in their honor in Ames, but they would later recall how a lot of college students and Ames youngsters cheered them as they struggled through Ames.[5]

A large crowd had been standing around awaiting the arrival of the American car. Some had expressed disappointment when they observed how slowly the cars were moving. Local auto enthusiasts, however, explained that the object of the great race was intended to be "endurance" more than speed.[6]

A boy of eighteen was in that crowd in Ames that day. He lived on a farm 12 miles south of Ames, and his father had a two cylinder Reo but refused to use it in the mud.   The young man had heard about the expected arrival of the racing cars, so he drove a team of horses to Ames.   He recalled waiting six hours to witness the arrival of the Thomas Flyer; he never forgot the excitment of that day and his wish that he might join the crew of the famous car.[7]

The Italian car, Zust, arrived in Ames the next day at about 8 P.M. having covered the distance from Marshalltown in four hours.   It was driven into L. R. Morris Livery where it was overhauled thoroughly. The car was washed down removing several hundred pounds of mud.[8]

The French car, the De Dion, passed through Ames on the evening of March 11.   The driver and

The American Thomas Flyer shown at the Duff Avenue and Main Street corner on March 2, 1908.   Munn Lumber yard is in left background. Monty Roberts was the driver, George Schuster was the mechanic. George Miller was added to the crew at Buffalo. The sideboards apparently were added to carry their luggage as well as repairs for the car. This car was declared the winner when it entered Paris, France on July 30, 1908. Photo courtesy of the Iowa Department of Transportation.   ID No. 212.1263.3-4-5

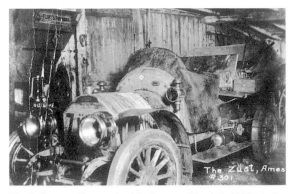

The Italian car, Zust, arrived in Ames on March 3, 1908 missing the big banquet and celebration in the Ames hotel on Main Street the day before. This photo taken of the Zust when it was in the Morris Livery on Main Street in Ames where it had just been completely washed and "serviced." Note the advertisement on the wall for "FLINTS POWDERS for horses and cattle." Photo cortesy of Carl W. Allen, Nevada, Iowa. ID No. 212.1208.2-4

The German Protos required repairs when it arrived in Ames on March 16,1908. The Sigma Nu fraternity entertained the German crew, made up of Lieutenant Koeppen, Ernest Maas; and Hans Knape, with lodging and meals until their car was repaired. The crew rewarded the fraternity by sending them one of their tires as a souvenir. Photo taken when car was in Story County near Colo. Photo courtesy of Carl W. Allen, Nevada, Iowa. ID No.213.1210.2-4

The French car, De Dion, came through Ames on March 11, 1908. This car passed through Ames making no stops. The crew had their evening meal in Boone reaching Jefferson by moonlight that same day. This pictire taken in Mechanicsville, Iowa a day or two earlier Photo courtesy of Carl W. Allen, Nevada, Iowa. ID No, 212.1206.1-2

crew spent no time looking over the town and apparently made no stops to converse with anyone. They were reported to have stopped for a meal in Boone and continued on, reaching Jefferson by moonlight.[9]

The German Protos arrived in Ames on March 16, requiring extensive repairs that tied up their crew in Ames over Sunday. The Sigma Nu fraternity boys took the men to their house where they royally entertained them at dinner and put them up for the night. At that time the Sigma Nu fraternity was located on the northwest corner of Ninth Street and Douglas Avenue in downtown Ames. When the Germans left the next day they assured the young men that

they might expect a souvenir of the race. Several weeks later, the Protos burst one of its huge tires at Salt Lake City. The old tire was immediately shipped to the Sigma Nus where it was prominently displayed in their fraternity house.[10]

The last of the international cars to come through Ames was the second French car, the Moto Bloc. It came along on Monday, March 16,1908. Local photographer Hart took a picture of the car as it stood in front of a cafe on Main Street, and college photographer Colburn caught it with his camera as it went up the hill on Boone Street near the campus. Local comment was that the Moto Bloc was a "handsome car and far better equipped for the hardships of the long journey than the German car that had preceded it from this city by a few hours."[11]

The French Moto Bloc came though Ames on March 16, 1908. It is shown here as it went west on Boone Street. Photo was taken as the car went up the hill west of Beach Avenue on Boone Street (Lincoln Way after 1914). Today, Linden Hall is at left, and fraternity houses line the street on the right. Its crew of three were M. Goddard, M. Hue and M. Livier. Photo courtesy Iowa State Univerisy Archives / Parks Library. ID No. 210.1193.5

[9] *ibid,* March 12, 1908, p.3, "French Car Went Past."
[10] *ibid,* April 16, 1908, p.2, "Souvenir Of The Race."
[11] *ibid,* March 19, 1908, p.1 "The Last Car Sails Past."

At that point it was reported that the American car was two weeks ahead of the last three cars to pass through Ames. As far as Ames was concerned, the New York to Paris automobile race was about over![12]

Much to the surprise of some Ames people, the second car to drop out of the race was the French Moto Bloc; its driver found Iowa's winter weather too severe.

The eyes of the American public continued to follow the remaining cars in their battles with blizzards in the midwest, sandstorms in the west, and the unbelievable problems that they endured in driving the cars across almost uncharted portions of their route. In 1908, there were places where roads seemed to not exist. Interest in their progress remained high. The racers continued to receive excited attention. A crowd of cowboys yelling like Comanche Indians, and 100 automobiles, escorted the American car into Cheyenne, Wyoming where they drew the attention of the entire population.[13]

Four of the original cars that left New York on February 12 succeeded in reaching San Francisco. When the American car, still in the lead, went by boat to Alaska it became apparent that the terrain and conditions there were not at all suitable to automobile travel. Changed route plans were devised that brought the car back to Seattle and then all the contestants were directed by boat to Japan. The race continued across the island then again by boat to the China mainland and on to the Russian Siberian plains.

The French De Dion dropped from the race at Vladivostok, the last of the original starters to leave the race. The remaining cars experienced bad weather and primitve roads in Siberia where at one point they resorted to travel on the track of the Trans-Siberian. The American car finally entered Germany on July 21.

Finally at 8:00 on July 30, the American car drove into Paris to be declared the winner of the longest automobile race ever. The German Protos had arrived in Paris at 6:15 on July 26; however, the Protos had been officially penalized 30 days some days earlier because it had omitted the 1,100 mile segment connected with the American car's jaunt to Alaska.

The Thomas Flyer arrived in Paris 169 days after the race had begun at New York. It had traveled 13,341 miles, which was 3,246 more miles than the German Protos. The Italian car, the Zust, arrived in Paris on September 17, 1908. Of the six cars that left New York City on February 12, three had attained the goal.

The stamina of both the American automobile, and the human personnel involved, had established the potential for the automobile in the world of transportation. The world had begun to get smaller. Better roads would soon be coming, at least in parts of the world.

It may have been coincidental; however, the race that had begun in New York on Lincoln's birthday in 1908, had blazed a trail across the United States much of which, five years later, became the Lincoln Highway.

September 15, 1998

---

[12] *Iowa State College Student,* March 16, 1908, p.4, "Auto Race About Over."

[13] *New York to Paris, 1908,* by Floyd Clymer, p. 19.

CHAPTER 13

We Ride Our Shetland Ponies

Before I had a bicycle, I had a Shetland pony. That was in 1919. At least five of us in downtown Ames had ponies. We ranged in age from nine to the mid-teens. I was the youngest.

Gwen Edwards,[1] Conrad Stephenson, Loren Bower, Harold Knight, and I were the five that I recall having ponies. Gwen's father was the minister of First Methodist Church. Conrad's father was a part of the Tilden Store operation, and was associated there with my father. Loren's father was with the post office. Harold's father operated the popular Knight's Pony Farm on north Grand Avenue. He had lots of ponies.

Knight's farm was located on the quarter section of land just north of Thirteenth Street and west of Grand Avenue.

Harold Knight's sister Gladys and his brother Lloyd were pony enthusiasts ahead of my time. Gladys Knight, the oldest of the Knight children, rode her pony in the Memorial Day Parade in 1913. Gladys graduated from Ames High School in 1922. Harold and I were classmates in Ames High's class of 1929. Conrad Stephenson and I rode our ponies together a number of times. Most of us rode alone around our own neighborhoods. The Knight children did most of their riding right on their farmstead.

My neighborhood buddy, Olin Stoddard, didn't have a pony; he had a bicycle, a small-sized wheel made for boys of about age ten. I had my pony. I had no bicycle. When I had asked my father to get me a bicycle, his response was that I already had the pony-didn't I think that was sufficient?

Olin wanted a pony; I wanted a bicycle. We had a solution to that problem: I rode Olin's bicycle and he rode my pony! We rode all over downtown Ames together. It seemed a good deal to both of us at the time.

Loren Bower "outgrew" his pony before I did. After I acquired his pony cart, I took my friends for

Gladys Knight, on her pony, leads the children in the 1913 Memorial Day parade. The parade formed in front of the Methodist church. The old post office on southwest corner of Kellogg and Fifth Street is in background. ID No.105.576.1

This was my pony, Betty, shown when I was about nine years old. Photo taken in the driveway of our home at 1011 Kellogg Avenue in 1919. ID No.197.1117.1-2

---

[1] Gwen is thought to have been her first name. F. C. Edwards was pastor of the First Methodist Church, 1918 -1924. Gwen Edwards graduated from Ames High School in 1922.

Olin Stoddard rode my pony while I rode his bicycle. Olin is shown here on the pony as he was about to ride down into the street. Olin was the only other child that Betty would "allow" to ride her. ID No.188.1063.1

rides. It had wooden-spoked wheels with steel rims and a seat with low sides. It wasn't fancy, but was sturdy.

Outgrowing a Shetland pony meant that as a boy's legs got longer, his feet would drag on the ground when he rode. We could ride around in that cart for a time after that.

The pony's soft tread and a near quiet ride down Kellogg Avenue in that cart added a bit of tranquility to the day for a ten-year-old boy and his friends.

Shetland ponies are not shod. Most of our cross streets were dirt which made for comfortable trotting for ponies. The soft sound of pony hooves on pavement was a part of the fun.

Having a pony when I was a boy meant taking care of it. Our ponies had names. Mine was Betty, Connie Stephenson's was named Ginger, and Loren

The pony cart that I had after Loren Bower "outgrew" it. Bower lived on the corner of Clark Avenue and Ninth Street at the time. Loren is shown here about 1917 with reins in hand. His younger sister, Ula, then age five, is one of the chldren enjoying the ride. I acquired the cart about 1920. ID No.190.1080.1-5

---

[2] Give Betty the benefit of the doubt, however, and credit that stomp to the fly that may have just bitten her leg!

Bower's was Daisy. We had a pony shed out in back of our house with a fenced pony run between it and my father's car garage.

That shed was originally built to serve as storage for kindling wood, cobs, and coal for the kitchen stove of earlier days. We converted it into a stable with manger and storage for hay, oats, and straw. I kept the pony supplied through the pass-through between the manger and the storage area.

Shetland ponies were lots of fun but a lot of work. There were challenges. Betty was smart. She was not about to let just anyone ride her. Except for me, and usually Olin Stoddard, she was stubborn transportation! She had tricky ways to prevent others from riding her.

A boy who lived several blocks from us begged me to let him ride my pony. I explained that the pony might not accept him; he still wanted to ride her. Once on the pony, he rode down into the street. After trotting a short distance, Betty turned and galloped into our front yard where she promptly laid down and rolled over, depositing the would-be rider on the gound.

When a neighbor girl persisted in wanting to ride my pony, I warned her, but told her how to control Betty. She got to the Kellogg and Tenth Street corner where the pony suddenly reversed direction and galloped at top speed right back into our yard. Darting under the low branches of the nearest apple tree, the pony unceremoniously brushed the girl off onto the ground.

Betty once took a neighbor boy on the run to the pony yard. Rushing through the shed door, she rudely brushed off her unwanted rider.

That pony never tried those tricks on me, perhaps because I was the one who cleaned her stable, fed her hay, oats, and, once in awhile, a lump of sugar for her good conduct. But one time, while I was putting her bridle on, she saw an opportunity to even a score with me. Without warning, she stomped her right front hoof down hard on my bare foot! Ouch![2]

My pony got out of her fenced run one day. We found her not far from home grazing in someone's yard. The staples that held up the woven wire fence on one side of her yard had been pulled. That was a puzzle. Only a human being could have done that.

A day or two later, I found her lying down, backed up to that same fence, rolling back and forth with her back pulling that woven wire fence right down to the ground! Each roll saw more staples fly. We found a better way to hold that fence in place.

We had great fun when there was snow on the streets. In the 1920s, streets were not cleared as they

Only once did my pony stomp on my bare foot when I was changing her halter or bridle. Probably that stomping action was her reaction to flies biting rather than having any "get even" intentions directed toward me. This picture taken about 1920 when I tethered Betty around much of our half-block yard in order to keep the grass mowed. ID No. 187.1061. 5

Knight's Pony Farm was located north of Thirteenth Street and west of Grand Avenue. This picture is from an aeriel photograph taken in about 1945 after residential development had begun in that area. The farm house located facing Grand Avenue can be seen adjacent to the large barn standing near Harding Avenue that by that time had a few homes north of Thirteenth. Grand Avenue's paving was still just two driving lanes. The Knight family children were Lloyd, Gladys, and Harold. Harold, the youngest, was an Ames High classmate of mine in 1929. ID No. 188.1068.2-5

are today. Instead the snow was packed down under wheels of cars and under the runners of the bob sleds that farmers brought to town. That was when we tied our sleds on behind the pony.

I'd hitch my sled to the pony. With reins in hand, I'd head for the snow-packed streets. Neighbor kids would join ranks, each lying belly down on his sled, grasping the rear runner struts of the rear sled forming a "sled train" behind the pony. We'd go around our part of town after a good snow. Traffic was not a problem.[3] Few cars were parked on the streets in those days.

If too many sleds came on board, it made it hard for the boy nearest the front to hang on. When that happened, I would coax the pony to trot faster. Then we'd make a quick turn at a street corner creating a crack-the-whip effect. Several tail-end sleds would usually "let go."[4]

These memories suggest that living in Ames in the teens and twenties provided some exciting advantages. It did. But when we had ponies in town, remember that we still had horse-drawn bob sleds every winter and farmers tied up their teams down by our city park on Fifth Street. The city still employed a street cleaner on Main Street.

When I got my pony in 1919, it had been only two years since our fire wagon was horse-drawn and we had a manure pile in the alley on the south side of our city hall.

August 11, 1996

---

[3] The residential section north of Main Street.
[4] Too many sleds made it harder for the pony as well.

Chapter 14

Thomas MacDonald

He Standardized Our Nation's Highway System
1881-1957

He would become the first chief engineer of the Iowa Highway Commission. In 1904, the thirtieth Iowa General Assemble had designated the Iowa State College to act as a Highway Commission. That action had been the direct result of the efforts made by two of Iowa States College's deans, Anson Marston and Charles F. Curtiss. The two deans were then appointed by the trustees to serve as the first commissioners. Thomas MacDonald, who had just gradu-

Tom MacDonald, Iowa's first chief highway engineer, 1904 - 1919, and early chief of the U.S. Bureau of Roads, 1919 - 1953. Photo courtesy of Iowa Department of Transportation.   ID NO. 156.861.4-6

[1] *Trasnportation In Iowa; An Historical Summary* by William H. Thompson. 1989. Iowa Department of Transportation.
[2] *America's Highways 1776 - 1976* Federal Highway Administration. Biographical account of Thomas Harris MacDonald. pp 176 - 179.

ated from Iowa State, and was an assistant professor for highway engineering was appointed as an assistant in charge of field operations.

The Highway Commission's operations at that point were a part of the college's engineering research program. Its first biennial appropriation in 1904 was $7,000.[1]   MacDonald's salary was $100 a month, with $50 of that amount provided by the Iowa Good Roads Association.

"Rugged integrity," "honesty," "fairness," "inspirational," "sound, far sighted leadership," and "dedicated public servant" were expressions used by many who came to know Thomas Harris MacDonald.[2]

MacDonald was born in Leadville, Colorado, in 1881. His family moved to Iowa when he was three and he grew up on a farm in the Montezuma area. He graduated from Iowa State College in 1904 with a degree in civil engineering. Under the supervision of Dean Anson Marston, he did his undergraduate thesis on the highway needs of Iowa farmers.

MacDonald was 26 in 1907 when he was appointed state highway engineer. In 1913, with the appointment of a three man Highway Commission, his title became "chief engineer."

During MacDonald's 15 year tenure with the Iowa Highway Commission, Iowa became one of the first midwestern states to develop a system of main roads. By 1919, about one third of Iowa's designated 6,400 miles of road network was permanently graded, drained, and provided with bridges. MacDonald had developed a plan for hard-surfacing Iowa roads. His success attracted the attention of highway officials and of the automobile industry. He had become a leader among highway officials and was active in the American Association of State Highway Officials.

In 1919, Tom MacDonald was called to serve as chief of the U.S. Bureau of Public Roads, chosen by President Wilson on the basis of the recommendation of the American Association of Highway Officials. As an early chief highway engineer at the federal level, MacDonald became the guiding hand for the development of the most extensive road building program in history.

In 1953 when he retired, millions of hard-surfaced, efficient highways had been constructed across the nation and the national system of interstate highways was about to begin.

During his career, Tom MacDonald received many honors. Awarded an honorary degree in engineering by Iowa State College in 1929, he received the "Marston Medal for Achievement in Engineering" in 1939. He received the "Medal of Merit" for outstanding service during World War II. He received the "Chicago Alumni Award." In 1931 he received the "George Bartlet Award," and was designated an honorary member in the American Society of Civil Engineers.

In the international field, his advice was sought, and given, all over the world. Among the honors that he was given by foreign governments were the "Cross of the Legion of Honor" by the French government, and "Knight of the First Class, Order of St.Olav," by the King of Norway.

In 1934, the Oskaloosa, Iowa, newspaper suggested that new federal Highway 63 be named MacDonald Highway in honor of their distinguished native son. Commenting on that suggestion, Fred White, MacDonald's successor as Chief Engineer of Iowa's Highway Commission, said in a *Des Moines Register* report that "He did a wonderful work here in Iowa in the early days of our road development, and during the past 16 years as chief of the Bureau of Public Roads he has performed a marvelous service to this nation."

MacDonald is considered by many to have been a leading personality in launching Iowa's Highway Commission on the course that established it as the premier highway department in the nation.

Following his retirement, MacDonald accepted the position of distinguished research engineer in the Transportation Institute of Texas A & M College. He died there on April 7, 1957.

From the Washing*ton Post* editorial of Tuesday April 16, 1957, we have these words:[3]

"It was Thomas MacDonald who persuaded Congress to pass the first Federal highway legislation under which the National Government shared costs and set specifications for major road construction. He administered the expenditure of these funds with uncompromising devotion to the public interest, and with an absolute avoidance of politics which kept him at his post under seven Presidents and 17 Congresses. In 1950, he appealed to the Congress for a vast program of highway modernization and development, which at last took form in the 50 million dollar National Highway Act adopted last year. Everyone who drives a car or truck, for business or pleasure, across the face of America stands indebted to this quiet, forceful public servant who earned the title "the father of all good roads in the United States."

January 15, 1997

---

[3] *Washinton Post*, April 16, 1957, editorial page.

Chapter 15

Conde McCullough, Bridge Engineer

(An Original with the Iowa Highway Commission)
1887 - 1946

Conde McCullough graduated from Iowa State College in 1910 with a degree in civil engineering. In 1913, he married a college classmate, and they started housekeeping at 1010 Kellogg Avenue, next door to my home. My father often spoke of McCullough in those days, so that when his name came up recently in connection with the history of the Iowa Highway Commission, it brought back a few memories of my own.

Conde McCullough was to become a nationally known and highly regarded bridge engineer. Though in Iowa but a few years, it was here that he established the foundation for his reputation. The influence of his Iowa experience can be seen throughout his career.

Born in Redfield, South Dakota, May 30, 1887, McCullough's piblic schoolng had been in Fort Dodge.[1] He graduated from Iowa Sate College in 1910 with the degree in Civil Engineering. When McCullough graduated from Iowa State, its enrollment totaled less than 2,000. He had a close association during his college days with Dean Anson Marston, whose reputation and influence in the engineering profession, especially in the field of highway development, was nationally rocognized.

McCullough's first employment following graduation from Iowa State was with the Marsh engineering firm of Des Moines, a major regional bridge designing and building firm. His experience with John B .Marsh, who was also an Iowa State engineering graduate, further influenced the development of McCullough's philosphy of bridge design.[2]

Conde Balcom McCullough, in the 1940s became an adminstrator and writer.

In 1911, McCullough became an assistant engineer with the Iowa Highway Commission. Established in 1904, the commission at that time was an arm of Iowa State College with the deans of Engineering and Agriculture serving as the official commissioners. Its mission was that of an advisory agency providing guidance on road building matters to the counties and cities within the state.

In 1913, the state legislature enlarged the commission's responsibilites. Chief Engineer, Tho-

---

[1] *The Oregon Statesman*, Salem, Oregon, May 7, 1946, p.2, "Death Ends Career of Famed Highway Engineer."
[2] *Pacific Northwest Quarterly*, Vo.82, no.1, January 1991, p.8, Robert W. Hadlow, "C.B.McCullough, The Engineer and Oregon's Bridge Building Boom, 1919 - 1936."

mas MacDonald, an Iowa State graduate of 1904 and an original Marston appointee, then named McCullough to the position of design engineer. Federal engineers were soon reporting that Iowa had what were described as the "best bridge and culvert designs of any state in the union. Much of the credit for that reputation went to Conde McCullough."[3]

There had been no standardization of bridge designs in use in the state prior to 1913. An out-of-state bridge engineer by the name of Daniel B. Luten held patents on bridge designs, making them available through agents to a number of Iowa counties. Between 1907 and 1913, about twenty Iowa counties had built Luten patented bridges. In 1913, the commission, having acquired jurisdiction over the construction of roads and bridges in the state, began to evaluate those bridge designs.

McCullough and the Iowa Highway Commission engineers were soon contending that the payment of royalties to Luten for his bridge designs was unnecessary since his designs were, in fact, based upon engineering principles that were in the public domain.. The major objection, however, to the Luten-patented bridge designs was their non-conformity with engineering practices then established by the Iowa Commission. It was believed his designs did not provide sound structures. Too often, patented plans were selected on the basis of cost rather than suitabilty to the conditions under which they must function.[4]

The Luten firm circulated charges of infringements on their designs with the result that the Iowa Attorney General employed Wallace R. Lane, a patent attorney, to investigate the firm's claims. Commission engineers prepared a detailed report on the construction of reinforced concrete bridges. The patent attorney found no evidence of infringement in any of the commission's plans.

In 1911, litigation over infringement of patented Luten bridge plans was instigated by Luten against the Marsh engineering firm of Des Moines.[5] The Iowa Attorney General was called upon to defend the construction firm. Conde McCullough, by then the commissioin's bridge engineer, was assigned by Tom MacDonald, the job of assisting Mr. Lane and Mr. Sampson in the defense of the suit.[6]

While the case had begun in late 1911, its defense did not begin until 1913.[7] McCullough's key research during the trial was monumental. Over six hundred pages of testimony resulted. One hundred and fifty exhibits were introduced, and fifteen miniature bridge models were made for use in the trial.

On January 3, 1918, after many months of research and testimony, Federal Judge Martin J. Wade, for the Southern District of Iowa, rendered his oral opinion holding a number of Luten patent claims on concrete bridge construction invalid and dismissing the petition of the plaintiff in the case of Daniel B.Luten versus the Marsh engineering firm.

Five month later, on the last day of June 1918, the Lincoln Way bridge in Ames over the Squaw Creek collapsed.[8] The Ames bridge had been a Luten-designed bridge; it had been built ten years earlier[9] under the juisdiction of the Story County supervisors.

The story of the Squaw Creek bridge interestingly illustrates the problem with the early day use of the patented designs. The Story County supervisors had received bids ranging from $10,630 to $10,900 that were based upon design plans submitted by the Iowa Highway Commission for the Squaw Creek bridge in Ames. The low bid had been submitted by Marsh Engineering of Des Moines.[10] The supervisors opened the bids on May 7, 1908. On June 1, 1908 they rejected all bids, stating that they were "too high."[11]

On August 3, 1908, having discarded the recommendations of the Highway Commission engineers, the supervisors contracted with the Stark engineering firm of Des Moines to build the Squaw Creek bridge in Ames for $6,485 based upon a design plan provided by Luten.[12] That was $4,145 less than Marsh's rejected bid.[13] Dean Marston would pronounce the bridge's failure in 1918 as being the result of inadequate footings and reinforcement.

McCullough's involvement in the technical

[3] ibid. "Soon federal engineers reportedly commented that Iowa had the best bridges and culverts of any state in the Union. McCullough deserved much of the credit, prompting MacDonald, soon to become chief of the U.S.Bureau of Public Roads, to promote him assistant highway engineer."
[4] Prior to 1913, part of the problem was the lack of engineering competence at the county level where decisions were often made.
[5] This involved the design and construction of a bridge at Albert Lea, Minnesota.
[6] The Iowa Engineer, Vol 18, No.4, (January 1918), p. 122
[7] ibid, pp. 117- 127. Provides details of this federal case.
[8] Ames Tribune, July 1, 1918, p.1, "Squaw Creek Bridge Collapsed."
[9] The Intelligencer, December 31, 1908, p.1 "Squaw Creek Bridge Completed."
[10] The Marsh firm also had submitted a bid of $8,180 based on their own design.
[11] Story County Supervisors, Minute Book "F," page 86.
[12] Intelligencer, December 31, 1908, p. 1, "Fine Structure now Completed." Confirmed the $6,485 cost.
[13] Ames Evening Times, April 28, 1908, p.1, "Cement Bridge Over Squaw Creek." The City Council agreed to pay for grading for the new bridge. County to pay contract cost of bridge construction.

preparation for that federal litigation proved to have been a significant factor in his developement as a bridge designer. It had added to his experience acquired with Marsh Engineering where he first undertook experimental work with reinforced-concrete bridge design. "By compiling a persuasive body of evidence that would win the suit for his old employer, McCullough acquired in-depth knowledge about the capabilities of concrete that served him for a lifetime."[14]

In 1916, McCullough had accepted a position as head of the Engineering Department at Oregon State College in Salem, Oregon. In 1919 he became the chief bridge designer for the Oregon State Highway Commission. He was destined to become interna-

tionally recognized as a bridge designer and engineer. An engineering historian recently stated that, "The Oregon Coast Highway has one of the great, perhaps unequaled collections of bridges in the United States. That Conde McCullough built ten major bridges on it, no two alike, in the space of eight years, during the heighth of the depression, is nothing short of amazing."[15] Another example of his work was the Dr. John D. McLaughlin Bridge in Portland which won the 1933 award of the American Institute of Steel Construction for beauty of design.

In 1935, McCullough's former Iowa associate, Tom MacDonald, who, in 1919, had left Ames to become the Chief Engineer and Director of the U.S.Bureau of Roads in Washington, D.C., called upon McCullough to design the bridges on the Pan American Highway in Central America. McCullough received a year's leave of absence from Oregon to carry out that assignment. MacDonald would turn to McCullough's talents on other similar assignments as well.[16]

---

[14] *"Bridges, A History of the Worlds Most Famous and Important Spans,"* Judith Duprey, New York: Black Dog & Leventhal Publishers, 1997.

[15] *ibid.* Eric DeLony, from conversation with Judith Dupre.

[16] McCullough had received a law degree from Willamette University in 1928 and an honorary engineering degree from Oregon State College in 1934. He authored several books on engineering.

The Conde B.McCullough Bridge at Coos Bay on the coast of Oregon. Designed and built by McCullough in 1936, it was dedicated in his memory and renamed in ceremonies held on the bridge on August 27, 1947. Courtesy of Iowa State University Archives / Parks Library.

McCullough suffered a stroke and died shortly before his 59th birthday at his home in Salem, Oregon, on May 6, 1946. A year later, on August 27, 1947, a tribute to Conde McCullough was held on the Highway 101 mile-long Coos Bay bridge which he had designed and built in 1936. All members of the highway commission with McCullough's widow, their son and his wife were present for the ceremonies. Fifty others stood at the south approach to the bridge to listen to talks lauding the accomplishments of McCullough, who had served Oregon as a faculty member of Oregon State College, as the state's bridge engineer, and was the assistant state highway engineer at the time of his death.

"Conde McCullough was more than a bridge designer," R. H. Baldock, state highway engineer, told the assembly, "He was an artist and a genius. The beautiful span here is also pleasing to the aesthetic sense." The name of the bridge was officially changed and dedicated to be known as the Conde B. McCullough bridge.[17] Iowans who sense the full context of McCoullough's life experience would agree with Baldock's assessment.

McCullough's career began in Iowa. His early association with Dean Anson Marston, a recognized leader in the field of engineering, and especially his continued association with John Marsh,[18] and Tom MacDonald both Iowa State graduates, suggests his strong Iowa professional roots.

Iowa State College's Engineering Dean, Anson Marston, taught a special course for his students entitled *"Engineering Aesthetics."* Marston would have been proud of McCullough's bridges which were described at the time of his death as "The monuments of his genius....the beautiful bridges which fit as smoothly as steel and concrete can be made to do into the grandure traversed by Oregon highways."[19]

August 24, 1998

---

[17] "Spanning the tide rivers of the Oregon coast, the snow fed Clackamas of the Pacific Highway, the dark gorge of Crooked River, stand the strong and graceful monuments to C.B.McCullough, assistant highway engineer whose death Monday halted a great engineering career. The monuments of his genius and his unsparing work for the people of Oregon are the beautiful bridges which fit as smoothly as steel and concrete may be made to do into the scenic grandure traversed by Oregon highways." — from Conde McCullough's obituary, the *Oregon Statesman,* (Salem, Oregon), May 7, 1946.

[18] *The Oregonian*, Portland, Oregon, May 7, 1947, p. 18, "Span Dedicated to Builder Conde Balcom McCullough."

[19] See footnote No. 17.

Chapter 16

Lincoln Highway Memories

The Lincoln Highway was dedicated as the great national roadway on October 31, 1913. Celebrations were held on that day in many towns on the transcontinental route. In Ames, the Lincoln Highway was routed on Boone Street[1] from the east edge of town on through Campustown to Pike Street (now Sheldon Avenue) then north to North Hyland Avenue and on north to Ontario Road. The Highway followed Ontario Road west to the Boone County line one mile west of Ontario.

In late April, 1914, the Ames City Council officially changed the names of respective portions of those local streets to become the unified "Lincoln Way."[2]

By October, 1914, the city, with the cooperation of the good roads committee of the Ames Commercial Club, had a paint crew out putting up Lincoln Way street signs. They placed Lincoln Highway markings on poles, beginning at a point half way between Ames and Nevada continuing to the Boone County line. In town, signs were placed at street intersections, especially at corners where the highway made a turn. At Duff and Grand Avenues, large signs were placed giving directions to the Ames business district.

Referred to as the "Main Street of America," the Lincoln Highway was soon bringing "good roads" promotions of all kinds through town. Sponsored by the Lincoln Highway Association and often, jointly or independently, by the manufacturers of automobiles, tires, or motor oils, the objective was to promote highway improvement and to demonstrate the advantages of the transcontinental highway. For example, there was a cross country excursion through Ames sponsored by the Packard Motor Car Company in July 1914.

On a Monday evening of mid-June 1914, two young men, driving what the *Tribune* called a "migit"

This is one of the concrete Lincoln Highway markers installed by the Boy Scouts in the Ames area in 1928. It is today on the southeast corner of Lincoln Way and Beach Avenue in Ames. Relocated to this spot as an historical reminder, it commemorates the earlier day existence of the official Lincoln Highway. These markers weighed about 270 pounds and were very durable. ID No.209.1185.2

car, arrived in Ames reporting to Parley Sheldon, Ames's official Lincoln Highway consul. On June 4, they had dipped the wheels of their little car[3] in the ocean at Coney Island, New York, expecting to arrive in San Francisco in time to take part in the Fourth of July parade down Market Street, and dip their wheels in the Pacific Ocean and then pour into the ocean a bottle of water that they had carried all the way from the Atlantic. The *Tribune* reported, "that was the first small car to make the entire trip across the continent on the Lincoln Highway and no doubt

---

[1] Boone Street is today Lincoln Way. Originally it was known as Boone Road.

[2] *Ames Tribune*, August 26, 1929, p.1, "Lincoln Way Route Changed." This remained the route until the change in 1929 that took the Lincoln Highway straight west from the Sheldon corner, thus eliminating the railroad crossing west of Jordan.

[3] *Ames Tribune*, June 18, 1914, p.1, "Migit Car Crosses U.S. On Lincoln Way." (Assumed to mean a "midget" car?)

will be the forerunner of thousands of others who will make the trip later."

On November 28, 1914, Mayor Parley Sheldon, with Fire Chief Lynn Morris, made a trial drive on the Lincoln Highway from the Marshall County line to the Boone County line. Proving that the drive across Story County could be made in less than an hour (their time was 55 minutes), Sheldon reported that they drove at a normal speed and that the road was "in pretty good shape, though in some places it needed some dragging." Sheldon's trial drive was a part of a coast to coast study requested by Lincoln Highway officials.[4]

Anita King, "the Paramount Girl," came through Ames driving her Kissel car from San Fancisco enroute to New York City in September, 1915. She carried a message from the San Francisco mayor to the mayor of New York City. The Lincoln Highway was sort of the "internet" of its day. The *Tribune* reported that King was the "first person, man or woman, who had ever passed over the Nevada and Utah deserts alone and had lived to tell the story."[5]

Anita King, the "Paramount Girl," drove her Kissel car from San Francisco to New York City on the Lincoln Highway, passing through Ames on September 23, 1915. Her car is shown here in front of the Princess Theater at the east end of Main Street. ID No.135.745.1-3

4 *Ames Tribune,* December 3, 1914, p.1, "Crosses County In Less Than An Hour."
5 *Ames Evening Times*, September 24, 1915, "The First To Cross The Desert Alone."
6 *Ames Tribune,* July 8, 1915, p.1, "Ames In Movies To Show Advantage of Lincoln Highway."
7 *Ames Tribune,* January 14, 1915, "Story To Gravel Lincoln Highway."
8 *Ames Tribune,* July 27, 1922, p.1, "Wednesday a Big Day For Ames Tourist Camp."
9 *Ames Evening Times,* August 2, 1922, p.1, "Tourists From All Over Stop In Ames."
10 *Ames Evening Times,* August 3, 1922, p.1, "50,000 Mile Hikers Go Thru Ames Today." (Walked Lincoln Highway full length twice). It wasn't just cars that traveled the Lincoln Highway!

One more example will further demonstrate the way the Lincoln Highway held our attention in those earlier days. The July 8, 1915, *Tribune* expressed great enthusiasm about the "Film Caravan" that was filming the Lincoln Highway coast to coast. Two days were spent filming in Ames. The Commercial Club had seen to it that business places were spruced up and important people were seen on the streets. Main Street, Ames High School, the railroad depot and, of special importance, the Iowa State College campus, were all filmed for public showing across the entire nation as examples of attractions along the Lincoln Highway. The caravan traveled in four cars, a Stutz, a Packard, a Studebaker, and a Buick. Included in the party were Lincoln Highway Consul-at-large, H. C. Osterman; E. A. Holden, civil engineer and secretary; Leon Loeb, official photographer; C. M. Reiling, road viewer and statistician; T. A. Stalker, of the Packard Company; and R. C. Sackett, of the Studebaker Company.[6]

The first graveling of Lincoln Highway began, I believe, in 1915 when Sam Stiegerwalt, Story County Engineer, announced that four gravel pits had been secured between Ames and Nevada.[7]

Lincoln Way was paved from the east city limits of Ames to Squaw Creek in 1916. It was 1921 when the first paving was installed west of Squaw Creek. Before that first paving project in west Ames, the summer dust in campustown area must have been almost unbearable. The shrubs at the Knoll, for example, were a murky gray rather than green, most of the summer months.

By 1920, many towns on the Lincoln Highway had established "tourist camps" for the driving public. Ames provided one of the most popular such tourist facilities in this part of the state when Maxwell Park, maintained by the Chautauqua Association, was made available. Adequate plumbing facilites as well as a beautifully wooded camping area were provided there. The Ames *Tribune* carried stories about tourists who camped at the "Ames Tourist Camp."[8] In those days the local paper carried daily lists of the names of tourist campers,[9] including their home towns, and also similar lists of those who stayed over night at the Sheldon Munn Hotel. A majority of those travelers came off the Lincoln Highway. It was common for local youngsters to report on how many "out of state" car licenses they had seen each day down on Lincoln Way.[10]

By the late 1920s, the Lincoln Highway was well established across the nation. Standard highway marking had been developed, but it was in 1928 that the Boy Scouts of America undertook the project of installing the most professionally-designed highway signs of all. The project involved the Lincoln Highway from coast to coast.

In 1928, Ames scouts placed 29 Lincoln Highway cast concrete markers as a part of that national Boy Scout project. Fifty Ames scouts met at the corner of Kellogg and Lincoln Way on the morning of September 1, 1928. With National Deputy Scout Executive, Andrew Janson,[11] in charge of the special ceremony, speeches were made by Dr. L. H. Pammel, head of the Botany Department at Iowa State College; Fred C. Tilden, veteran of the Civil War; and

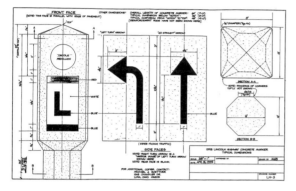

Working drawing of specifications for construction of those Lincoln Highway markers.

Parley Sheldon, banker and for many years the mayor of Ames. Sheldon lifted the first shovelful of earth as a marker was dropped into its hole. Others present were A. H. Fuller of the Rotary Club, Earl Weaver of the Lions Club, and Joe Robinson of the Kiwanis Club. Harry Brown and E. C. Potter represented the Story County Council of the Boy Scouts.

Concrete markers were placed in Ames at Kellogg Avenue, Grand Avenue, Hazel Avenue, and at West Gate. Steel markers were placed on the Squaw Creek bridge. That day, Ames Boy Scouts placed markers along Lincoln Highway from a point two miles east of Ames to a point three miles east of Boone.[12]

Those attractive concrete markers weighed about 270 pounds. I vividly recall the feeling of satisfaction (and some relief) when we installed the last one that day at an intersection east of Boone.

Today, with the passing of those famous marked or designated highways, those very special Lincoln Highway markers have become collectors items.

[11] *Ames Tribune,* August 9, 1928, p.5, "Boy Scout Manual Illustrator Doing Work at Iowa State."
[12] *Ames Tribune,* Sept. 1, 1928, p.1, "Boy Scouts Place 29 Hiway Markers."

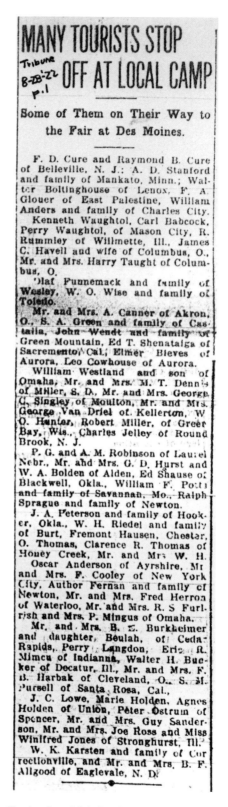

MANY TOURISTS STOP

Tribune 8-28-'22 p.1

OFF AT LOCAL CAMP

Some of Them on Their Way to the Fair at Des Moines.

F. D. Cure and Raymond B. Cure of Belleville, N. J.; A. D. Stanford and family of Mankato, Minn.; Walter Boltinghouse of Lenox, F. A. Glouer of East Palestine, William Anders and family of Charles City.

Kenneth Waughtol, Carl Babcock, Perry Waughtol, of Mason City, R. Rummley of Willmette, Ill., James C. Havell and wife of Columbus, O., Mr. and Mrs. Harry Taught of Columbus, O.

Olaf Punnemack and family of Wesley, W. O. Wise and family of Toledo.

Mr. and Mrs. A. Canner of Akron, O., S. A. Green and family of Castalia, John Wendt and family of Green Mountain, Ed T. Shenataiga of Sacremento, Cal., Elmer Bieves of Aurora, Leo Cowhouse of Aurora.

William Westland and son of Omaha, Mr. and Mrs. M. T. Denn's of Miller, S. D., Mr. and Mrs. George C. Singley of Moulton, Mr. and Mrs. George Van Driel of Kellerton, W. O. Hunter, Robert Miller, of Green Bay, Wis., Charles Jelley of Round Brook, N. J.

P. G. and A. M. Robinson of Laurel Nebr., Mr. and Mrs. G. D. Hurst and W. A. Bolden of Alden, Ed Shause of Blackwell, Okla., William F. Potts and family of Savannah, Mo., Ralph Sprague and family of Newton.

J. A. Peterson and family of Hooker, Okla., W. H. Riedel and family of Burt, Fremont Hausen, Chester, O. Thomas, Clarence R. Thomas of Honey Creek, Mr. and Mrs. W. H. Oscar Anderson of Ayrshire, Mr. and Mrs. F. Cooley of New York City, Author Fernan and family of Newton, Mr. and Mrs. Fred Herron of Waterloo, Mr. and Mrs. R. S Furlrish and Mrs. P. Mingus of Omaha.

Mr. and Mrs. B. E. Burkheimer and daughter, Beulah, of Cedar Rapids, Perry Langdon, Eric R. Mimcu of Indianna, Walter H. Bucker of Decatur, Ill., Mr. and Mrs. F. B. Harbak of Cleveland, O., S. M. Pursell of Santa Rosa, Cal.,

J. C. Lowe, Marie Holden, Agnes Holden of Union, Peter Ostrum of Spencer, Mr. and Mrs. Guy Sanderson, Mr. and Mrs. Joe Ross and Miss Winifred Jones of Stronghurst, Ill.

W. K. Karsten and family of Correctionville, and Mr. and Mrs. B. F. Allgood of Eaglevale, N. D.

"Many Tourists Stop Off At Local Camp" The Ames Tribune kept the public informed about the tourists that patronized the Ames Tourist Camp in the 1920s. The Ames camp was located in what is now the north portion of the Ames Municipal cemetery. (News item dated August 28, 1922). ID No.209.1186.3-4

We need to remember just how important those old highway systems were in the development of our nation. The U.S. Army motorcade that came through on the Lincoln Highway in 1919, that included Dwight. D. Eisenhower among its personnel, is recalled because of its ultimate bearing upon our present day Interstate Highway System.

We might well recall that in 1915, the Aero Club of America designated the Lincoln Highway as their official transcontinental air route.[13] The Lincoln Highway was indeed vital and versatile in its day.

April 11, 1998

---

[13] *Ames Evening Times*, July 2, 1915, p.8, "Lincoln Way To Be An Air Route."

Chapter 17

Tom Rice, The Veterinarian Who Filled Teeth - For People

1871 - 1947[1]

Tom Rice graduated from Iowa State with a degree in veterinary medicine in 1895. He was the team manager for the football team that defeated Northwestern University in 1895 by a score of 36 to 0. When the *Chicago Tribune* described the team from Ames as having played like a cyclone that day, the name stuck. Iowa State teams have been the "Cyclones" ever since. Rice practiced veterinary medicine in Harmony, Minnesota, from 1895 till 1897 when he joined the United States Department of Agriculture as a specialist in the animal industry section.

During the Spanish American War, Rice spent seven months with Teddy Roosevelt's "Rough Riders" as a veterinary surgeon. Following his service with the famous calvary regiment, Rice entered Northwestern University where he graduated with a dental degree in 1905.

He opened his dental office in Ames in 1905. While it was true that Ames had a veterinarian who was practicing dentistry, most Ames people soon forgot that Dr. Rice had originally been a veterinarian. In 1900, he married Harriet McCarthy, daughter of Dan McCarthy, a prominent pioneer Ames lawyer. Tom Rice and his wife lived for many years on the southwest corner of Grand Avenue and Sixth Street, the site today of "Shops on Grand."

Rice was a member of the Ames City Council in 1914, and had been chairman of the Story County Republican committee.

Elected Ames mayor in 1920, Rice served two two-year terms. Ames adopted the city-manager form of government during his first term. Known for his strong leadership abilities, he did not back away from controversy. In 1923, Tom Rice publicly

supported Charles Mayser, the Iowa State College athletic director, who had become embroiled in a dispute with President R. A. Pearson. That incident was credited by some with being a factor in delaying a decision on extending Sixth Street between downtown Ames and the campus.[2]

Dr. Thomas Lester Rice, 1871 - 1945, served with Teddy Roosevelt's "Rough Riders" in the Spanish Amercian War as a veterinary surgeon and in World War I as a dental surgeon. He served Ames as councilman and mayor. He was comander of the local American Legion in 1934. Photo courtesy of the Ames Chapter of the American Legion.

---

[1] *Ames Dairy Tribune,* June 7, 1947, obituary for Thomas Lester Rice.
[2] See the account in the story of "The War of The Road."

In 1924, Rice built the Rice Building located at 323 Main Street. Younker's Department Store once occupied Rice's building, and Dr. G. E. McFarland had his office on the second floor there before the McFarland Clinic was founded on Fifth Street in 1946. Rice died June 6, 1947 at the age of 76.

February 15, 1998

Chapter 18

Winifred R. Tilden

Directress of Physical Culture
1880 - 1948

W inifred R. Tilden played an important role in the development of women's physical education at Iowa State University. The daughter of George and Lydia Tilden, Ames pioneers, Winifred attended Ames schools, then entered Mt. Holyoke College, her mother's alma mater in Massachusetts, where she graduated in 1903.

Winifred Tilden in 1921, at her desk in Margaret Hall on the Iowa State campus. Miss Tilden was a proficient golfer and also a good tennis player during most of her years as director of women's physical education at Iowa State. ID No. 12.53.2

Picture taken in 1925 of Winifred R. Tilden, first head of women's physical education at Iowa State College. She served in that position from 1904 through 1939. ID No. 194.1101.1-5

In 1904, she became the first professionally-trained director of physical education for women at Iowa State College when it was a part of the Department of Speech. Her title then was "Directress of Physical Culture."

She has been described as a no-nonsense person, but a fun loving, creative person as well. She once invited several of her eastern college friends to

spend Christmas in her home in Ames. In 1901, eastern girls thought that Iowa was still a wild western country. Before coming to Ames with her friends, Winifred wrote to her brothers asking them to meet their train decked out with war paint and feathers prepared to whoop it up when they got off the train. Her brothers complied and took the young ladies to the Tilden home in a hay rack to further impress her friends.

Winifred Tilden brought to the Iowa State campus ideas that she had acquired through travels and observations of physical education programs in countries such as England and France. She introduced the May Day pageant and May pole dances in 1911 that were to become a part of VEISHEA after 1922.

In 1918-1919, she was on leave to direct recreational programs for American soldiers in France. She served on a number of national physical education committees where she was a pioneer in advocating competitive sports.

During her tenure she introduced competitive sports which in 1915 were organized as the "Girls Athletic Club." She developed a progressive curriculum of developmental and corrective gymnastics. She organized the Women's Athletic Association and the Women's "A" Club, which later became the "I"

Club. Hockey, basketball, tennis, swimming, archery, and golf were among the activities offered by the department.[1]

Tilden's competent and enthusiastic instruction combined spontaneous recreation with definite physi-

Miss Tilden was on leave in 1918 to direct recreational activities in France during World War I. The program was sponsored by the National Y.W.C.A. ID No.194.1102.2-5

Win Tilden instructs a golf class in 1906. Photo taken on the practice course that she developed on the hill located in the southeast corner of the campus. As this picture was taken, she was driving the ball southeasterly toward the intersection of Lincoln Way and Beach. Today, this site is the location of several dormitories. Photo courtesy of the Iowa State University Physical Education Department. ID No.194.1103.1-5

Win Tilden with her bicycle in 1898. On August 11, that year, she and Tot Bigelow rode their bicycles to Des Moines. Both young ladies became students of physical education for women. ID No.177.990. 1-3

cal benefits. Her students numbered less than a hundred in 1904 and in the thousands when she retired in 1944.

Until 1938, women's physical education was centered in Margaret Hall, the first women's dormitory on the Iowa State campus. The large dining hall in that building was converted into a well-equipped gymnasium. In 1913, the basement area was expanded for lockers and showers, and in 1915 a swimming pool was added.

"Hammill Swats Gym" was the headline in the Ames Tribune of December 31, 1928. President Pearson had given high priority to Miss Tilden's plans for up-to-date physical education facilities only to have the Governor intervene! ID No. 199.1126.4-5

---

[1] *Christian Science Monitor,* March 10, 1922, "Women At Ames Enjoy Athletics."

One of Tilden's dreams came true in 1939[2] when a long-standing request for a well-designed, well-equipped women's physical education building became a reality. She had presented detailed plans for a new women's building in 1925[3] during President R. A. Pearson's term. In 1928, President R. M. Hughes made the request for funds for a women's gym a priority, only to have Governor Hammill remove the item from the appropriation,[4] a frustrating event in Tilden's long effort to obtain suitable facili-

ties. After the threat of another setback in the appropriations process, the efforts of Miss Tilden, her staff and the students themselves won the legislature's approval of the necessary funds.[5] The building, dedicated in 1941, is the south unit of today's much enlarged Physical Education Building.

Winifred Tilden died July 4, 1948, having contributed to the lives of ten college generations of Iowa State coeds. In 1997, Winifred Tilden's name was placed in Iowa State University's "Hall of Honor."

Miss Tilden with her golf clubs in front of Margaret Hall, the primary dormitory for Iowa State women prior to 1920. The large dining hall in this building was equipped to also serve as a women's gymnasium, complete with a basement level swimming pool. Miss Tilden's office was in this building until it burned in 1938. ID No. 12.53.1

May 15, 1997

[2] *Iowa State Daily Student,* March 9, 1939, p.6 "New Hopes For Women's Gym" by Rachel Roewe.

[3] Nine years earlier she had informed President Pearson of the women's needs. His report to the state board at the end of 1916 included her recommendations: "A modern up-to-date gymnasium for the young women of the college is needed. Such a building would include exercise floors, locker and shower rooms, swimminmg pool, consultation and examination rooms and a room for the accomodation of those interested in athletics. The present exercise room does not provide sufficient space for basketball contests and other physical tests to which the public is admitted. The new gymnasium should also provide space for a running track." Fourth Biennial Report (1915 - 1916) pp.242-243.

[4] *Ames Tribune* December 31, 1928, p.1 "HAMMILL SWATS GYM" (headline). After the death of Budget Diretcor E. L. Hogue, the Governor had asssumed budget authority and struck the Women's Gym from Iowa State's request.

[5] *Mount Holyoke College Quarterly,* 1944, "Winifred R.Tilden '03" by Mary Cook Fuller.

Chapter 19

When The Coeds Lobbied The State Legislature

"**A**pparently all that you have to do to get $300,000 is to go over to the senate with two girls from Ames and back it goes into the bill." A state representative had just

The Women's Physical Education Building was dedicated in 1941. This building was the result of long and extensive efforts on the part of Miss Tilden, her staff and her students. After the building had been enlarged in the 1970s a University publication noted, "Under her direction the south wing of this building was constructed. Her astute planning allowed the wing to become an integral part of the new facility 33 years later." Photo courtesy of the Iowa State University Library / University Archives.

---

[1] *Iowa State Daily*, April 26, 1939. Rep. Robert Blue may have been the source of that reference.

[2] A southwest Iowa legislator suggested that he did not want his son to marry an Iowa State girl because they were educated to expect too high a standard of living. See: *Iowa State Daily* April 21, 1939, "Iowa Staters Protest - T'aint True."

[3] *Iowa State Daily*, April 18, 1939, p.1, "House Votes Against Bill for Coed Gymnasium."

[4] *ibid*, April 21, 1939, p.1, "Coeds Lobby in Legislature."

[5] *Iowa State University Campus and Its Buildings* - 1859 - 1979, H. Summerfield Day, p.338

[6] *Iowa State Daily*, March 9, 1939, p.6, "High hopes for Women's Gym."

asserted that there were better places to spend the taxpayers' money than to put it into a "playhouse"[1] for the girls on the campus at Ames.[2]

On April 17, 1939, the Iowa House rejected the State Board of Education's request for funds for a women's gymnasium at Iowa State College,[3] and now, here they were, again debating the matter. After the house originally deleted the item from their bill, the senate had acted favorably on the behalf of the gym request; but the house refused to reconsider.

At that point the word on the Ames campus was that getting the appropriation for the women's gym was a lost cause.

That is when those "two girls from Ames" entered the discussion.[4]

That legislator arguing against the appropriation on April 25, miscalculated a bit when he mentioned the two coeds as having influenced the senate on the matter. It had been three coeds, not two, and they had stacks of petitions signed by over 1,000 Iowa State coeds.

In 1939, the student enrollment at Iowa State was 7,900; 1,900 of them were women. Winifred Tilden, founder and first head of women's physical education at Iowa State, had held that position since 1904. She had developed programs in sports such as hockey, basketball, tennis and swimming as well as special developmental and corrective exercise programs. Such programs were well established in the daily schedules of Iowa State coeds.

Women's physical education facilities were centered in Margaret Hall, the first women's dormitory on the Iowa State campus. The original dining hall had been converted into a gymnasium. In 1915, a swimming pool was added to the building.[5]

In April of 1938, Margaret Hall was totally destroyed by a fire. Iowa State women then had no physical education facilites.[6] Women students had no pool, no basketball floor, no adequate area for indoor exercise. Staff offices had been temporarily relocated in Botany Hall.

Jean Vieth, from Oakland, Home Economics, class of 1939.

Mary Bush, of Ames, Institutional Management, class of 1940.

Gaynold Carroll, of Des Moines, Journalism, class of 1940.

These three coeds carried the message and the petitions to the state legislature. Petitions signed by over a thousand Iowa State coeds convinced the legislators to approve the appropriation for the women's gym on the Iowa State campus. ID No.191.1081.2-3 ID No. 180.1016.3-4-5 and IDNo.191.1081.4-5

Margaret Hall, the first women's dormitory on the Iowa State campus. It was the center for women's physical education until the 1938 fire. Locker and shower faciltities were added in 1913, and a pool was added in 1915. ID No.37.188A.1

Margaret Hall, or all that was left of it, on April 8, 1938, the day after it was destroyed by fire. Iowa State women lost their gym, most of their equipement and their swimming pool that day. Gone, also in that fire, were Miss Tilden's office and that of her staff. ID.No.38.191B.1-2

Word that the legislature was turning down the funds for a women's gymnasium was an unacceptable development in the eyes of every Iowa State coed.[7]

The Cardinal Guild, the student-elected governing body, went to work. Home economics coeds headed for the women's dorms and sororities with petitions directed to the state legislature. Their message was loud and clear: the girls in Ames were in real need of those facilities. They deserved them.

After all, the men had had a modern gymnasium facility since 1913.

The facilites that were destroyed in the 1938 fire had been barely adequate as it was. It was time to deliver a wake-up call to those state legislators.

Miss Tilden had been asking for better women's physical education facilities since 1925. Beginning that year. the State Board of Education requested funds for a women's gymnasium. President Pearson had stated that it was near the top of his list for funding.

Mary Bush, a senior from Ames in institutional management; Jean Vieth, home economics senior from Oakland; and Gaynold Carroll, a senior from Des Moines in journalism were soon on their way to Des Moines where they presented petitions to Senator Doran of Boone.

Senator Doran escorted the three coeds on a tour of the state house offices and introduced them to Governor George Wilson and Lieutenant-Governor Bourke Hickenlooper.

[7] The Women's Athletic Association was also involved.

Returning to Ames the young women expressed optimism. They had had a great day; their reception by legislators had been positive.

The bill was revived in the house on April 25. Fourteen representatives spoke against the inclusion of the women's gym. Eleven spoke in favor of its inclusion.

That was when one of the representatives referred to the proposed gym as a "playhouse."[8] There was a bit of manuvering. The proponents were gaining votes.

The $300,000 appropriation stayed in the bill when the final vote was taken; the girls had won.

Those Iowa State coeds deserved the credit. The legislature had gotten the message.

Those three coeds made their dramatic visit to the State House on April 20; the Senate approved the appropriations for the women's gym on April 21; and the house came through with a favorable vote on April 25.[9]

Gaynold Carroll Jensen, one of the three Iowa State coeds who carried the petitions to the state legislators in 1939, today resides in Minneapolis. She recalls that day in the Iowa legislature as one of her most memorable college experiences. In a recent phone conversation, she described the event as a "very exciting time."[10]

March 25. 1996

---

[8] *Iowa State Daily,* April 26, 1939, p.1, "Gym Proposal Passes Senate."

[9] *ibid,* April 26, 1939, p. 1, "Representative Sanction Given to Gymnasium."

[10] Telephone conversation with Gaynold Carroll Jensen, February 13, 1996.

Chapter 20

Eleanor Wilkins

A.K.A.
Martha Duncan
1896 - 1975

Martha Duncan's voice went out over the air waves of WOI radio for twenty eight years.[1] She was really Eleanor Wilkins, the widow of Professor F. Scott Wilkins, who had died in 1936. In 1939, she was invited to become the hostess of the WOI "Homemaker's Half Hour." Andy Woolfries, the station manager and main announcer, gave her the name

Eleanor Wilkins (1896 - 1975) was known to thousands of WOI radio listeners as "Martha Duncan." She kept her audience appeal through three generations, sustaining her program through a complete transition in broadcast methods. Photo courtesy of the Iowa State University Library / University Archives.

---

[1] *Ames Daily Tribune*, June 20, 1966, "I Can Do It And She Did," by Marilyn Sealine.
[2] *News of Iowa State, Vol. 19.1,* September - October, 1966, p.3, "Softened with a Feeling of Human Interest."

"Martha Duncan." That name became synonymous with the program.

Under the leadership of Martha Duncan, and with the help of Iowa State College's home economics staff and of the WOI staff, the "Homemaker's Half Hour" was enlarged and formatted to represent the entire College of Home Economics. It was said to have been the earliest women's radio program in the Midwest. It featured home economics information and had been broadcast continuously since 1925, three years after WOI radio received its license.

"Martha Duncan" was a native of New York state but had a degree in home economics education from Oregon State College where she had met and married agronomist F. Scott Wilkins in 1919. They came to Ames and the Iowa State campus in 1921 when Prof. Wilkins joined the Agronomy Department staff.

Martha Duncan developed an extensive audience during her years broadcasting over WOI, years that included the transition in 1950 to television. It was estimated that she conducted 30,000 interviews on the air. Her warm, down-to-earth manner always came through to those she interviewed and to listeners as well. Of her interview with Eleanor Roosevelt in 1944, she said that it was "one of the high points of my whole professional life. Mrs. Roosevelt was such a delightful person."[2] Her interviews included hundreds of campus visitors and students.

She conducted a new program, beginning in 1942, known as the "Women's Forum," beamed to an audience of mostly women. It provided well-rounded and intellectual content covering current events and political comment. Duncan made a special effort to bring foreign student interests into the programming.

One of Martha Duncan's favorite programs was called "The Book Club," a half-hour program featuring someone reading a book to the audience. The first book to be tried was *A Man Called Peter*. The response was very positive.

In addition to her on-going work at WOI, Martha

Duncan spoke to audiences all over the Midwest, and her fan mail over the years "speaks eloquently of her appeal to many." Her listeners found her to be an inspirational, deep thinking, and vital woman.[3] In 1930, her fan mail totaled 13,060 letters. By 1948, the total was reported at 150,000.[4]

Martha Duncan received many honors. In 1966, she was presented with a plaque by the College of Home Economics inscribed "To Martha Duncan, for her cheerfulness, friendliness, loyalty, and confidence in us as we shared the microphone." She was given the "Matrix Award" in 1966 from Theta Sigma Phi, national women's journalism sorority in recognition of her "vast contribution to the field of women in journalism."

When she retired on July 1, 1966, a news release stated that "Given the name 'Martha Duncan,' she kept her audience appeal through three generations, sustaining her program through a complete transition in broadcast methods."

When she retired, WOI retired both the name "Martha Duncan" and the program title, "The Homemaker's Half Hour." The home economics information program would continue, but that title had long been identified with her personality.

Eleanor Wilkins died in January, 1975. Writing about her in the Iowa State Alumnus of April, 1957, Bess Ferguson said that Mrs. Wilkins, "has a journalist's nose for news, an actress's flair for the dramatic and a business woman's way of doing things."

That was "Martha Duncan."

January 10, 1997

---

[3] *Ames Daily Tribune*, June 20, 1966, "I Can Do It; And She Did."

[4] *Des Moines Register*,- January 28, 1948, "Radio Homemaking Gets Top Rating"

Chapter 21

Dr. Margaret Sloss, D.V.M.

First Woman To Receive D.V.M. Degree at Iowa State
1901 - 1979

Margaret Sloss was a pioneer among women in the professional field of veterinary medicine. Born in Cedar Rapids on October 8, 1901, she grew up in Ames where her father, Tom Sloss, was superintendent of buildings and grounds at Iowa State College.

She graduated from Ames High School in 1919. She received her B.S. degree from Iowa State in 1923 followed by a M.S. degree in veterinary anatomy in 1932. She attained the D.V.M. degree in 1938 - the first woman to receive that degree at Iowa State.

Her career was devoted fully to the veterinary college. Starting in 1923 as a technician, she ultimately became a full professor in 1965. Always an excellent student, she received many honors both as a student and in her field of veterinary pathology.

In college she was recognized by, and active in, the highest honorary organizations. She also excelled in campus activities. She loved athletics and was outstanding in women's basketball, tennis and hockey. She was a member of the Women's Athletic Association and the Woman's I Club.

Above all, Margaret Sloss is remembered for her personality. Displaying a keen sense of humor, she was always ready to assist her professional asso-

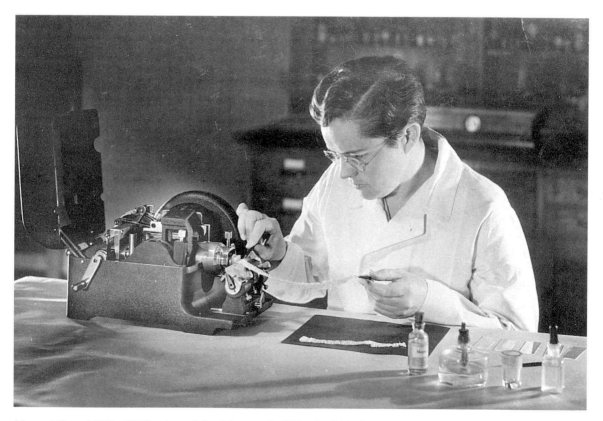

Margaret Sloss (1901 - 1979), shown in her laboratory in 1935. In 1940, she was personally invited by Carrie Chapman Catt to attend the Women's Centenniel Congress in Washington, D.C. to be honored as one of 100 U.S. women who successfully followed careers in 1940 which were unheard of 100 years earlier. Photo courtesy of the Iowa State University Library / University Archives. ID No. 118.652.2

ciates and her students. Graduate students, not only in veterinary medicine but in related academic fields, found her a vital source of counsel.

She authored, or co-authored many articles and books in her field. Among those she wrote were *Women in the Veterinary Medical Profession*, and *Women In Science.*

In 1940, Dr. Sloss was named by the Women's Centennial Congress as one of 100 women in the United States who successfully followed careers in 1940 which were not practiced by women 100 years earlier. Carrie Chapman Catt, an Iowa State graduate of 1880 and president of the congress, wrote a personal invitation to Dr. Sloss informing her of the honor.[1] Another Iowa State woman receiving that honor at the same time was Millie Kalsem, an Iowa State graduate of 1921, who was the executive dietician of the Cook County Hospital in Chicago. Others receiving that honor in 1940 were Eleanor Roosevelt, Frances Perkins, and Ruth Bryan Rohde, U. S. Minister to Denmark.

She received several awards from her alma mater including the Distinguished Chicago Alumni Award in 1964.[2] She was invited by Eleanor Roosevelt to attend a luncheon at the White House for "women in science," a memorable recognition.

Dr. Margaret Sloss in 1965 viewing the inner courtyard of the former Veterinary Quadrangle. Photo courtesy of the Iowa State University Library / University Archives. ID No.118.652.1

A champion of the cause for women in the veterinary medical profession, she is represented today by a growing number of young women graduating from the I.S.U. Veterinary College, entering that field in every area of specialization.

Dr. Margaret Sloss retired in 1972. She died December 14, 1979.[3] She was buried in the University Cemetery.

October 1996

---

[1] *Ames Tribune,* December 3, 1940, p.1, "High Honor to Dr. Sloss."

[2] Originated in the 1930s by the Chicago Alumni of Iowa State to commend alumni who have made a major contribution to society. See June, 1964 *Alumnus Magazine.*

[3] *Ames Tribune,* December 11, 1979, p.16, obituary for Margaret Sloss.

Chapter 22

Katharina Diehl

In Charge of Everything At Mary Greeley
1875 - 1959

According to the September 26, 1916, *Ames Evening Times*, "Miss Diehl is delighted with the hospital and its arrangement and looks forward to entering upon her new work here with a great deal of pleasure." "I will give every moment of my time and every ounce of my strength to make the hospital a success in every respect," Miss Diehl said.

Katharina Diehl (1874 - 1959), matron supervisor of Mary Greeley Hospital (1916 - 1945). Her twenty-nine years service helped establish the local hospital on a solid foundation. Photo courtesy Ames Chapter of Eastern Star ID No.161.891.4-5

Katharina Diehl arrived in Ames on September 21 to become the first matron supervisor of the Mary Greeley Hospital. She held that position for 29 years maintaining her resident apartment in the hospital during that period. She retired in 1945 at the age of 71.

Miss Diehl was born in Germany and came to the U.S. in 1884 when she was about nine years old. Her family settled in Boone. Following her high school graduation, she trained in the field of nursing in Des Moines where she had graduated from Iowa Methodist Hospital School of Nursing.

Mildred Judge of Ames, who was on the Mary Greeley nursing staff from 1930 through 1935 remembers Miss Diehl well. "Miss Diehl was superintendent, but that included about everything that went on in the hospital. She was director of nursing, manager of the kitchen, took over duties, herself, wherever needed in the nursing schedules. She kept every nurse busy somewhere in the hospital. She never let a nurse go because she was out of work. Instead she found places for them to stay busy."

In those days, nurses moved around to the floors or sections of the hospital as needed. Miss Diehl "worked everywhere." She was in charge of preparing the operating room, then she was the surgical nurse, directing the kitchen, handling nurse supervision and everything else in the hospital, all during the same day. It was all in Miss Diehl's schedule.

Katharina Diehl was efficient and a disciplinarian who expected hospital staff to follow her orders. It was said that some almost feared her; but most staff, and patients as well, recognized that Miss Diehl usually was right. She was highly respected by the doctors and nurses who worked with her at Mary Greeley.

She died March 4, 1959, at the age of 84.

October 1996

---

[1] *Ames Daily Tribune,* March 5, 1959, p.1, obituary for Katharina Diehl.

Chapter 23

Ada Hayden

A Champion Of Prairie Preservation
1884-1950

"Throughout the season from April to October, the colorful flowers of the grassland flora present a rainbow-hued sequence of bloom." Ada Hayden wrote those lines about one of Iowa's endangered natural treasures. As a child, she developed a deep interest in Iowa's dis-

Ada Hayden (1884 -1950), professor of botany, plant pathologist and conservationist. An Ames native, she was the first woman to receive the Ph D degree at Iowa State College. Photo courtesy of Iowa State University Library / University Archives. ID No. 178.1003.1-3

1 The Hayden farm was located north of what is now Top O' Hollow Road and west of the Hoover Avenue intersection. The original prairie growth has been entirely converted to residential property.
2 *Ames Tribune,* August 14, 1950, p.1, "Funeral This Afternoon for Dr. Ada Hayden."
3 *Iowa Conservationist,* July 1987, pp. 22, 23, "Ada Hayden Pioneer of Iowa Prairies."

appearing virgin prairie. She had recognized the beauty of a small tract of native prairie that her father had preserved on the family farm located at the north edge of Ames.[1] As a child and later as a student, it was there that she studied the characteristics and learned to cherish Iowa's native prairie land.[2]

Born on her parent's farm at the north edge of Ames August 14, 1884, Ada Hayden graduated from Ames High School in 1904 and from Iowa State College in 1908, with a bachelor's degree in botany. She continued her education with a master of science degree at Washington University in St. Louis. Following further graduate work at the University of Colorado and at the University of Chicago, she returned to Iowa State where, in 1918 she earned the fourth Ph.D. degree to be granted by Iowa State. Even more significant, perhaps, she was the first woman ever to receive that degree at Iowa State College.

Hayden's entire professional career was at Iowa State. Her early work was closely associated with Dr. L. H. Pammel, a pioneer botanist who was often spoken of as the father of Iowa's state park system.

Dr. Hayden worked as a professor of botany and plant pathology from 1918 until her death in 1950.

Beginning in about 1940 when she was chair of the Conservation Commission of the Iowa Academy of Sciences, Miss Hayden wrote a number of articles pointing out the necessity for preserving the few examples of native prairie still existing. She surveyed and described the location of 6,000 remaining acres of prairie scattered throughout the state. As a direct result of the determined efforts of Ada Hayden, there have been twenty-six native prairie tracts set aside by the state of Iowa to be preserved for future generations of Iowans to enjoy and to study.[3]

Following Ada Hayden's death August 12, 1950, in recognition of her contribution to the conservation movement, the state named a preserve acquired in 1946 in her memory. The Hayden Prairie consists of 240 acres of virgin prairie located in Howard County near the town of Lime Springs.

Ada Hayden devoted much of her time to the

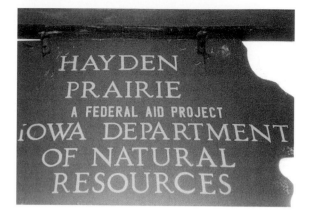

The Hayden Prairie, a native prairie located in Howard County, was acquired in 1946 and named in Ada Hayden's honor to recognize her contribution to conservation in Iowa. (1997 photo of large plaque located on the north side of the Hayden Prairie.) ID No. 176.985.5

study of prairie grasses. She was an ardent member of the Conservation Commission at the time of her death. She was curator of the herbarium at Iowa State College. She was well known and highly respected in her field of activity. Her memberships in scientific organizations included: the Botanical Society of America, the American Society for the Advancement of Science, American Society of Plant Taxonomists, and the Grassland Research Association.

Hayden's friends and associates said that the outstanding characteristic of Dr. Hayden's life and career was her unusual devotion to duty and to her friends. From her birth on a farm at the north edge of Ames, to her lifetime in her chosen work, Ada Hayden left us the legacy of the preserved prairies that otherwise would have been forever lost.

October 1996

Chapter 24

Dr. Jennie Ghrist, M.D.

First Female Medical Doctor In Ames

D r. Jennie, as many of her patients called her, came to Ames with her husband, Dr. David Ghrist, in 1899. That year they purchased a home on the southeast corner of Douglas Avenue and Seventh Street.

For most of the twenty-six years that the Drs. David and Jennie Ghrist practiced medicine in Ames, they maintained an office above the Fair Store on the south side of Main Street. Today, that would be approximately above where the Lazy M Shoe Store is located.

A 1905 professional ad for the Drs. Ghrist shows their specialty was the treatment of "Diseases of Women and Children." They seem to have been quite advanced for their day, since in that ad they stated that they provided X-ray treatment in their offices.

It was uncommon for women to obtain an M.D. degree in those years when Dr. Jennie and her husband began their practice in Ames, and it was significant that she and her husband provided a man and wife medical team in Ames at that early date.

In 1925, the Drs. Ghrist moved to Glendale, California. They were in their sixties and approaching retirement age. Dr. Jennie and her husband had been among the doctors consulted by Capt. Wallace Greeley when he was planning the Mary Greeley Hospital. Their move to Glendale was motivated by the fact that their son, Orie Ghrist, and his family had settled there. Orie Ghrist, an Ames High graduate of 1912, became a well known ophthalmologist in Glendale. His wife, the former Eva Kurtz of Nevada, Iowa, and an Oberlin College graduate in music, was on the music staff at Iowa State at the time of their marriage.[1]

After the senior Ghrists established their home in California, Dr. Jennie Ghrist continued to practice medicine a few more years, specializing in the care of women and children. Dr. David Ghrist later limited his practice to the field of anesthesiology.

Dr. Jennie Ghrist, M.D. was the first female medical doctor in Ames. A favorite with many Ames women, Dr. Jennie practiced medicine with her husband, Dr. David Ghrist, from 1899 until they moved to Glendale, California in 1925. ID No.174.977.1-4

D. M. GHRIST.   JENNIE G. GHRIST.

DRS. GHRIST & GHRIST,
Physians and Surgeons.

Especial attention paid to diseases of women and children.   Glassess Fitted We are also prepared to give Static Electrical Treatment and X-ray work.

Office in Budd block over Millers Store.
Res. 3 blocks north of postoffice.
Telephone in office and residence.

*This professional advertisement for the **Drs. Ghrist and Ghrist** appeared in the February 6, 1902 Ames Intelligencer. ID No.209.1184.4-5*

---

[1] Orie Ghrist graduated from Ames High School in 1912. He obtained both the A.B. and M.D. degrees from Stanford University.

There is more that we would like to know about these particular practitioners, especially Doctor Jennie. Those today who remember her, do so quite favorably. I make this comment, in part, because I recall the reliance that one of my aunts placed upon Dr. Jennie, the first female medical doctor to practice in Ames.

While Jennie Ghrist was the only female medical doctor in Ames during those years, she represented a percentage of the total number of Ames doctors of that day that probably is no greater today.

November 1996

Chapter 25

Mary Beaumont Welch

Home Making Was More Than Cooking
1841 - 1923

Mary Beaumont Welch came to Ames in 1868 with her husband, Adonijah Welch, when he became Iowa Agricultural College's first president. In 1872, Mary developed and began teaching the domestic economy curriculum, the first such course to be offered west of the Mississippi and one of the first in the nation.

The Trustees of the Iowa Agricultural College had set the environment for the development of Mrs.

Mary B. Welch (1841 - 1923), wife of the first president of Iowa State. She developed and taught the first home economics course to be offered in a land grant college in this country. Photo courtesy of the Iowa State University Library / University Archives.

---

[1] *Century of Home Economics At Iowa State University*, Ercel Sherman Eppright and Elizabeth Storm Ferguson, published by the Iowa State University Home Economics Association, Iowa State University Press, 1971, Ch. 1, p.1.
[2] *Ames Daily Tribune* , January 13, 1923, p.1, "Mrs.Welch Dead; Wife of First I.S.C. President."

Welch's ideas when, in May, 1868, they decided the new college would be coeducational. Mary B. Welch took an active interest in the welfare of the young women enrolled at the college, and was unhappy about the absence of special courses for the women students. "Why not teach the ladies as we do the men, some of the industries that directly concern them as women," Mary may have asked her husband. That question led to the action of the college trustees when, on December 8, 1871, they adopted the "ladies course" as "laid down in the President's report."[1]

Nowhere was Mrs.Welch able to find precedents for the kind of course work she desired to provide for the Iowa girls. Her ideal was to instruct them in homemaking and not merely cooking. The courses that she designed grew into the largest school of home economics in the world.[2]

There were no text books available so Mrs.Welch developed her own. A copy of her handwritten volume is in the Iowa State University archives. In the front of that book is a list of essays or topics, such as: (1) "Necessity of culture for the Model Housewife," (2) "My Library and the values it yields," (3) "When I shall wash - My Expedients for making wash day endurable for my family," and (4) "Slovenliness is a sin." Mrs.Welch developed the curriculum to include the same science and cultural courses available to the young men. She taught the course for twelve years.

From those beginnings, when the course was known as "Domestic Economy," has evolved the highly developed College of Family and Consumer Sciences.

At the time of Mrs. Welch's death on January 2, 1923, O. H. Cessna, a member of Iowa State's first graduating class in 1869 and its first college chaplain remembered her this way: "Mrs. Welch in her wise suggestions to Dr. Welch helped to shape the early policies of this young institution. Upon her good judgment the President could always rely. She was the first home economics teacher in a land grant college in this country, and to her the state and nation owe a debt of gratitude for planning a course in which the practical and theoretical sides of Home Economics were equally important. It was her idea that the course should be so planned that a woman could have a well rounded education including both cultural and practical training. She realized the importance of fitting women to meet the problems of the day in the home and in society."

October 1996

Chapter 26

Carrie Chapman Catt
1859 - 1947

She was an Iowa State graduate of 1880, a world leader of the woman suffrage movement who became an international promoter of peace among the nations. Acclaimed and honored by the educational and political leaders of our nation, she continued to "possess the qualities that endeared her to her classmates and friends"[1] in Ames. The following calls attention to some of her Ames connections following graduation from Iowa State.

Carrie Chapman Catt (1856 - 1947), Iowa State graduate of 1880 and world leader of women's suffrage movement. She was acclaimed one of the greatest women of her day. This 1890 photo courtesy of State Historical Society of Wisconsin. ID No.199.1128.1-4

Carrie Lane was born January 9, 1859 on a family farm near Ripon, Wisconsin. When Carrie was seven, the family moved to a farm near Charles City, Iowa. She came to the Iowa Agricultural College in 1877 in spite of her father's belief that women did not need a college education. From her Iowa farm background that included teaching in an Iowa one-room school, she brought determination and strength of character with her to the Ames campus. From the beginning, she was a woman with a purpose — a mission in mind.

As a member of the Crescent Debating Society at Iowa State, and as a campus activist of her day, Carrie Lane was an exceptional student. Advancing the position of women in society was central to her nature, even in her student days at Ames. It was here on the Iowa State campus that she developed the special talents that would make her one of the best known and respected women of her generation in the entire nation. To many, she would eventually be one of the best known women in the world.

She became the women's suffrage movement's ultimate leader - the one who would take the action all the way to final success with the establishment of the nineteenth amendment granting U.S. women constitutional voting rights. It was a long and arduous battle that faced the young woman from Iowa. Tough and bitter fights were ahead. Carrie Chapman Catt proved equal to the task.

Following graduation, she continued to demonstrate leadership abilities. Becoming a school superintendent at Mason City while still in her twenties was but one example.

Marriages

She married Leo Chapman, a Mason City newspaper editor. Her advancement as a public activist continued its upward direction. The untimely death of Chapman and her later marriage to her Iowa State classmate, George Catt, were significant chapters in her life.

In 1890, just ten years following her graduation from Iowa State, the *Ames Intelligencer* on April 24 announced, "Mrs. Carrie Lane Chapman, the well known Iowa writer and lecturer will be in Ames the evening of the 25th and deliver an address in the Congregational Church under the auspices of the Women's Suffrage Association." The May 1, 1890 *Intelligencer* had this commentary, "Mrs. Carrie Lane Chapman gave a lecture in the interests of equal suffrage in the Congregational Church last Friday

---

[1] The *Ames Milepost,* June 12, 1930, p. 4. Editorial (col. 2), See Footnote No. 12.

evening. All were pleased with the speaker. Her subject was pleasantly but forcefully presented and abounded in sparkling and interesting points which made it well worth hearing."[2] While in Ames, Mrs. Chapman was a house guest of Mrs. Rowena Stevens.[3]

By 1900, Carrie Chapman Catt had assumed a lead position in the women's movement. On April 26, 1916, she spoke again in Ames where she was greeted by her many friends on the Iowa State campus and by townspeople, as well.

Warm Welcome

The *Ames Tribune* of April 27, reported, "Mrs. Catt has been received with a warm welcome by the citizens of Iowa, both male and female, but she has not received a warmer welcome at any point than she has received in Ames. She was a resident of this city at one time, attended the Iowa State College, and married a man who was a student at the same college. Her heart beats just a little faster for good old Iowa State, and the hearts here are always for her."

The *Tribune* continued, "It is particularly fitting that an Iowa woman should be at the head of the world suffrage movement when her native state is engaged in a campaign to give the ballot to its women. The work that Mrs. Catt has been doing in behalf of the suffrage cause has stamped her as a world's citizen of more than ordinary prominence. She is the dominant figure in the suffrage world today."[6]

Referring to a recently publicized statement by Mrs. Phillip Snowden, the distinguished English woman, that Mrs. Catt was the first and greatest woman of the English-speaking world,[4] the *Tribune* observed that "such sentiment met with the hearty approval of all Ames people."

As a prelude to her speech that day, Mrs. Catt stated how much pleasure it gave her to return to Ames. She pointed out that in every state where a campaign had been waged to get the vote for women there had been a secret influence, an influence that was manifested in many different ways. Deceptive letters and gross misrepresentation of facts had to be dealt with. Even sincere opposition to granting the vote to women was based upon imagined fears.

"By her own gracious charm, by her genius of leadership, by her executive ability and her power for constructive service, Mrs. Catt has achieved the place she holds today," concluded the *Tribune*.[5]

Details of Mrs Catt's remarks from that April 26, 1916, address are found in the *Ames Evening Times* of that same day. Referring to the huge crowd that was present that morning in State Gymnasium, the *Times*, in a headlined story, stated that, "For more than an hour the assembly listened attentively to the words of the speaker and were fully rewarded for their attendance. Mrs. Catt's address was not the hysterical outburst of an agitator but the sane, forceful arguments of a brainy American woman whose efforts for the recognition of American women are bound to be successful sooner or later."[6]

The *Times* observed further, "The quiet dignified bearing of Mrs. Catt, the impressiveness with which she spoke, and the **unexpected lapses into the comical aspects of the topic** held their attention throughout the lengthy discourse." She cited the example of how easily immigrant **men** were granted the right to vote — while native born American **women were denied the right to vote.** (The point of such comparisons was always the injustice of denying women the right to vote!)

Skilled in Debate

From reading her early-day addresses made here in Ames, we recall how Carrie Chapman Catt excelled during her debating society days at Iowa State. The ability to make it precisely clear to her audience just how ridiculous it was to discriminate against our women citizens was a skill that she had acquired in the days of her college English language studies and debate activity. A sharp sense of humor served her well in making her points.[7]

2 The *Intelligencer*, May 1, 1890, p.1.

3 Details of her talk at the Congregational Church were not published. Rowena Stevens, mentioned as Mrs. Chapman's hostess, was an 1873 graduate of Iowa State. Stevens was a local leader of the suffrage movement.

4 *Cosmopolitan* (magazine), February 1916, "One of the World's Great Women," by John Temple Graves. "Carrie Chapman Catt may fairly be regarded as the woman who best represents the women of the civilized world at the present time." - Cutline below the photograph of Mrs. Catt.

5 *Ames Tribune,* April 27, 1916, p.1, "Mrs. Carrie Chapman Catt."

6 *Ames Evening Times,* April 26, 1916, p. 1, "Large Audience Hears Suffrage Leader at Gym."

7 W*oman Suffrage by Federal Amendment*, compiled by Carrie Chapman Catt, 1917. Chapter Six - Note her response to **southern** congressmen and state legislators who were asking their people to vote against woman suffrage because it would "**Interfere with white supremacy in the South.**" Catt spelled out the fact that the population figures in all but two of the southern states demonstrated that white women outnumbered black women. She expressed doubt as to the sincerity of the southern politicians, "If the South **really** wants white supremacy, it will urge the enfranchisement of women," she said. She had thrown their argument right back at them - a **debating skill** she had learned right here on the Iowa State campus. By "reversing" **their argument** she had taken the wind out of those southern racists' sails. A sense of humor can be seen in that procedure.

"No country has ever repented giving the vote to women," Mrs. Catt said. "The best thought of the land knows that woman suffrage works no ill to women or children, but where tried, has been a blessing to their state." Mrs. Catt spoke of the victories won in Canada and the Scandinavian countries. "Finland's women have had a voice in their government longer than in any other country in the world, and the women of America, admittedly the equal of those of any other nation, are **still denied the right to vote.**"

She closed her remarks with a plea for the men voters of the state to recognize the intelligence of their women - and give them the right to vote.

By 1920, Carrie Chapman Catt had led the suffrage movement to a final victory with the ratification of the Nineteenth Amendment. Mrs. Catt's insistence upon acquiring the right to vote for American women by the Constitutional method had been a monumental example of her unwillingness to bow to a state's-rights approach. With the Ninteenth Amendment to the U.S.Consitituion, all women acquired a **basic civil right** no matter where they lived in the United States.[8] In a real sense, the Nineteenth Amendment was Catt's answer to southern racism.

Commencement Speech

On June 20, 1921, Carrie Chapman Catt was again in Ames, this time to become the first woman to deliver the commencement address at an Iowa State College graduation. On that occasion, she received the honorary degree of Doctor of Laws from her alma mater.[9]

The *Ames Tribune* of June 21, 1921, gave front page attention to Mrs. Catt's address. "Speaking intimately and directly to the graduates before her in this 50th commencement of the college, Mrs. Catt gave a message of encouragement and inspiration drawn from the varied activities of her own life."

The *Tribune's* account continued, "Challenging her hearers to the unfinished work of reconstruction, Mrs. Catt told the Iowa State College graduates that it is their job, and the job of other graduates of American colleges this June, to grasp a vision of what the world should be and work unremittingly toward that goal."

Courage and Strength

"Vision," declared Mrs. Catt, "is the comprehension of something of benefit to the world, not a burden, but an inexhaustable source of courage and strength." "As she elaborated this idea her audience heard behind her words the echoes of her own achievements. They caught a glimpse of the clarity and intensity of the vision which she had as a young woman and to which she had devoted her life," stated the *Tribune*.

"Mrs. Catt did not deliver a set address, but passed on to the young men and women, where she sat forty-one years ago, the ideals and convictions which she has gathered in her unusually full life," the *Tribune* observed.

"We face a bigger problem than our forefathers dreamed when they declared that all men are created equal," Mrs. Catt declared.

"The time when a parochial outlook on life was enough is past. I believe that one of the great weaknesses of our country is that we have forty-eight different states and we are wont to think of them rather than the country as a whole. I urge you, first to think nationally, but even that is not enough. You must think internationally; you are members of the human race. You must extend your hands across the seas to men and women all over the world. Let us grow closer together for greater happiness in the world at large. Let us be a nation with sympathy enough to put war out of the world."

"The most serious result of wars," she said, "is the wild, ill considered demands of radicalism at one extreme and over conservatism at the other extreme which constitutes a reaction in thought and leads to pessimism in politics. We face this result in our own country today."

"Find your vision and stand fast. You graduates will have to take your place as directors of the nation," That was her advice to Iowa State graduates of seventy-six years ago. That was exactly what she had attempted to do when she had graduated and left the Iowa State campus forty-one years earlier.

International Interests

Carrie Chapman Catt called the first conference on the Cause and Cure of War that met in Washington, D.C, January 18-24, 1925. Her continued international interests and efforts toward world peace had become for her a driving force. Her address, delivered in 1926, on "The Outgrown Doctrine of Monroe"[10] and her support of the League of Nations following the First World War and later of the United

---

8 *ibid,* published by the National Suffrage Publishing Co. Inc.
9 *Ames Tribune*, June 16, 1921, p.1, "Mrs.Catt Urges Graduates Grasp Vision for World."
10 The *World Tomorrow*, November ,1926, p. 193

Nations, are examples among many of her expanded activity.

On June 9, 1930, Mrs. Catt was back in Ames again at the invitation of her alma mater to deliver the commencement address.[11] The occasion was also the fiftieth anniversary of her own graduation from Iowa State.[12]

Two days later, on June 11, Mrs. Catt addressed more than 1,600 Iowa 4-H girls and their leaders assembled on the Iowa State campus for their third annual convention.

"The farmer has made the world," was her theme, stated the *Ames Tribune*.   "I was a farm girl," she

prefaced her words about her own childhood.   For more than forty years she had been a prime mover in the cause of woman suffrage, the *Tribune* observed. "She has seen equal suffrage spread through thirty-two of the sixty-four civilized nations of the earth." Today, her word is: "the task is never done."

The *Tribune* described Mrs. Catt as speaking "with the characteristic vein of rich humor which lights all her words and highlights the appeal of her beautiful speaking voice."   She told the girls, "I left the farm, but always I have been thinking of the farm. As a child I loved everything that grew."[13]

Carrie Chapman Catt was back in Ames on special occasions in her later years.   During Alumni Reunion days in 1933 she received Iowa State College's Alumni Award in recognition of "preeminent service in advancing human welfare."   The list is long of the honors that this Iowa girl, this 1880 graduate of Iowa State, who died in 1947 at New Rochelle, N.Y., received during her lifetime.   In 1975, Carrie Chapman Catt became one of the first inductees into the Iowa Women's Hall of Fame.   In 1992, she was named one of the ten most important women of the century by the Iowa Centennnial Memorial Foundation.

November 12, 1997

---

[11] *Ames Tribune,* June 9, 1930, p.1. "Mrs. Carrie Chapman Catt, a graduate of Iowa State College in 1880, who has been prominent in the National Women's Suffrage Movement since 1892 and who has been president of that organization since 1916, gave the commencement address at the exercises Monday morning."

[12] The *Ames Milepost,* June 12, 1930, p.4. Editorial comment stated, "The most notable member of the State College alumni at the commencment this year was Carrie Chapman Catt. She was a member of the class of 1880, and received the gold 50 year medal with the rest of her class present. The distinction that has come to her as being one of the outstanding workers for the betterment of government and welfare of the women of her day and generation has not affected her attitude toward associates of her youth. She still possesses the qualities that endeared her to school companions and friends of her youth."

[13] *Ames Tribune*, June 11, 1930, p.1, "Mrs.Catt Gives Counsel To Iowa 4-H Girls."

Chapter 27

Jack Trice Story

a chapter in the historic record.

"**P**ayment of a small mortgage and presenting the balance of the fund to his widow and his mother marked the closing chapter in the story of the death of Jack Trice, Iowa State College football player, in the Fall of 1923," stated a front page story in the *Ames Tribune* January 3, 1924. A recent chapter in that same story has been the naming, in 1983, of Iowa State's football field in the memory of Jack Trice, who suffered fatal injury in a 1923 football game. In 1997, still another chapter was recorded: the Iowa State University stadium was renamed the Jack Trice Stadium.

The 1924 account represented what then appeared to be the final word on community response to a tragic event.

In 1923, a call to the general public had been made for contributions to aid the widow of Jack Trice and his mother. Mrs. Anna W. Trice, his mother, of Ravenna, Ohio, had negotiated a mortgage of several hundred dollars on her small home so that she could send Jack to Iowa State. Prof. William H. Pew who had been the head of the Animal Husbandry Department at Iowa State, and had later located in Ohio near the Trice family, administered the fund. After paying off the mortgage and funeral expense

Jack Trice's name became permanently associated with Iowa State football tradition because of his tragic death in 1923. He was a man of high character and a role model in the game of football. Photo courtesy of the Iowa State University Library / University Archives. ID No. 105.572.2-4

The caption on the statue of Jack Trice reads, in part: "This statue was erected by the students of Iowa State to memorialize the ideals of ethical competition so embodied in the story of Jack Trice." The sculpture was completed in 1987 by Christopher Bennett. It was recently moved from central campus to the northeast corner of the stadium. ID No.210.1195.1-2

balances, there remained $1,160 which was divided equally between Jack's wife, Cora Mae, and his mother.

The Iowa State Athletic Council then announced the awarding of an honorary "A" to Jack Trice. (It was not until 1929 that Iowa State athletic teams would be referred to as "Iowa State.")

A published excerpt from a letter written by Jack Trice's mother acknowledged the recognition accorded her son following his tragic death. "I sincerely thank you for the many kind expressions of good will for the memory of my son. If John had lived, the athletic association of Ames would have always had a warm spot in his heart. The spirit in awarding him his "A" is wonderful. I am asking his wife to let me keep it during my lifetime. It is sacred."

August 12,1997

Chapter 28

Martin Luther King's Ames Address In 1960

"We have allowed our mentality to out run our morality and our civilization to outpace our culture," was the key note statement made by Dr. Martin Luther King, when he spoke on the Iowa State Campus on the evening of January 22, 1960.[1]

The occasion was the closing session of the Religion In Life Week program sponsored by Iowa State University that year. King was the featured speaker of the series. The student body turned out in large numbers to hear him. His visit to Ames had been anticipated by many.[2]

He spoke at a social science discussion at the Memorial Union at 4 p.m. and was a dinner guest at the Delta Delta Delta sorority house.

I have never heard a more inspiring speaker. He demonstrated an ability to clarify emotional issues in intellectual and objective terms. Fifteen-hundred people were on hand in Great Hall that evening to hear King speak. I heard him from the balcony with the rest of an overflow crowd.

King spoke again the next morning in the Gallery of the Memorial Union. King's sincerity, his deliberate, clear enunciation of every word, and his deep feeling again came through. Today, I can not recall much of what he said, but I will never forget how he said it. More important, perhaps, is the fact that I had heard a man who had insight and a timeless feel for his message.

Lynn Dreeszen, an Ames High graduate of 1957, and a junior at Iowa State at the time,[3] has corresponded with me with reference to Dr. King's visit to Ames in 1960.[4] In a recent letter to me, he recalled hearing Dr. King speak. "We must have gotten to Great Hall just before the address began, because we sat or stood in the balcony. It was a cold night, but I recall getting uncomfortably hot - even sweating. I know that my sweating was due to King's dynamic delivery rather than the temperature of the Great Hall."

Dreeszen continued: "I picture him behind the Great Hall podium, his deep voice with its unmistakable inflection, gesturing with his arms, and speaking to an audience that was 99% Caucasian. Great Hall was packed for his address."

Dr. King spoke of the "Moral Challenges of a New Age." "We have seen the old order of our nation in the form of segregation and discrimination," he said. "The Emancipation Proclamation freed the slave from slavery, and established him as a legal fact, but not as a man," he continued. "The Negro had to rise above crippling illiteracy,"[5] he said. "The new Negro realized, then, the basic thing about man was not his specificity but his fundamentalism."

Advocating non-violence in bringing about a revolution in race relations, Dr. King stated that he was not interested in rising from a "position of disadvantage to a position of advantage."

"We are challenged," King stated with emphasis, "to rise above individual concerns to the concerns of all humanity."[6]

December 6, 1997

Martin Luther King, Jr. (1929-1968) is recognized as a member of the American pantheon. A man of great talent and unrelenting commitment, his work and dedication to the civil rights movement will continue to inspire future generations.

Photo: Martin Luther King, Jr. Center, Atlanta, GA

---

[1] *Ames Tribune*, January 23, 1960, p.1 "Mentality Has Outrun Morality."
[2] The *Iowa State Daily*, January 22, 1960, "Civil Rights Leader Will Speak Tonight."
[3] Dreeszen lives in Scotts Valley, CA.
[4] Lynn Dreeszen to Farwell Brown, letter dated October 30, 1997.
[5] The *Iowa State Daily*, January 26, 1960, p.1, "King Asks for Broader Ideas." King drew oveflow crowds. 1,500 heard him the evening of the 22nd with an overflow crowd hearing him by the public address system in several locations in the Mcmorial Union.
[6] Martin Luther King, Jr. was born January 15, 1929, at Atlanta, Georgia. He died April 4, 1968, the victim of an assassin's gunshot at Memphis, Tennessee.

Chapter 29

Saved By A Little Tree

And help from her grandmother and the mayor

A little tree changed her life, Geraldine Koss explained in her letter written to me in December of 1980.[1]

She retired as an art teacher in Richland, Washington. Her memory trips had brought her back to Ames, Iowa. Would I be able to assist her in reconstructing an important detail of her early years when as a small girl she had lived with grandparents in Ames?

She said that it had been a little tree that grew near the Ames & College Railroad's depot on the Iowa

State College campus that had been so decisive in the course that her life had taken when she was a very small girl.

Do you have a picture of that little tree? That was her question.

The death of Geraldine Koss's mother occurred when Geraldine was only a few months old. Her father had promised her mother that Geraldine would be raised by her mother's parents. She lived with her grandparents in Ames for the next four and a half years.

One day her grandmother received a phone call from her father who had remarried and had come to Ames unannounced to take Geraldine to live with him and his new wife in California. Her father called from

---

[1] Based upon correspondence with Geraldine Koss, dated December 1, 1980, and March 19, 1981.

The Dinkey steam train at the campus terminal located north of the College Main building in 1905. Geraldine Koss says her grandmother took her behind the little tree at the right when her father arrived on the train from downtown. Her father left the car to enter the depot waiting room at the left. Geraldine and her grandmother then boarded the car from the far side for the ride to downtown Ames. ID No.45.225.3-4

downtown Ames, and directed her grandmother to bring the little girl over to the Ames & College depot on the campus where he would come to pick her up.

Her grandmother packed up Geraldine's belongings and they hurried over to the campus depot of the "Dinkey" as her father had directed. The little depot was then located north of the "Old Main" building on central campus.

Geraldine's grandmother took the little girl with her to stand behind a small tree that stood a short distance to the north of the depot. She was trying to think of some way to keep Geraldine in Ames. She was certain that the little girl's father, who had opposed the idea of girls being well-educated, would not provide the best environment for the child.

From behind the little tree, they watched the Dinkey arrive at the depot. The father, leaving the train, proceeded to walk to one side of the tree enroute to the street. The grandmother, acting on impulse, took the granddaughter around the tree in the opposite direction.

They walked over to the train, unseen by Geraldine's father. Boarding the train for its return run to downtown Ames, the grandmother decided on a plan for a solution to their problem.

Reaching downtown Ames, Geraldine's grandmother found Mayor Parley Sheldon in his office at the Story County Bank, then located on the northeast corner of Douglas Avenue and Main Street. Parley Sheldon seemed to fully comprehend the situation.

He took the grandmother and the little girl immediately to an attorney's office across the street from the bank.

In her letter to me, Geraldine Koss told how Parley Sheldon and his attorney prepared adoption papers. There was a quick ride to Nevada to make necessary filings. It was Parley Sheldon's signature on those adoption papers that permitted Geraldine Koss to remain here in Ames with her grandparents.

The little tree and the timely help from the mayor of Ames, made a big difference in the life of that little girl.

Since she was allowed to remain in Ames, Geraldine acquired a good education including a college degree and special art training at the Chicago Art Institute. After a career in public school teaching, she retired in the state of Washington. She had always enjoyed recalling that little tree that stood on the campus in Ames and how it changed the direction of her life that day back in 1906.

Geraldine in later years met and talked with her father who frankly told her that he *might* have permitted her to finish high school.

I did have a picture of that little tree. It shows the campus depot with the Dinkey about to depart; the little tree can be seen in the background. Geraldine Koss wrote telling me that she had placed that photo in the center of a collage where it portrays an important chapter in the story of her life.

May 1996

Chapter 30

Former Governor In The Philippines Dies In Ames

From Success and fame to a life of anonymity

Christopher Ney was known in Ames only as a recluse.

He came to Ames in 1923. He lived in a corrugated metal-covered shack north of Thirteenth Street

Christopher Ney (1869 - 1927), former Philippine Island Governor. Ranging from a life of unusual productivity to that of a recluse, he died in Ames, Iowa, almost as an "unknown." From an "original photo."

---

[1] Summit Avenue was platted June 9, 1923.
[2] *Tribune*, Feb. 4, 1927, p.3.
[3] *Ames Tribune*, Feb. 8, 1927, p.3.
[4] John Ney had also been a member of the University of Iowa law faculty.

in the vicinity of today's Summit Avenue.[1] Today, when you drive north from the intersection of Thirteenth and Ridgewood toward Ames High School, you will be within a block of where his shack once stood. He looked like a typical "odd jobs" sort of man. In fact, "odd jobs" was just what he did do much of the time. He worked, when needed, on several farms near town.

Who was he really? In some ways it was apparent that he was not the ordinary "common man." He visited the college library, sometimes daily. He read many books at the library and also checked out books frequently. Librarians were well acquainted with his wide interests, and commented upon them to each other.

No one ever seemed to find out who he really was. There might have been clues. On several occasion he brought books, good books, academic-type books, and donated them to the library.

It happened on February 3, 1927.[2] Ney was helping Ernest Hunter cut down some trees on his farm located across the road west, and a bit south, from today's Ames Golf and Country Club. A falling limb struck Ney on the head knocking him unconscious. He was rushed to Mary Greeley Hospital, where he was diagnosed with concussion and probable skull fracture. On Monday February 5, 1927, Christopher Ney died from that injury.

Three days later, the headline spread across the top of the Ames Tribune revealed what very few people in Ames had known before about Christopher Ney. It read: *"Former Island Governor In the Philippines Dies Here."* [3]

His life story eventually came to light. His brother, Marshall Ney, an Omaha attorney, came to Ames when he heard the news of the accident. Funeral plans were announced as soon as his sister arrived from Alamo, Texas. He had been predeceased by one brother, Judge John J. Ney of the Tenth Judicial District of Iowa.[4]

Christopher Ney was born in Arcola, Indiana,

on Oct. 28, 1869,[5] and came to Iowa with his parents in 1884, settling in Buchannan County near Independence.

Ney attended Iowa State College in 1889/1890, enrolled in civil engineering. He next "read law" in a law office in Waterloo. He then entered the University of Minnesota Law School where he attained a law degree. He passed the Iowa bar in 1895.

When the war with Spain broke out, Ney enlisted and saw service in the Philippines. Mustered out in Manila, he then founded and edited the *Manila Tribune,* the first American newspaper in the Philippines. Forceful editorials from his pen attracted the attention of William Howard Taft, then the civil governor of the Philippines. In 1901, Taft appointed Ney the treasurer of the province of Ilocpa; and a few months later, he appointed him the Governor of the province of Luzon.

In 1908, while still holding his responsibilities in the Islands, Ney married his sweetheart from Minnesota. She came to the islands to teach in an American school. Later that same year when they were visiting in the United States, Ney's wife contracted pneumonia and died. Completely overwhelmed by his wife's death, Ney stayed in the U.S. for a short time, but returned to Manila where he practiced law until 1913.

At his death, he still carried the gold watch bearing the inscription, "Presented to C. W. Ney in token of the esteem in which he is held by the lawyers of Manila, April 20, 1913."

Returning to the States, he attended Columbia University, earning a doctorate in law degree. With the outbreak of World War I, he again enlisted, participating in many important military engagements on the Hindenburg line.

Ney reentered the law practice in New York for a short time after the war, but his ambitions faded. It was at this point that he made his way back to Ames.

Why did Ney abandon his profession? Why did he choose to live the life of a recluse?

Those who knew him best when he was in the Philippines felt that a profound change came over him after the death of his wife.

A year before his death, Ney wrote these lines to a friend: "My giving up the law was due to no one thing in particular but rather to a combination of circumstances."

The tin-covered cabin that Ney built and in which he resided when he returned to Ames in 1923. Located north of Thirteenth Street in the vicinity of Ridgewood and Summit avenues, it was possibly the first habitation in that area of Ames. Drawn by Dianne Mumm from 1927 newsprint photo. ID No. 188.1063.2-4.

His comments continued, "I was footloose, I did not have a little family of the average professional man. Too much idealism on my part, and too much realism in the practice of law might therefore be the first and main part of my answer for leaving the profession."

Those who had known Ney best right here in Ames detected a sense of Ney's disappointment in the directions that society had taken following World War I. Ney expressed a poetic, idealistic nature. Some thought that he had been working on a manuscript of his life's philosophy; but no one today has any knowledge of its existence.

Ney had been befriended by Father LeRoy Burroughs of the Episcopal Church in Ames . Marguerite Burroughs Righter, now living in New Hampshire, recalls going with her father for visits with Ney. She remembers his telling fascinating stories. Her father felt that Ney had much to offer and that his self-imposed isolation was a tragedy.

Ney's tiny shack in north Ames was almost devoid of furnishings. He had made his own furnishings, except for a single chair, a decrepit cabinet and a stove. A box and a straw tick mattress, without springs, served as his bed.

The De*s Moines Register's* front page story of February 13, 1927, summed it up this way: "When the buglers sounded taps and the soldier's rifles cracked in salute over the fresh grave of Christopher W. Ney in St. Boniface cemetery in St. Paul [6] yesterday, it was the last honoring of a man whose life had been a blending of success and tragedy into a philosophy."[7]

Who was Christopher Ney? A part of the answer would be: A college graduate with an advanced de-

[5] *National Encyclopedia of American Biography.*(1929)
[6] *Ames Tribune,* Feb.10, 1927, p.1.
[7] *Des Moines Register*, Feb. 13, 1927, p.1

gree, an attorney, a newspaper editor, an army of-
ficer, a government official, and finally, a recluse who
had assigned himself to anonymity.

On the day of his funeral, the American flag flew
at half mast on the flagpole that stood next to his tin-
covered shack in north Ames, the flagpole that Christopher Ney had made.

June 26, 1996

Chapter 31

The Greatest Agricultural Fair In The Nation

It was *supposed* to be Iowa's wasn't it?

Current banter between the governors of Iowa and Minnesota[1] as to the relative merits of their respective states is a no-win game, and it is old stuff at that.

For example, Iowans of my vintage will recall that the Iowa State Fair was sometimes billed as the largest agricultural fair in the country-or words to that effect. After all, Iowa was the greatest farm state in the nation. Iowa has a fourth of the nation's grade-A land within its borders; its state fair would have to be the greatest and best in the country.

That was the direction my thinking took me many years ago when I became involved in that kind of "my state vs. your state" conversation.

I graduated from Ames High School in 1929. That September I entered Oberlin College in Ohio. My roommate in the freshman dormitory was Aikin Gortner from Minnesota. His father was a chemistry professor at the University of Minnesota. As we walked across the campus that first day, he mentioned that his family lived in St. Paul, since his father's teaching was on the farm campus of the university, and that they lived just one block from the state fairgrounds. With that opening, I naturally informed him that one of Iowa's claims-to-fame was that it had the lar*gest agricultural fair in the country.*

He was quick to inform me that *Minnesota, not Iowa*, had the largest and best agricultural state fair in the land. I had him there, I thought, as I explained to him that the *Des Moines Register*, the largest paper in Iowa, had just a few weeks earlier described the Iowa fair as the premier agricultural fair in the nation. Was that not proof plenty?

At that point, we caught up with a freshman by the name of Holmes who hailed from Fremont, Ohio.

The Iowa State Fair: "The World's Greatest Agricultural and Livestock Fair." That was the caption on the advertisement for the Iowa Fair that appeared in the Des Moines Register in August 1928. That was my proof that I was right about what I told those college boys in Ohio!

I had conversed with him earlier that same day and had found him to be a reasonable fellow. As we began our conversation, I suggested that he might settle a bit of a dispute between my roommate and myself.

Holmes listened to our question about the state fairs. He seemed to give it careful consideration for a moment. Then he said, "You are both wrong *Ohio has the best, the largest, and greatest agricultural fair in the country.* I know that to be a fact since the Columbus paper, and also the Cleveland paper, made that claim this fall."

For some reason the three of us found something else to talk about. Our respective state fairs were never again discussed.

February 26, 1997

---

[1] Reference to the January, 1997, statement by Minnesota's governor that Des Moines is a "dead city" compared with Minneapolis. Iowa's governor's demand for an apology was refused, and the topic has been in the news ever since with no indication of resolution.

Chapter 32

He Climbed To The Top Of The Sheldon Munn

(On The Outside That Is)

"Human fly will entertain Ames audience Tuesday." That was the headline of an *Ames Tribune* front page story on July 28, 1924.

You may recall a recent news story about a daredevil who climbed the Empire State Building in New York City. He didn't get advance permission to make the climb, so he was in trouble with the law when he got to the top. That fellow used some sophisticated equipment in accomplishing his fete.

Billy Brine, as announced in the Tribune, did climb the Sheldon Munn Hotel and he had everyone's permission at the time. I was in the crowd that day and remember it well.

Fifteen years earlier, Brine had worked on farms near Marshalltown. In 1924, while visiting in

Illustration courtesy of the Daily Tribune.

Sheldon Mun Hotel as it appeared in a 1919 postcard photo. ID No. 32.158.4

Marshalltown, he took up his brother's challenge to climb the Sheldon Munn in Ames.

A big crowd filled the street in front of the hotel. The climb was made on the Main Street side. Brine went right up the side of building at a point above the hotel entrance. He prefaced the climb with a lot of fanfare and some theatrics. He used no equipment, but he did have an accomplice on the inside of the hotel. Climbing from window to window, Brine was able to climb to an open window on each floor as he moved upward. His accomplice was kept busy opening and closing windows. Because his assistant would pull both panes of each window into the down position after the human fly had reached still another window sill, Brine could then thrust himself upward by climbing onto the tops of the frames.

When you are next down on Main Street, take a look at the hotel and see just how hard it would be for an ordinary man to do what he did that day. He must have had exceptional strength in his arm and leg muscles; once he got his hand on the brick window sill above him he would literally lift himself to a point where he could wiggle into the open window space.

Brine frightened the crowd several times by pretending to slip, each time catching himself just in time. I recall that he was thrown the flagpole rope from the top of the building and made use of that in scrambling to the top edge. Reaching the top of the building, he proceeded, then, to climb the flagpole where

he balanced himself on the gilded ball at the top. As the crowd hushed, he shouted out the name of his usual sponsor. "CHEVROLET CHEVROLET" he called out. I presume that it was the Chevrolet Company that sponsored his climb that day.

We don't hear of "human flies" today, but in 1924 the Tribune story explained that Brine was one of six "in business" at the time. Brine had been climbing buildings for 11 years by 1924. His record had been 161 building climbs in 1921. Brine was reported to have climbed a 24-story building in Pittsburgh, Pennsylvania in 33 minutes. Unlike the recent case of the man climbing New York's Empire State Building, Brine, except for his accomplice inside the building and the use of the flagpole rope, had used only his strength and agility in that 1924 climb on the Ames hotel.

Before Brine made his climb, there were two attempts by itinerate climbers who announced plans to climb the Sheldon Munn. In both cases they failed.[1] One of those, a man named E. T. LeBouef, had attempted to climb the building on July 28, 1921. He made his attempt on its southeast corner where the brick design offered a more textured surface. After ascending but a few feet the attempt was abandoned. There was some grumbling that day among spectators because the man had passed the hat collecting about $24 before he attempted his climb. He left abruptly, taking the loot with him.

The day after Brine's climb in 1924, the *Ames Tribune* reported that several Ames youngsters had acquired a few bruises when they attempted to emulate Brine by climbing to the tops of their family garages or front porches.

May 18, 1994

---

[1] *Ames Tribune*, June 26, 1920, p.2, advertisement announcing, "Jack Williams, The Human Fly" would climb the Sheldon Munn Hotel at 7 p.m. that day. There is no indication in the news that he ever arrived!

Chapter 33

In 1932, It Was "Ride 'Em Cowboy"

As a part of my six-months' "on-the-farm experience" required for a degree in agriculture at Iowa State, I worked most of the summer of 1932 on the Iowa State College Dairy Farm. Ag students from the farm met that requirement automatically, but I had always lived right here in the town of Ames.

Prof. Henry H. Kildee became Dean of the Agricultural Division at Iowa State in 1932. He was a nationally known dairy livestock judge. In fact, he was internationally known as an authority on livestock matters. One afternoon in mid-July, Prof. Kildee brought to the Dairy Farm a group of visiting specialists. I believe he had in mind showing off the farm's facilities and some of the select, pure-bred milk cows and calves. Making a good impression would have been considered important.

Lindley Finch, another of the student farm workers, and I were called upon to select some of the better calves that had crowded into the rear of the calf shed to escape the heat of the day. We were to drive those calves out into the open lot where they could be seen by the visitors.

That shed was a rectangular, lean-to structure located south of what was then a horse barn located to the west of the drive entrance to the farm building area. The opening along the south side of that lean-to was perhaps twenty feet in width and had a long burlap curtain hung along its entire length. The curtain was to darken the inside of the shed and keep it as cool as possible.

The lot south of the calf shed was next to the cindered drive and had a white board fence along its east and south sides. The dean and his visiting group

The lot at the Dairy Farm looks like this today - sixty-six years later. There was a board fence where the wire fence and feed bunk arrangement is seen here in the forground. The barn near the road was a horse barn then. The shed at far left may have been about in the location of the calf shed that day in 1932. ID No. 209.1189.1-2

115

were lined up along that fence when Lindley and I went behind the burlap to drive out the calves. After a few calves had run out under the curtain into the lot, Lindley, who had gone to the rear of the shed, suddenly called to me to detain a not-too-good-looking calf. "Don't let that one go out." I was near the front of the shed at that moment. That calf was definitely headed out, and it was angling away from me. Thinking I could divert the calf, I made a lunge in its direction hooking my left arm around its neck.

The momentum of the calf threw me off-balance just as we reached that burlap curtain. What happened next will explain why the event was to be one that I remember so well.

A hole in that burlap was just large enough and in just the right location to fit into the forthcoming sequence. I was positioned with my arms around the calf's neck and my head above it so my head went right through the hole in the burlap. Down came the burlap, breaking loose all the way across the shed's entrance.

The excited calf bounded out into the lot. The burlap covered the calf entirely, it covered all but my head. What the dean and his dignitary guests saw was my head bounding around on a big stretch of burlap. They broke into hilarious laughter. I don't think they ever saw the calf.

Lindley and I made quick work of rolling up the burlap, and I imagine there was no more calf selection that day.

The dean seemed to be in a good mood when he spoke to me later and no reference to the special event of that day was ever made.

January 17, 1996

Clhapter 34

Hey, Now!
Cow In The Hay Mow!

When I attended Iowa State College in the 1930s, one requirement for obtaining a degree in agriculture was to be either from the farm or to acquire a minimum of six months "on-the-farm experience" before graduation. Since I was a town boy myself, I spent three summers on farms in central Iowa. One of those summers I spent on a large livestock farm in Dallas County. It was there that an especially adventurous farm animal provided some special "entertainment" one morning.

Most Iowa barns in those days provided substantial overhead hay storage and were often referred to as "mow barns," mow rhyming with *cow,* with that upper barn area known as the "hay mow." Since World War II with changing technology in the hay handling and storage, mow barns have almost disappeared from the Iowa farm scene.

This story took place in one of those traditional two-level barns common to Iowa farms in the 1930s.

In the summer of 1933, Howard Hill and his wife were providing me with room and board on their Dallas County farm. Howard, his hired man, and I arose each morning at about five. Our early morning activities were often referred to as "barn chores." The main stock on that farm were feeder cattle and hogs. There were only two milk cows on the place. Howard milked one cow, and his hired man milked the other one while I harnessed the two teams of draft horses for the day's field work.

As each finished his milking, he would release his cow from its stanchion and it would then saunter out the north door of the barn to the open lot. One morning as I was finishing harnessing the second team, Howard called out to me to come to his assistance: "We've got something going on down here!" He had discovered that the hired man's cow had not gone out into the lot. Instead, it had wandered down to the center part of the barn. Here there was an enclosed stairwell that led to the hay mow above. The door at the bottom of the stair had been left open.

Was it the hay up in the mow or was it just curiosity? The cow never explained, but she made a nice start up that narrow flight of stairs. That was when Howard came along. He tried to coax the cow out of the stairwell. Instead she had just gone up one more step.

I hurried to the hay mow by means of a ladder near the other end of the barn. Coming down the stairs I confronted Bossy head-on. I attempted to put some backward pressure on Bossy's head and shoulders while Howard worked from the other end. I learned that morning that milk cows are called "bossy" for good reason. That Bossy had only her forward gears under control. Howard then said that we would have to handle her on her own terms; so we let her stay in the forward mode and led her step by step on up into the hay mow above. Slowly, but surely, she cooperated in a clumsy stair climb.

She was one bewildered milk cow! Once she was firmly established on the floor of that hay mow, we broke the news to her. She was now to show us how a full grown cow can go downstairs. Turning her around was no problem. What happened next might have been taken on the road as a sideshow attraction.

*This "mow barn" located on the Taylor farm at the north edge of Ames resembles the one on the Dallas County farm where this story took place. Notice the **extended hay lift track** at the front peak of the barn. Most of the track has been removed since it has been years since hay was stored in this barn. A few days after I took this picture, this barn was torn down. The traditional Iowa barn with the hay mow or "loft" is becoming an endangered species. ID No.182.1031.2-3*

I do not recall whether Howard or I took the lead on that narrow stairwell that morning. With one to guide and one to add persuasion, we began. There was a right-angle turn in those stairs to add to the thrill of both cow and mankind, especially in the downward direction. Bossy's forward gear still functioned. A stiff-kneed cow on a downward slant is even more fascinating than on the upward climb. Start down she did. The scramble of a cow going downstairs, negotiating a right-angle turn to boot, sounded like a whole herd of cattle. It also took less time than going up. Our Bossy was more resigned, and probably gravity was in her favor.

She was as willing to conclude the escapade as we. Also, the stairs being both narrow and enclosed prevented some directional distractions.

We were late for breakfast that morning but plenty hungry. Just how difficult it was to explain our delay, I do not specifically recall. I have also wondered what our Bossy said to that other cow about the whole matter.

Feb.16, 1996

118

Chapter 35

They Ate Dean Curtiss's Blue Ribbon Pig

On February 6, 1919, at about 11:30 p.m., ten initiates of the Beta Fraternity at Iowa State College went out on a "raiding expedition," the purpose was to find a pig to expedite a planned pig roast. They caught a pig down on the Rockwood farm, located about two miles south of the campus.

Dean Curtiss's farm located on South State Street is today owned by Iowa State University. The ISU Press operation and warehouse is today on this property. ID No.203.1147.1

It was never explained whether or not any of the ten Beta initiates involved in that expedition knew that it was Dean C. F. Curtiss's farm. However, that fact soon became well known to them since, as it turned out, they had selected one of the dean's prize purebred boars.[1]

Dean Curtiss, of course, was the dean of the School of Agriculture at Iowa State.[2]

The students killed the pig on the spot and hauled it home leaving blood stains all the way to the fraternity house. Curtiss's farm manager followed the trail and notified F. W. Willey, the town marshall, who found the freshly butchered hog in the Beta's icebox the next morning.

Those ten Betas were called before the Board of Deans. Each man willingly signed a full confession. Those confessions covered every detail of their mid-

Charles F. Curtiss, Dean of Agriculture, Iowa State College -(1897 - 1932). Photo courtesy of Iowa State University Library / University Archives. ID No.88.463.5

night expedition. Following their deliberations, it was the unanimous decision of the board that all ten of the men be indefinitely suspended and that the college should be slow to consider reinstatement.[3]

That is the end of the story except to add that, according to reports, Dean Curtiss received $500 as restitution for the loss of his thoroughbred pig.[4]

A check of the record reveals that of the ten college men that had been suspended, three of them did later return to Iowa State and graduate. One of the men[5] who returned and graduated became the head of one of Iowa's leading wholesale hardware firms located in Des Moines. Many of the employees of that firm, in later years, would hear at least a "selected version" of that infamous night raid on the Dean's hog lot and the "big trouble" that resulted.

August 3, 1996

---

[1] *Ames Tribune* of February 10, and 16, 1919.

[2] *Ames Tribune* of March 3, 1919.

[3] Board of Deans action dated Feb.11, 1919, I.S.U. Archives.

[4] *Ames Tribune*, March 3, 1919. Apparently no indictment.

[5] Louis C. Kurtz. Jr., I.S.C. ME, 1920. The others were Robert P. Moscrip, Chem.E., 1922, and George G.Schilling, Vet.Med., 1921.

Chapter 36

Alpha Zeta Pledges Make The News

I t happened at three o'clock in the morning of March 6, 1939.[1]

During those fateful early hours in the springtime of many years ago, some Alpha Zeta pledges at Iowa State College were on their way over to the horse barn located on the northeast corner of the campus. They had been led to understand that it was their assigned objective to pull off a stunt that would aggravate Iowa State's engineering students. In so doing they would prove their qualifications to be members of the Agricultural College's prestigious honorary on the campus.

The point was to be fully proven. Soon after daybreak, when students began to come on campus to attend classes the next morning, the word was out fast.[2]

A team of large Belgian draft horses was bedded down in the main entrance lobby of Marston Hall.[3] Just inside the main floor entrance the fully-harnessed team of Belgians was tied up to the wall radiators. The horses stood on a bedding of straw. A manure spreader, full of straw, was sitting outside of the entrance doors. The latter, probably was to serve as a tip-off as to what was to be found inside.

Word reached Dean Henry H. Kildee. Alpha Zeta men were contacted and told to bring the pledges to the dean's office later that morning.

From Agricultural Hall the young men were sent directly to President Charles E. Friley's office in Beardshear Hall.[4] Friley seemed overwrought! "It has taken years for us to get rid of the "cow college image," he was reported as saying, with a display of displeasure. "You have undone all our efforts in one night."

A manure spreader, full of straw, was sitting outside the entrance doors of Marston Hall - probably as a tip-off to what was to be found inside. Photo from the 1939 VEISHEA issue of the Green Gander. ID No. 169.941.1

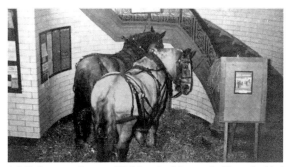

A fully harnessed team of Belgian draft horses had been bedded down inside the Marston Hall entrance. Photo from the 1939 VEISHEA issue of the Green Gander. ID No.169.941.2-3

Photos appearing in the VEISHEA 1939 issue of the Green Gander.

The Alpha Zeta honorary was placed on probation by Iowa State's administrative board as a result of their outrageous prank. The initiation of the pledges scheduled for that night at a banquet was cancelled, and no initiation of new members was permitted that term.[5]

The story continues. It seems that an active member of the Farm House fraternity had an early tip on the prank being perpetrated on the engineers by those Alpha Zeta pledges. Early that morning he had taken his camera over to Engineering Hall and had taken pictures of the Belgian horses bedded down in the lobby and of that manure spreader at the building's entrance.[6] What a "scoop" he must have

---

[1] Much of this account was related to me by Dallas McGinnis.
[2] Knute Hegland, I.S.C. night watchman, discovered the horses bedded down in Engineering Hall on his early morning rounds that day.
[3] Known as Engineering Hall in 1939.
[4] Known as Central Building until 1948.
[5] *Iowa State Daily,* March 7, 1939, p.1.
[6] Both pictures are found in 1939 VEISHEA issue of the *Green Gander.*

thought, as in an ambitious move he had immediately forwarded those photos to *Life* magazine with his hastily written story. Word of those pictures got back to Dean M. D. Helser who sent for the young student photographer.

"Get those pictures back, young man," was the gist of the dean's advice. "If *Life* publishes those pictures, you had better believe it, *you are out of here!!*"

Good luck of sorts then set in. *Life* returned those pictures to the Farm House fraternity photographer. "Thank you for sending them," they wrote, explaining that they would not be able to publish them since they did not fit any of the magazine's current themes.

Everyone involved in that elaborate fraternity prank in 1939 did live to graduate from Iowa State. And those pictures taken of the Belgian horses in Marston Hall are collector's items today.

August 1, 1996

Chapter 37

One College Prank That's Tough To Top

Guess what? There's a dead horse in the living room!

Something like that was the exclamation one early morning in November of 1949 when the active members of the Iowa State College fraternity Sigma Alpha Epsilon went down stairs for breakfast at their house on Lynn Avenue in Ames.

This is a true story. A DEAD HORSE was lying on the floor of the parlor of the fraternity house. The perpetrators of what was a "prank for all occasions" had also turned loose a pen of pigeons to help greet their fellow fraternity brothers that morning.

No doubts existed as to who the perpetrators were. It had been the pledge class that had taken off on a traditional "skip day" the night before. The dead-horse act had been the result of their attempt to play

---

WEDNESDAY, NOVEMBER 23, 1949

Dead Horse Hauled From SAE Fraternity

Chapter President Says 'No Comment'

A dead horse was hauled away from the back yard of the Sigma Alpha Epsilon social fraternity house Tuesday afternoon. The horse reportedly had been found by fraternity members in their living room Tuesday morning.

But Alden C. Noble, fraternity president, when asked about the incident, replied firmly, "No comment."

This statement was made Tuesday afternoon in the fraternity house at 140 Lynn Avenue. Two reporters and several fraternity members were present.

Donald Hansen, a fraternity member, added, "It's just between us and the pledges."

He explained that the fraternity's pledges had staged a walkout Monday evening. He said they left about 50 pigeons in the living room of the fraternity house.

"It was a good walkout," Hansen added. "It proves the pledge class was unified."

"Then you don't want to say anything about the horse?" a reporter asked.

"What horse?" Hansen replied.

However, Ed Sorenson of the Ames Rendering Company said that a dead horse was picked up at 140 Lynn Avenue about 1 p.m. Tuesday.

The driver of the rendering plant truck, contracted later, said he had been at the plant when a call came in that morning asking that he come and get a horse.

A few minutes later, he said, a second call was received. "Don't come after all," he quoted the person telephoning. "The horse isn't dead yet."

Then, the driver added, there was a third call instructing him to come and get the horse.

George MacBride, a worker employed in construction of the First Baptist Church immediately north of the fraternity house, reported that he saw what he thought was a horse behind the residence.

"But maybe this is just a half eyewitness report," he added. "I know I saw a glossy brown hide and some legs sticking out so I thought it was a horse. There was a crowd of fellows around it at the time and I couldn't see too well."

MacBride said that a rendering plant truck came to the house early in the afternoon and picked it up from the back yard.

WEDNESDAY, NOVEMBER 30, 1949

Horse Still Dead; Persons Involved Just Won't Talk

The Sigma Alpha Epsilon fraternity's dead horse story is not dead yet- only dormant.

The horse reportedly had been found lying dead in the chapter room, by the actives when they came down to eat breakfast early Tues. morning.

Since that time, rumors have been circulating around the campus concerning the incident. Many different versions of the story have been heard. Previous attempts to uncover the facts of the story have resulted in "No comment" replies from the chapter officers.

Dean M. D. Helser, when contacted yesterday regarding the incident said, "A very thorough investigation of the whole matter is being made," but when asked for further statements, he only answered, "No comment!"

Not only were the fraternity members confused by the whole affair; but also the Ames Rendering Works. They received three phone calls concerning removal of the horse; the first and last, asking them to come to remove it and the second stating not to come, because the horse wasn't dead yet. It was finally picked up by the rendering truck at 1 p.m. Tuesday.

Alden C. Noble, president of the fraternity, gave two reporters the traditional "no comment" statement Tuesday night. He added that any further information concerning the incident would be released from Dean Helser's office.

DECEMBER 10, 1949

Fraternity Accepts Conduct Probation

The active and pledge chapters of Sigma Alpha Epsilon social fraternity in formal meetings on Nov. 28, 29 have voluntarily considered themselves to be on a conduct probation status beginning Nov. 28 and ending June 1, 1950.

On Nov. 22, a dead horse and 50 live pigeons were found in the living room of the fraternity when the active members came down to breakfast. The horse and pigeons had been placed there the night before when the pledges "walked out." The horse was hauled away that afternoon by an Ames Rendering Works truck.

As a result of the incident, all initiation privileges for the SAE's have been suspended until June 1, 1950. This action prevents immediate initiation of about one-third of the pledge class who are upper classmen and holdovers from the previous pledge classes.

All house dances, dance exchanges, and dinner exchanges of the chapter have been suspended until the close of winter quarter, March 17, 1950.

According to Dean M. D. Helser, of the junior college, the episode has been given much consideration by various committees. The faculty-student fraternity committee and the Inter-fraternity Council are continuing their investigations.

Since the time of the incident many rumors have been circulating about the campus. Various versions of the story have been heard. Previous attempts to uncover the story resulted in "no comment" replies from the chapter officers.

"The committees investigating the issue are satisfied that the death of the horse was instantaneous," Helser said.

He expressed hope that the issue would be completely settled soon after the beginning of winter quarter.

---

*The Iowa State Daily's Stories: carried on **November 23, 1949**; **November 30, 1949**, and **December 10, 1949** - arranged in a collage.*

a joke on the active members, a joke that would go down in fraternity history as one that would be hard to top.

The pledge group had gone about the project in a most professional manner. With several veterinary students in their group, they had talent. First, they found a horse that was an immediate candidate for the rendering plant. Next, they chose to electrocute the old horse in the best-accepted way. With one side of a 110-volt line clipped on one end of the horse's digestive tract, and with the other side of the circuit clipped onto the other end of the horse's anatomy, the instant that the switch was turned on that horse was dead and lying flat on the SAE living room floor.

The *Iowa State Daily,* the college newspaper, ran the story: "DEAD HORSE HAULED OUT OF THE SAE FRATERNITY - Chapter President Says No Comment" The story was out, and it began to sound bad. Reports had it that the national president of SAE was soon on his way to Ames.

The phone rang constantly. The Society for the Prevention of Cruelty to Animals (SPCA) was not happy. A hearing was promptly underway in the administration office of the college. A local newspaper editorial charged the fraternity with cruelty to animals specifically to "that poor old horse."[1]

With Dean M. D. Helser presiding over the proceedings, the facts came out. The horse was to have been disposed of at that same time it became a party to the SAE pledge class's prank. Veterinary staff people testified that, in fact, the way in which the horse had been dispatched had been in the accepted and humane way. The SPCA backed off, satisfied at that point. Questions remained about how the fraternity brothers got the dead horse out of the living room. It must have posed a special problem; but, no doubt, the fraternity's veterinary students were instrumental in the corpse's removal and disposal.

The Iowa State *Daily,* December 10, 1949, carried this front page headline: "FRATERNITY ACCEPTS CONDUCT PROBATION." No one was individually disciplined. The fraternity, however, was prohibited from holding any social events and was not permitted to initiate any new members until after the end of the winter quarter in 1950.

The *Iowa State Daily* summed up what happened by saying, "On November 22, a dead horse and 50 live pigeons were found in the living room of the fraternity when the active members came down for breakfast. The horse and pigeons had been placed there the night before when the pledges walked out."

The horse was hauled away that afternoon by the Ames Rendering Works truck.[2]

The best guess is that no one will ever want to pull off a prank like that one again!

August 4, 1996

---

[1] The *Ames Milepost* December 1, 1949, p.6, "Guilty Should Not Go Unpunished."
[2] *Iowa State Daily* November 23, 1949, p.1, "Dead Horse Hauled From SAE Fraternity."

Chapter 38

With Two Feet In The Grave!

Youth and good health are among the factors involved in obtaining life insurance on favorable terms. This story might seem to present an exception to the rule. I should explain that it took place during my years selling life insurance so that I can vouch for the facts of the case.

A young farmer who lived with his family on a farm located northeast of Ames had expressed interest in acquiring some life insurance. He made an appointment with me to come to his farm home on a Saturday morning to discuss the transaction. It was in late spring and the year must have been about 1945.

It was mid-morning when I arrived at his farm; his wife explained to me that he had been called over to the Pleasant Grove Church, a short distance north and west of their home, to do some work in the churchyard. He had left word for me to come over there. Proceeding to the church, I parked my car in the front of the little frame church building that stood in a wooded area near the old Soper's Mill.

I found several men working in the churchyard. Two of them were cutting the grass and raking the lawn. The man with whom I had the appointment was not in view at first. One of the men directed me to the cemetery area that lay nearby, east of the church. My man was digging a grave. He had dug that grave perhaps three-fourths of the required depth such that his head and shoulders were still well above ground-level.

"We can talk right here," he told me as he leaned his shovel against the side of the grave. I proceeded to show him the outline that I had prepared for him. In order to discuss the matter and to answer his questions, I was down on my knees while he stood there in the grave.

We had talked about the type of insurance in an earlier interview, so that morning he had a good idea

The Pleasant Grove Church appears today just as I recall it when this story took place. The church is on the north side of the county road about two and a half miles east of the Gilbert corner north of Ames. Located about half mile east of the old Soper's Mill site on the Skunk River, it remains in good condition today. The cemetery where this story took place is to the right of the church. ID No.196.1116.3

about what it was that he wanted. "If you have the papers with you we can just take a few moments and take care of it right now," he said. I asked the necessary questions, filled out an application, then handed it to him with my pen. He signed the application and the transaction was concluded.

Driving back to my office, I amused myself thinking of the circumstances under which I had just written that $5,000 life insurance policy.

My man passed the physical and I delivered that policy to him a week or ten days later. He had that life insurance policy for many years. I withheld from the insurance company the fact that I had written that insurance on a man who really did have two feet in th*e grave!*

February 25, 1997

Chapter 39

Mrs. Hicks Gets Her Groceries

Escott Hicks was a fine tailor, I am sure. He lived on the corner of Douglas Avenue and Seventh Street here in Ames and had his shop in a little square building that he built next to his home. You entered his little shop directly from the sidewalk on the Seventh Street side[1].

But it is not about Escott Hicks that I am writing. My story is about Mrs. Hicks whose first name I probably never knew.[2] After all, I was only about fourteen years old when the event I'm about to relate took place. I had seen Mrs. Hicks a few years earlier when I visited my fifth grade classmate, Wayne Conkey, whose parents lived in an upstairs apartment in the Hicks home.

One late afternoon, I was down at my father's office which at the time was located in the building located on the west side of Douglas Avenue across the street from where the Ames Pantorium is today. As I was looking out the window of my father's second-floor office, I saw Mrs. Hicks come out of the Norris Grocery Store across the street. The Norris Grocery was in the building now occupied by the Alliant-IES Utilities office on the corner of Douglas and Main streets. Mrs. Hicks came out of the store by way of the Douglas Avenue entrance that was located at the northwest corner of the building. She was carrying two big sacks of groceries.

What transpired next was almost equal to a special feature at a Tom Mix movie, and I had a front-row balcony seat.

Mrs. Hicks was a strong-appearing lady, and I would judge that she had a commanding personality. She likely would have had no difficulty carrying those two rather large sacks of groceries to her house located three blocks up Douglas Avenue from the Norris Grocery Store.

The building occupied by the Norris Grocery was originally the Story County Bank building shown in this picture. Parley Sheldon moved his bank to the Kellogg corner in 1916, and Norris later opened his grocery store here. This story about Mrs. Hicks and her grocery bags took place on the walk in front of one of the large display windows seen at the left. ID No.20.100.6

Mrs. Hicks had a different idea. The Norris Grocery had three large plate glass windows on the Douglas side of the store. Those windows had a setback ledge that provided ample width for Mrs. Hicks to set her two grocery bags upon, one on each side of her, as she proceeded to stand with her back to the side of the building and just WAIT.

Curiosity kept my eyes fastened upon Mrs. Hicks. My hunch was that she was up to something. I would soon know what it was.

It was late in the five o'clock hour when Main Street folks were beginning to leave for home.

Around the corner came Mr. Fisher. Earl Fisher was in the real estate and insurance business and had an office on Main Street. He was heading north up Douglas. He lived several blocks to the north and east of the Hicks home. Just as he reached the spot where Mrs. Hicks so patiently stood, it happened!

"Oh Mr. Fisher," she exclaimed, as she stepped out right in front of him. "You are going right past my house," she continued, as she placed sack num-

---

[1] Escott Hicks appears in the Ames telephone book in 1916 at 700 Douglas Avenue. His tailor shop is given a Seventh Street address. It was on the same lot with the Hicks home. The Hickses last appear in the telephone book in 1937, and apparently left Ames after selling their home in September, 1937. This story took place in about 1924.

[2] The deed record, dated September 1, 1937, gives Mrs. Hicks's given name as Belle.

ber one on his left arm. Turning and picking up the second sack from the window ledge, she placed that one under his right arm. "Just leave these at my door as you go by."

Fisher was startled, confronted without warning - sandbagged might be the better description. In the space of a few seconds, he found himself in full involuntary possession of both of Mrs. Hicks's big grocery bags.

Fisher was a large man, and you might say a jovial man I last saw him that day heading north up Douglas toward the Hicks home carrying those two big sacks of groceries. He was mumbling to himself, but seemed to have taken it all in good stride. For some reason, I can believe that he never headed for home up Douglas Avenue after that without first looking ahead to be sure that Mrs. Hicks wasn't standing by at some point along his line of travel.

From my vantage point I had seen the entire episode. I may not have heard their words, but I understood every bit of what was said. The action was that clear.

January 16, 1997

Chapter 40

When Smoking Was Banned On The Iowa State Campus

Today we have state laws that govern smoking in public places, and Iowa State University buildings now provide a "smoke-free environment" for students.[1]

Just how new is that idea?

The *Ames Times* of April 14, 1913, announced that Iowa State College students would, on the following day, be voting whether or not to ban smoking on the campus. The vote had been called for by the Cardinal Guild, the student governing board.

On April 15, 1913, the *Iowa State Student* carried a story about Dean Edgar Stanton. A few years earlier Stanton had become acting president after President A. B. Storms had resigned.[2] Stanton, it may be recalled, was the donor of the Stanton Memorial Carillon on the Iowa State campus.

Stanton's office had a good view of the campus. Anyone he saw smoking on the campus was given an urgent invitation to call at his office. The guilty party found the Dean ready to talk about smokers in general and one smoker in particular.

Some smokers discovered that Dean Stanton had quite a range of vision. He had the ability to see out of both sides of Central Building (later named Beardshear Hall). Some smokers, the story reported, had resorted to smoking on the north side of the Hub. An interview with Professor Fred Beckman, head of the Journalism Department, appeared in the same issue of the *Iowa State Student*. Beckman came down hard on smoking, explaining that he spoke as a former smoker himself. He made reference to "tobacco heart" and to "susceptibility to cancers in the mouth and throat."

Beckman felt that the real issue was "shall we allow the word to go out over the state to our homes and even the world, as far as Ames graduates may go, that we have broken down on a time-honored tradition that we now allow smoking on our campus?"

---

[1] Includes dormitories. Two dormitories allow smoking in private rooms only.

[2] *Iowa State College Student,* "Dean Stanton Started Things," April 15, 1913, p. 1.

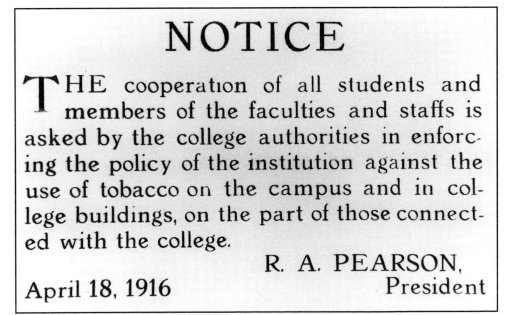

NOTICE

THE cooperation of all students and members of the faculties and staffs is asked by the college authorities in enforcing the policy of the institution against the use of tobacco on the campus and in college buildings, on the part of those connected with the college.

R. A. PEARSON, President

April 18, 1916

Iowa State students and staff received this notice in April 1916 requesting their cooperation in connection with the ban on tobacco use on campus.   ID No. 160.890.1-5

"MAJORITY AGAINST SMOKY CAMPUS" read the headline of a front page story in the April 19, 1913, issue of the *Student*. It was the largest vote ever polled by an Iowa State student body.[3]

A majority of the voters favored abolishing smoking on campus. Of the 1,358 votes cast, a hundred nonsmokers had voted for unrestricted smoking on campus while a hundred and sixty-seven smokers had voted in favor of the ban. Based on the votes of men students alone, a majority favored banning smoking on campus.

The smoking issue was referred to the faculty for ratification, after which a ruling was issued prohibiting smoking on the campus.[4]

Then came World War I. With the establishment of the Student Army Training program and the Army's subsidized distribution of cigarettes, the ban was forgotten.

That is, until 1922.

Following the Armory fire on December 16, 1922, Tom Sloss, Superintendent of Buildings and Grounds, requested that smoking be banned in campus buildings because of the fire hazard. The Board of Deans then passed a special ruling positively forbidding smoking in any college building.[5] President Pearson spoke to the janitors enjoining them to see that the ruling was enforced.

In 1913, when action was taken at Iowa State on the "smoking on campus question," a survey of other college and university campuses indicated that there was general agreement on the matter. Three schools, the University of Nebraska, Kansas State College, and the University of Illinois, had established outright smoking bans on their campuses. Nebraska's Board of Regents had been responsible for the action at their state university. Faculties had instigated the ban at the other schools.

At the Universities of Wisconsin and Minnesota, tradition was relied upon to prevent smoking on campus. However, Minnesota was reporting that tradition no longer as strong because of the recent change in administration at the school. The Universities of Missouri and Kansas were permitting smoking, but at Missouri it was permitted only on the entrance steps of buildings.[6]

By the 1930s, college and university campuses had succumbed to the influence of returning war veterans who had become addicted because of the wartime distribution of cigarettes and to the postwar social acceptance of smoking. Added to this, was the peer pressure of fellow students.

Free cigarette distribution then came directly to the campus with tobacco companies paying students to hand out sample cigarettes to students as they exited Beardshear Hall. The trend noted earlier on the University of Minnesota campus was then in widespread evidence; it was to be further entrenched by the effects of World War II in the 1940s.

Much of what was known back in the teens and twenties about the effects of smoking has again been emphasized and has been fortified by medical research. Many campuses are now governed by state laws in the matter of smoking in public places.

Added to the personal health factors, today there is an emphasis upon one's right to breathe fresh air. Health and environmental interests are much more in evidence than before.

Stronger evidence is available today than before World War I. However, Iowa State's student body was more "on target" than they knew when they voted that ban in 1913.

July 5, 1996

---

[3] *Iowa State College Student,* April 19, 1913. 1,358 votes cast.
[4] *Iowa State College Student,* April 18, 1916 Pearson's post card request to faculty and students.
[5] Minutes Board of Deans December 21,1922. Also: *Iowa State College Student,* January 3, 1923
[6] *Iowa State College Student,* April 15, 1913.

Chapter 41

Joe's New Theater

Harold Loughran graduated from Ames High School in 1920.[1] A few years ago I had an opportunity to talk with him about some of his memories of Ames. He was in that group of young men who entered military service during the world war before they graduated from high school; as a result they were older than the usual high school seniors at the time of their delayed graduation. It is important to get that fact in mind since the story that I wish to relate took place before World War I when Harold was perhaps a freshman in high school.

It seems that Joe Gerbracht had taken over the management of the Scenic Theater in 1913. Joe will be remembered by many, because he became the primary theater owner and manager of Ames theaters for a good many years. Harold's story had to do with Joe's announcement sometime along in 1913, that he was going to build a new theater on the northwest corner of Main Street and Kellogg Avenue. That was, of course, before the Sheldon Munn Hotel was built in 1915 and 1916. According to Harold, Joe publicly announced plans for his new theater on more than one occasion, but he made no move to carry out such a plan.

Harold and his friends were inclined to joke about Joe Gerbracht's new theater-to-be. Then Halloween 1914 rolled around, and these same boys were entertaining an ambition of their own-namely, to carry out a Halloween prank that might be worthy of real comment. One that might even go into the record book somewhere!

Harold didn't tell me that the idea had originated with him; however, he sure knew the details. The boys looked at that still-vacant corner at Kellogg Avenue and Main Street where all there had been of recent time was a signboard or two. Here is where the idea struck!

A little sign painting on the part of one of the boys who had that special talent and the rest was easy.

When folks came down to Main Street in the morning, there it was: Gerbracht's New Theater! Drawing made by Dianne Mumm.

In those days there was still in downtown Ames a fair supply of yet in use old fashioned facilites best known as outhouses or privies. You may by now have guessed the rest of the story.

Halloween seemed quiet enough around town that year, but the next morning, when folks came down to Main Street, there it was!

On the northwest corner of Main Street and Kellogg Avenue sat a perfectly good outhouse with its front facing the corner at an angle. Posts had been set in front to support an overhang with a couple of "coming attractions" posters attached to it. Above the door of that privy (a privy no longer!), a nice big sign announced that "**Here is Joe Gerbracht's New Theater!**" Still another sign appeared on the door of the structure with the words "**Main Entrance.**"

Not long after that, Parley Sheldon announced his plans to build the Sheldon Munn Hotel at that corner. I guess that let Joe Gerbracht off the hook on that whole matter. As for the boys, Harold told me that not even his father[2] ever knew who the boys were who had "built" **Joe's new theater** on Halloween night in 1914.

April 19, 1998

---

[1] Harold Loughran grew up in Ames. His family lived in the Octagon house at one time. For many years he was the dispatcher for the Des Moines City Railway Company. His sister, Lolly Loughran, was a home economist with the Iowa State College Extension Service.

[2] Tom Loughran owned the Rexall Drug Store on Main Street.

Chapter 42

Man In A Fog!

This is a story that I know to be true. It was a front page story in one of our local newspapers sometime in the 1920s. Several years ago I inquired of some longtime local residents as to their recollections of the event.[1] Bob Williams, once a shoe repairman on Main Street, recalled the story just about as I do. Neither Bob nor I could put an exact date on it.

A young fellow had driven to Ames from northern Iowa to see his girlfriend who was a student at Iowa State College. He had never before been in Ames. The day was overcast; he drove through rain and fog that afternoon. His girlfriend was expecting him to arrive at her dormitory around 7:30 that evening, so he made his way to Main Street to get something to eat. As I recall the story, he next stopped at the police station on Fifth and Kellogg to ask directions to the campus. That is really where this story begins.

The young man drove his Model-T Ford Runabout west on Sixth Street.   I suspect he had been

Looking north from point under the railroad bridge toward the Squaw Creek foot bridge. Built in 1908, the bridge provided pedestrian access to the cinder path to the campus for those who lived north of the railroad in downtown Ames. ID No.119.654D.2-3

---

[1] My search of the newspaper microfilms has not yet located that story. Eventually I expect to find it.

[2] There were then footbridges on both sides of the C.& N.W. bridge so that pedestrians did not have to climb the railroad's fences to reach the cinder path.

[3] A Model-T Ford measures 56" from the center-to-center of the tires. Overall width therefore of the car would have been six feet. On that foggy night our "out-of-town visitor" must have had railing-to-railing car as he crossed the Squaw Creek on that footbridge!

told to make a turn to the south at Grand Avenue; but, remember, at that time Sixth Street was unpaved and Ames had no stop signs or traffic lights.   He failed to make the turn in the fog.   For whatever reason, he continued on Sixth Street in a westerly direction.

This story took place twenty-five to thirty years before Sixth Street was extended to the campus. Sixth Street went over the railroad tracks then as it does today, by way of a viaduct. But in the twenties that viaduct was the original wooden overhead that had been there since 1904. Sixth Street in those days ended with the Brookridge Avenue intersection. The fog must have been pretty dense by the time our visitor was approaching that point.

While there was then no street west of Sixth and Brookridge as there is today, that intersection was where the old cinder path began.   That cinder path was a very popular pedestrian walkway to the campus for Iowa State students and faculty alike. A footbridge had been placed over Squaw Creek, paid for by the railroad, as a matter of fact, back in 1908.[2] Located about where the Sixth Street bridge is today, the footbridge was an especially well constructed wooden bridge. It was little more than six feet in width. I think that it stood there until the 1940s when Sixth Street was extended and an automobile bridge was constructed at that same location.

The cinder path continued from the west end of that footbridge. It curved southwesterly under the railroad bridge then went up on the south side of the interurban tracks.   That well-maintained path continued on west to the campus, following along the south side of the streetcar tracks all the way to the heating plant.   It was wide enough for students to walk in pairs and to easily pass going both directions.

Knowing nothing of that cinder path, and having to operate in heavy fog, the young man continued past Brookridge Avenue on what he believed to be the road to the Iowa State campus.   He would eventually discover how mistaken he was.

Suddenly he was aware of a bridge.   A bit of a narrow fit, but his Model-T rumbled along slowly and without difficulty. He would learn later just how miraculous that part of the ride had been. The footbridge was only slightly wider than his car.[3]   He still thought that he was on the road to the campus.

It seemed difficult to follow the road after he got across the bridge. The "road" seemed to have curves in it, and it felt like his car was always right at its edge. He was proceeding with caution through heavy fog. He once was aware that he was under a railroad bridge when a train passed overhead. Several times he almost slipped off the road. He wondered why he met no cars. Could it be that he had taken a wrong road?

After it seemed that he had been on the road an eternity, he suddenly came upon another bridge. That bridge, over a small drainage ditch, was a short one but was too narrow for his car.

With confusion now adding to the fog, he moved away from the car a few feet to check out that bridge. It was then that he became aware that he had been following a footpath rather than a roadway. That little bridge was obviously limited to pedestrian use! He could neither proceed nor turn his car around.

At that point a very frustrated young man began his retreat on foot . He ended up walking all the way

Today, the tracks are gone. You are looking east along the old streetcar right-of-way from a point east of Ellwood Drive. That part of the old cinder path east of Elwood Drive is no longer in use. ID No. 208.1183.1

Looking east on the Cinder Path in 1974; that path was still there and only freight came over those former streetcar tracks at left. The little footbridge in the distance (about even with that box car) marked the spot where our "man in a fog" got stalled when trying to come this way that foggy night. Photo courtesy of Iowa State University Library / University Archives. ID No.208.1179.1-5

back downtown to the police station. Bill Cure was the chief of police at the time. He and the assistant fire chief returned with the young man to the scene of his predicament. Reportedly, they were in a state of disbelief about the turn of affairs — that is, until they found that Model-T astraddle the cinder path almost half way across the Squaw Creek bottoms!

It did not take long to determine that there was no way to turn that car around. In fact, there was no way to get the car out of that situation that night at all.

The next morning when the sun came up and the fog had dispersed, a city crew was sent to the scene. A portion of the fence along the cinder path next to the car was taken down and the car, pulled by a pair of Dragoun Transfer's draft horses, was taken across the pasture to Lincoln Way. Once on a good road, the car could again operate normally.

I have to assume that the young man ultimately did keep his date with his girlfriend at one of the college dorms and that all came out well on that score.

A portion of the old cinder path is still in use; it now has an asphalt surface instead of the old cinders. You are looking west from Elwood Drive. Our "man in a fog" never got this far that night in the 1920s! The heating plant is up ahead on the right, and the present day bus barn is on the immediate right.
ID No. 208.1182.5

But I wonder how he ever explained the entire matter to her — or to his friends back home!

There was quite a bit of conversation about the incident among the townsfolk for a few days. The consensus was that no one would ever attempt to drive a car over that Squaw Creek footbridge! Except perhaps, a young man in a fog. Like I said, this is a true story.

28 April 1998

Chapter 43

"...True To Stand For All Time"

The following were my brief remarks made at the dedication on Monday, July 14, 1997 of the the Youth and Shelter Services (YSS) Family History Plaza when the former Municipal Building, fully restored and renovated, became the YSS headquarters. This was the final event of a series in the dedication of the Youth and Shelter Services' new facilities that began on July 11, 1997.

"**B**UILT FOR THE FUTURE"[1] was the caption placed on one of the stories in the *Ames Evening Times* in February, 1916. Our new city hall was approaching completion, in fact, A. B. Maxwell, the City Clerk, had already moved into his offices on the north side of the first floor.

Since we are now situated in front of what originally was our fire station let me begin my comments by telling you about the fire wagon that stood in this fire station that first year that this building was open. The fire wagon was backed into the west door of the station. The horses were kept in the back of the station over by the alley. The harness for the team was kept in an "ever ready" position, suspended over the tongue of the wagon as it faced the open door. Harness tugs were hooked up to the double trees, and the horse collars were spread wide open at the bottom, being equipped with an hinged arrangement. Harness straps were also in a ready position, being suspended by an overhead pulley and rope system. When a fire call came, the horses were rushed to the front of the station and backed into their harnesses . The collars were snapped closed, and the harness straps buckled under the horses. In a matter of seconds, they were ready to head out of the station. Those horses were well trained. They were taken out on regular practice runs, so they knew exactly what was expected of them.

Serious talk about the need for a new city hall began back in 1913. The Chamber of Commerce in August that year had proposed a block long City Hall

and Civic Center complex to be located between Kellogg and Douglas, occupying the entire north half of the city block on the south side of Fifth Street.[2]

At the same time, Ames was having to make a major decision about its light plant. On February 12, 1913, Ames people had voted to build a new light

What was once the entrance to the fire station gets my attention while telling about the horses that once powered the fire wagon kept there. To my right is primary donor and campaign chairman Richard O. Jacobson, and Kathy Svec, president of the Ames Heritage Association. On my left is Mayor Larry Curtis. These people had just presented key thoughts in dedicating the center, and my assignment was to place the center in something of an historical perspective. Photo courtesy of Y.S.S.

Following the dedication of the Family History Plaza, Ruth and I visit with Richard O. Jacobson. Photo courtesy of Y.S.S.

---

[1] February 26, 1916, p.1, "City Hall Is Pride Of All Ames People." Sub-caption: "BUILT FOR THE FUTURE."
[2] A City Hall - Hotel and Business office complex that included a public auditorium was proposed.

plant over on Squaw Creek just west of the intersection of Sixth Street and Brookridge.

Mayor Sheldon was strongly opposed to relocating the light plant. You will recall the story how he kept the matter off of the agenda while the public could be "educated" on the subject. In October 1913, with Sheldon breaking two or three tie votes in the Council, the original light plant was improved in its original location, and the City Hall question moved up on the agenda.

In the meantime Mayor Sheldon announced his personal plans to put up $65,000 for a new hotel over on the Main and Kellogg corner, a project he was about to carry out with the Munn family. The City Hall project had thus been simplified.

A builder had been selected by April 1915 and the Big Day arrived in August 1915 with the laying of the cornerstone.

A parade began at the City Park, went down Main Street to Burnett, north on Burnett to Fifth and back on Fifth to the Kellogg corner where according to all news reports, two thousand Ames citizens waited to witness the proceedings.

General James Rush Lincoln, Iowa State's colorful military head, introduced Judge C. G. Lee[3] who gave the principle address of the day. Lee's father-in law, Dan McCarthy, Ames' pioneer lawyer and resident here even before the town was founded, sat on the steps of the Baptist church across the street watching over the proceedings.

Lee asserted that the attendance that day of 2,000 citizens was a guarantee of interest in the future welfare of the community. Insisting that the children of today are the assets of the community, Lee stated "We have philanthropists who build libraries, and who build hotels, and who endow hospitals, but there is a class that is doing more for the community, - the fathers and mothers of useful children. Ames has plenty of assets; the future of this town is assured."[4]

In closing his remarks, Lee stated that he should like to dedicate the new city hall to the "mothers of Ames who have done more for the city's welfare than any others."

As Sheldon prepared to lay the cornerstone, one of the workmen threw on some mortar and handed the trowel to Sheldon. The stone was about to be lowered and Sheldon said "Just wait a minute, I want to get this leveled up." "Oh, that won't matter," the workman responded, "we have to set it over again anyway, we always do."

"You won't this (one)," Sheldon uttered with finality, as he carefully laid the mortar so that when the stone was set, "it was laid true to stand for all time."

July 14, 1997.

---

[3] C. G. Lee was a district judge who later entered private practice. He was the donor of Emma McCarthy Lee Park in memory of his wife.

[4] *Ames Weekly Tribune,* August 12, 1915, p.1, "Thousands Help Lay Cornerstone Of New City Hall." Lee's address reported in detail.

Chapter 44

A Brief History Of Ames Camp Fire

Boys and Girls

Known as "Camp Fire Girls" for many years, it became a camping and nature lore training program for both girls and boys in 1978. The following is a summary of the founding and early days of the Camp Fire program in Ames.

The Camp Fire Girls organization began in about 1910 as did the Boy Scouts of America. In 1914, Dr. Luther Gulick, and his wife, Charlotte Gulick, national leaders of the Camp Fire program and pioneers in the development of camping programs for girls, were invited to Ames along with Ernest Thompson Seton, the renowned naturalist and a founder of the Boy Scouts of America, to conduct training sessions for leaders of both organizations. Sponsored by Iowa State College Extension, that 1914 program was the first such training program ever conducted in the midwest.

Prof. William (Bill) Gaessler, and his wife Myrtle, were present at each of the Camp Fire demonstrations that were conducted on the campus by the Gulicks and Seton in 1914. The demonstrations so impressed the Gaesslers that they became committed to a lifetime interest and support of the Camp Fire Girls program in Ames.[1]

According to local tradition, Dr. Luther Gulick had visited Ames in 1911 when he brought word of the new Camp Fire program to the attention of Ames people. However, the first organized Camp Fire group of record in Ames was formed at Central School in the fall of 1916, under the supervision of Daisy Lee Hummel, a seventh-grade teacher. Members of that group included Mevina Allen (Harpole), Blanche Belknap (Wyllie), June Bishop (Tate), Alice Clark (McCrillis), Ruth Cooper, Doris Gray (Nystrom), Ila Harris, and Elizabeth Hawley.[2]

The first president of the Ames Camp Fire organization was Margaret Freeman who served until 1918. Mrs. Margaret Hummel was president from 1918 to 1923. In 1924, the first Ames Camp Fire Council was formed with Mrs. L. C. (Ruth) Tilden serving as its first president and Mrs. Gaessler as executive secretary. Other council presidents have been Mrs. Charles Reynolds, Mrs. A. H. Fuller, Mrs.

Myrtle and William (Bill) Gaessler, long time active participants and supporters of the Camp Fire program in Ames. ID No. 204.1158.2-5

Gaessler Lodge, as it appeared after the improvements in 1956 and in 1971. The lodge in Camp Canwita had been made possible through the efforts of the Gaesslers starting as early as in 1925 when Mrs. Gaessler was chair of the camp committee. ID No. 203.1149.4

---

[1] *Ames Evening Times,* June 24, 1914, p.1, "Indian Council Near Campanile Last Evening."
[2] *Celebrate Friendship - Celebrate Camp Fire,* 1910 -1985, a history of Ames Camp Fire compiled by Mary Musgrove, Marjorie Pohl, and Sue Peters, p. 76.

Ethel Cessna Morgan, and Lt. Col. Harold Pride and Mrs. Pride. In 1929, Mrs. L. H. Wilson became the executive secretary of the council holding that position until 1945.[3]

In 1925, when Myrtle Gaessler was the Executive Director of the Ames Camp Fire organization, she chaired a committee that arranged with Walter Grove to set up a campsite for the girls in one of Grove's timbered pastures north of town.[4] The girls camped in tents that first year, naming their camp, "Camp Grove." The following year a new campsite was selected on Grove's farm closer to the Skunk River. Funds were raised, and with a major contribution in time and effort on the part of the Gaesslers, the construction of the the Camp Canwita Lodge was accomplished. Canwita Lodge still stands and is in continuous use. It is located just off north Duff Avenue in the northwest corner of Inis Grove Park.

In 1945, the Ames Camp Fire Council became a part of the Heart-of-Iowa Council in order to provide Ames access to Camp Hantesa, located near the

Bill Gaessler starts the 1973 candy sale by making a purchase from Susie Yager and Patti Mendenhall. The candy project is an important fund-raiser for the Camp Fire program every year.

Ledges State Park south of Boone. Mrs. Percy Carr became the first executive secretary of the newly formed Ames City Camp Fire Council, with Mrs. I. A. Merchant its first president.

In September 1956, an enlarged and improved Canwita Lodge was rededicated. Over 100 fathers of Ames Camp Fre girls were honored for their volunteer work on that project.[5] By 1971, the lodge was further improved by the addition of plumbing and heating, so it could be used for year-round camping.[6]

The full story of Ames Camp Fire includes the account of the many activites that have been provided for members. Today the organization is referred to as "Camp Fire" with boys included as members since about 1978, although, except for the younger ages, girls make up the larger membership. The traditional annual council fire that is held on the Friday before Memorial Day, and the candy and cookie fund raising activities have been vital to the volunteer part of the education of young people. The Canwita Lodge is the scene of activity four or five days a week and on many weekends for overnight group camping. It is there that nature lore is learned and outdoor life is experienced.

This account began with the story of the earliest interest in Camp Fire work with special reference to the influence of Bill Gaessler and his wife, Myrtle Gaessler; it will close with the account of the presentation, in 1981, to Bill Gaessler, of the plaque that now hangs in the Canwita Lodge in his honor. The lodge is appropriately known as Gaessler Lodge.

At the time of Mrs. Gaessler's death in 1965, the Gaessler Fund was created to provide support of the Canwita Lodge.[7] Bill Gaessler continued his interest and activity in behalf of the Ames Camp Fire Girls following his wife's death. In 1981, the Ames District Council of the Camp Fire Girls presented the

Bill Gaessler in 1981 received the plaque honoring him for his many years of effort and support for the Ames Camp Fire program. ID No. 209.1189.5

3 *Ibid,* p.77.
4 *Ames Tribune,* July 8, 1965, Obituary for Myrtle Bihl Gaessler.
5 *Ames Tribune,* September 17, 1956, Woman's Page, "Campfire Addition Dedication Will Be Held Sunday Afternoon."
6 *Ames Tribune,* February 6, 1971, p. 3, Article about growth and aim of Camp Canwita.
7 *Ames Tribune,* April 6, 1985, "A Tribute To Bill Gaessler." (Article refers to Gaessler Fund.)

Gaesssler's plaque today hangs on the wall in Gaessler Lodge on the Camp Canwita grounds. ID No. 183.1037.5

Fred Hopkins supervised the planting of trees at Camp Canwita on May 6, 1972.

plaque shown here, to Bill Gaessler for his many years of enthusiastic support of the Camp Fire program. In 1996, Gaessler's daughter, Ruth Gaessler Veltrop, of Skokie, Illinois, gave her father's plaque to be displayed in the Canwita Lodge.   Bill Gaessler died March 25, 1985.[8]   The 1981 presentation was as follows:

"It is with a great deal of pleasure that the Ames District Council of Camp Fire presents you with this plaque which reads:

"We together with thousands of others who have been Camp Fire members thank you for bringing Camp Fire and Canwita to us.

"Years ago, in 1914, when you heard Dr.Gulick speak at Iowa State about his new youth organization, you liked what you heard and had the vision to see the potential Camp Fire would have in the lives of its members.

"We thank you in 1981 for all that you have done for many years for our Ames youth. We love you for it."

Because of the devotion of the Gaesslers to the Camp Fire program, similar sentiments continue to flow to the many Camp Fire leaders in Ames who followed in their footsteps and to today's Camp Fire leaders who continue to make the work of that organization important to the Ames community.

16 January 1998

---

8 *Ames Tribune,* March 26, 1985, Obituary for William Gaessler.

Chapter 45

Girl Scouts - Scouting for girls too.

When Ernest Thompson Seton appeared on the Ames Chautauqua platform in 1910 he also brought the word of the founding of the Boy Scouts of America to our community. At the same time, plans were being developed along the same lines for the girls as well. It had been Lord Baden Powell, in England, who founded the first Boy Scout program. Powell's sister, Agnes Baden-Powell, organized a group for girls known as the Girl Guides. Assisting Agnes Baden-Powell was Juliette Low who later came to the United States where, on March 12, 1912, she organized the first Girl Scout program in America when she gathered together a troop in Savannah, Georgia.[1]

Programs for girls were appearing on the scene in Ames during that early time period. "Girl Guides" and "Girl Pioneers" for example, were early names for programs mentioned in local news stories. The *Ames Tribune* of January 25, 1912, announced a series of leadership training meetings for public school and Sunday school teachers interested in nature or camping activities for young people, between the ages of twelve and eighteen.

Later that same year, Mrs. Charles F. (Olive) Curtiss, the wife of Iowa State's Dean of Agriculture, with three daughters of her own, organized the first Girl Scout troop in Ames. It consisted of seven "campus girls" or daughters of Iowa State staff people. The Curtiss family resided in the Farm House on campus, thus providing the center of activity for that first Girl Scout group.

The girls are said to have made their own uniforms and to have engaged in camping out in the timber on the Curtiss farm south of the campus. Transportation for those first Girl Scouts consisted of a horse drawn farm wagon that transported them from the campus to the farm.

A second Girl Scout troop was formed in 1918 with Laura Niles as its leader. The Girl Scouts, on occasion, engaged in overnight camping at the Boy Scout cabin located northeast of Ames. That old cabin was reported to have been a bit too primitive for the

Olive Wilson Curtiss, wife of Dean Charles F. Curtiss, organized the first Girl Scout troop in Ames in 1912. Seven "campus daughters" were members of that first group. The Curtiss family then were residents of the Farm House on the Iowa State campus.

Dr. Niles's log cabin on his farm northeast of Ames where the early Girl Scouts camped in 1919.

---

[1] Priscilla Matt, Kattie Seidel, and Irene Crippen were consulted in compiling this brief account of the Ames Girl Scouts.

Esther Rawson (1889 - 1968), the first president of the Ames Girl Scout Council when organized in 1945. Miss Rawson was long associated with the Iowa State College registrar's office.

Irene Crippen, served as treasurer of the Ames Girl Scout Council from its founding in 1945 until it was merged into the Moingona Council in the 1950s. Photo taken in 1996 on her 90th birthday. Irene was business manager for Tilden's Department store in Ames. ID No.213.1212.5

girls, however. Mrs. Harold (Dorothy Miller) Giebelstein, Mrs. David (Grace Johnson) Peterson, Mrs. J. (Letha Seymour) Englehorn, Mrs. Thelma (Houghan) Nowlin, Mrs. Velma (Jensen) Kingsley, and Mrs. J. R. Christofferson were among members of that 1918 troop.[2]

The Girls Scout organization in Ames consisted of independent troops until 1945, when the Ames Girls Scout Council was formed with Esther Rawson as the first president. Irene Crippen was the first treasurer of the council, serving for many years in that capacity. Mrs. Lee (Alice) Rosebrook succeeded Miss Rawson in 1949 as president of the council. Mrs. Carl Sanford headed the council in 1952.

Ames Girl Scouts have traditionally engaged in public service programs ranging from assisting in such fund-raising projects as the March of Dimes, used clothing collections to visiting residents of the county care center and nursing homes. Summer camping is a big part of Girls Scouts, including day-camping in local parks when many local adult leaders participate in training projects with the girls.

In 1957, the Ames Girl Scout Council merged with the councils of a number of surrounding towns, including the Des Moines Council, to form the

Dining hall at Camp Sacajawea located on 262 acres, five and a half miles northwest of Boone. The camp, established in 1958, by the Moingona Council of the Girl Scouts, is where Ames Girl Scouts experience camp activity.

Moingona Girls Scout Council. Boone was included in 1958, Marshalltown, in 1960 and Ottumwa, in 1970. With the larger unit involved, the Ames Girl Scouts have been regular campers at Camp Sacajawea located on the Des Moines river north of Boone.

In March 1948, the Ames Girls Scouts conducted their annual celebration of the founding of girl scouting with 800 parents and friends in attendance. On April 12, 1987, the Ames Girl Scouts celebrated the 75th Anniversary of the founding of Girl Scouts by holding meetings on the local campus. On that oc-

---

[2] These are the married names; maiden names are added where available.

"Thank You " award presented in 1990 to Irene Crippen for her many years of service to Ames Girl Scouts that began in 1945. ID No. 213.1213.3-5

casion they moved from their meeting place at the Memorial Union to the Farm House where a touch of history was added to the occasion since the Farm House had been the site, in 1912, of the first Ames Girl Scout troop's founding.

Later that same day, over 1,300 Girl Scouts from around the state gathered at the Scheman building where "Ames girls were actively involved in an historical style show, crafts, films, songs, and other traditional activities."[3]

Today, over 300 Ames girls are active Girl Scouts.

---

[3] *Ames Daily Tribune,* April 18, 1987, p. 8, "Girl Scouts" - 75th Anniversary."

Tent area at Camp Sacajuwea.

Chapter 46

Camp Dodge - *brought World War I close to Ames.*

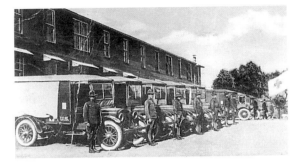

Ambulance company at Camp Dodge in 1918.   ID No. 187.1060.4-5

Panoramic views of Camp Dodge[1] show how extensive it was in 1918. Located northeast of Des Moines, the *Des Moines Register* once described Camp Dodge as having been built in sixty days at a cost of $3,500,000 to house 45,000 soldiers under training for democracy in the war trenches of Europe. Construction began in late June, 1917, and the first contingent of trainees arrived in camp in September, 1917. As many as 46,000 soldiers were in training at any one time. By the end of the war in November of 1918, a total of 150,000 soldiers had been trained and shipped out for active service overseas. The last discharged units left Camp Dodge in January, 1919.

Rail facilities were extended out from the city of Des Moines to service the camp. Barracks at one time extended several miles to the north. It was said that ten miles of concrete paved roadways were within the Camp Dodge training facility. Much reduced in size, Camp Dodge is now the headquarters for the Iowa National Guard. A full time staff of six hundred is today stationed at Camp Dodge.

Camp Dodge was a complete U.S.Army training establishment and included the best in the way of medical facilities. The ambulance company at Camp Dodge during World War I was fully staffed.

The United States Army Medical Corps and the Red Cross worked together at the training camps.

Thousands of the troops that trained at Camp Dodge passed through Ames on the troop trains traveling over the Chicago & North Western Line. The army arranged for the women of the First Methodist Church of Ames to provide meals for Camp Dodge soldiers changing trains in Ames at or near mealtime hours. 7,799 soldiers were fed in the basement of the church during 1917 and 1918. Advance arrival information was sent by phone or wire so that the women could organize food preparation in time for the soldiers.

Following the end of World War I, most of Camp Dodge was vacated by the U.S. Army,[2] a process that took a number of weeks and months. Many of the 2,000 buildings that had been hurriedly built in 1917 to house 40,000 troops, 1,400 officers and 15,000 horses and mules, were removed and the land area of the original training camp was reduced.[3] Lumber salvaged from barracks was obtained by Charles C. Stevens, an Ames real estate developer and home builder. In 1922,[4] Stevens subdivided a portion of the Nash's Division in the six hundred block on the south side of Lincoln Way where he built a number

---

[1]   *The Iowan Magazine,* September 30, 1987, p.29, "Camp Dodge" by Timothy Grover. "Camp Dodge was named for soldier, politician, and railroad builder, Grenville Dodge."

[2]   The federal government retained title to the headquarters units. Camp Dodge had been owned by the state of Iowa since 1907, and it had been the Iowa headquarters for the National Guard for many years.

[3]   *The Iowan Magazine*, September 30, 1987, p. 28, "Camp Dodge," by Timothy Grover.

[4]   *Deed Record Book,* No. 49, Story County, Iowa, p.558, Stevens' subdivision of Nash's Addition to Ames, Iowa. Consists of 12 residential lots on south side of Lincoln Way and on both sides of Maple Avenue.

Panoramic view of Camp Dodge looking east showing rail facilities. Beaver Drive and the main entrance to the establishment is on the rise in the background. ID No. 61.309.1-2

of small single family houses using salvaged lumber from former Camp Dodge barracks.

A number of those small homes, built by Stevens, remain today as a reminder of the World War I era.

Recreational time at Camp Dodge in 1918. Shows close-up view of barracks. Following the war, lumber from these barracks was used in construction of homes in Des Moines and in Ames. ID No. 214.1216.1-6

Chapter 47

The Farm House

The very root of the Iowa State University.

"When tillage begins other arts follow. The farmers, therefore, are the founders of human civilization." Daniel Webster, from his remarks made on January 13, 1840 in the Massachusetts State House in Boston.

Just twenty years later, in 1860, the construction of the Farm House on the native prairie near the western edge of Story County began. It was the first home of the farm manager and the base for the first farm operations essential to the founding of the Iowa Agricultural College. More than a symbol, it has

An 1868 map, taken from an early catalog and biennial report. It shows only three buildings on the land that is now the main University campus.

Artist's drawing, looking westerly with the Farm House largely out of view at far left, shows the first college barns that were built nearby. Today, the Hamilton journalism building is located in the foreground. Before 1893, Iowa State Agricultural College literature described the college as being located on a beautiful farm two miles west of the village of Ames.

The Farm House in about 1885 after it had served as the home of successive farm managers and was then the home of the head of agricultural teaching, Seaman Knapp. Knapp was later recognized as the founder of what became the extension service program of land grant institutions. The Knapp family shown in the photo are left to right: Mrs. Maria Knapp, Helen Louise, Arthur, Seaman, Minnie, Herman and Bradford.

1908 photo of the Farm House when the Curtiss family were residents (1896-1932). Curtiss took charge of the agriculture program at the college in 1897 when James "Tama Jim" Wilson took a leave of absence from Iowa State to become Secretary of Agriculture under President McKinley. The Wilson family had resided in the Farm House since 1891. Wilson served as Secretary of Agriculture for sixteen years, the longest tenure for a cabinet position to this day.

become the true example of Daniel Webster's words. What followed became the Iowa State University of today.

The Farm House today is a National Historic Landmark. It is maintained as a museum, preserving much of the physical evidence of what life was like during the "founding" years of the institution that was to develope around it. Perhaps the Farm House is symbolic of the entire state of Iowa, and of a special way of life as well.

December 24, 1997.

The Farm House as it appears in the 1990s.

Farmhouse photos from the collection of the University Museums, Iowa State University.

Chapter 48

The Canning Factory

A link in the food chain during World War I.

Ground was broken for the Ames Canning Factory in April 1918.[1] Shown here in 1919, it was located south of the railroad tracks at the corner of Third Street and Borne Avenue. Heralded as a promising new Ames industry, it had been encouraged to locate here by the Ames Commercial Club.[2] Parley Sheldon and Clyde Siverly ably represented Ames on the board of directors of the firm which was owned originally by Des Moines interests. By September, seventy people were employed and corn was being canned at the rate of 140 cans a minute. Forty to fifty loads of corn a day were being delivered at the factory. More employees were sought and greatly increased production was projected.

Twenty-five percent of the plant's production during its first years was contracted to the United States Army to feed the troops.[3] In 1919, Ames became the state headquarters for a team of canning factory inspectors. Many Iowa counties had canning factories at that time. Story County had canning operations at Story City, Roland, and Cambridge in addition to the one in Ames.[4]

Corn was king during August and September at the Ames Canning Factory. Sweet corn production was an early-fall cash crop for area farmers. Sweet corn was delivered in horse-drawn wagons until mid-to-late 1920s and later by truck from farms around Ames and area towns. By 1930, production of canned corn was up to 240 cans-per-minute and tomatoes and potatoes were being canned as well.[5]

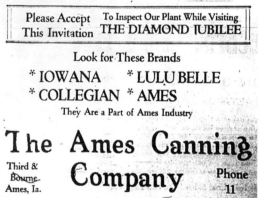

FARM TO MARKET
INDUSTRY——
LABOR——

THANKS for the encouraging reception you have given our products. This year marks our first packing of tomatoes. With your continued support we intend to expand in this field.

TO farmers of this territory will go checks for 235 tons of tomatoes – 2200 tons of corn. $3,200 worth of new equipment has been installed. $11,000.00 has been paid this season to local labor.

Please Accept This Invitation	To Inspect Our Plant While Visiting THE DIAMOND JUBILEE

Look for These Brands
* IOWANA   * LULU BELLE
* COLLEGIAN * AMES
They Are a Part of Ames Industry

The Ames Canning Company

Third &
Borne.
Ames, Ia.

Phone
11

Ames Canning Factory's advertisement on September 26, 1939. ID No. 201.1137.1-2-3

---

[1] *Ames Tribune,* April 24, 1918, p. 1, "Ground Broken for Canning Factory Today."
[2] *Ames Tribune,* Januarty 17, 1918, p. 1, "Meeting Favored Establishment of Canning Factory."
[3] August 26, 1918, p. 1, "Belching Smoke At Canning Factory."
[4] *Ames Tribune,* July 14, 1919, p.1, "Ames Headquarters For Inspections of Canning Factories."
[5] *Ames Tribune,* November 5, 1930, p. 9, "Ames Plant Now Canning Potatoes."

The Ames Canning Factory when new in 1919. ID No. 47.234B. 1-3

A 1939 advertisement lists some of the brand names used by the Ames Canning Factory. In addition, corn was probably canned and labeled for wholesale grocery firms.[6]

In November 1948, following the death of Henry Chavis, a major stockholder and manager, Mrs. Chavis sold the plant to the Minnesota Valley Canning Company of Le Sueur, Minnesota.[7] Operation continued through 1957, under the name of the Green Giant Company. After canning operations ceased, the Collegiate Manufacturing Company of Ames acquired the property converting it to the manufacture and warehousing of collegiate specialties and novelties. In June 1968, the building was the scene of a spectacular fire when it was struck by lightning, resulting in its total loss.[8]

The canning factories that once were a part of the life of many midwestern towns are only a memory today. A smaller farm population, and a more specialized and highly mechanized farm industry have been a part of the movement toward the centralized food processing of today. While sweet corn[9] is grown on a limited scale in Iowa, the idea of a five-to-ten acre planting of sweet corn as a commercial cash crop is no longer economically feasible in the Iowa farmer's operation.

November 5, 1997

---

[6] *Ames Tribune,* September 26, 1939, Jubilee Edition, p. 17, large advertisement gives brand names of local products.

[7] *Ames Tribune,* January 18, 1949, p. 1, "Canning Company Is Sold."

[8] *Ames Tribune,* June 10, 1968, p. 1, "Burn Firm's Stock, Building."

[9] The thousands of acres of corn that we see in the state of Iowa is the field corn grown largely for livestock feed.

Chapter 49

In The Days Of Picket Fences And Boardwalks

Happy memories from early Ames

Picket fences were distinctive. In a way, they were cozy because they defined one's private yard. They were a necessity in the early days because folks had livestock right in town. Each family had a driving horse. Just about everyone had a cow. Animals strayed or got "out" and were not welcome in a neighbor's garden or front yard. Farmers drove their cattle to market in town, and an occasional herd of cattle would be driven down a residential street on the way to the railroad yard south of Main Street. Picket fences were functional. Perhaps they were romantic as well. They are mentioned in song and in poetry, and they may make a comeback.

The J. L. Budd residence on the northeast corner of Kellogg Avenue and Eighth Street is today one of the Youth and Shelter homes. Our photo shows the Budd home when the plantings around the home represented the interests of its owners. Prof. Budd headed the horticulture department at Iowa State and at one time was acting president of the college. The picket fence protected Budd's yard plantings.

The Budd home was frequently the scene of happy social gatherings. Early in the college year of 1892, invitations to a "bouquet party" at the home brought together a large company of town and college people. The *Intelligencer* described the event: "At the entrance each guest was asked to take a bouquet, and later, in the parlor the ladies and the gentlemen having similar bouquets were partners for supper. The rooms were beautifully decorated and the evening passed rapidly and pleasantly."[1]

A famous graduate of Iowa State College, George Washington Carver, was a frequent guest in the Budd home during his student days, and was known to assist Mrs. Budd in preparing the home for those special occasions.

George Tilden's home with its extensive picket fence was on the west side of Douglass[2] Avenue in the nine-hundred block. Note the boardwalk in the foreground. A carriage house was located at the end of the drive. The gate shown open in this photo led to the carriage house. Tilden and his neighbors had at least one milk cow and a good driving team of horses housed on their home properties. In 1904, this house was cut into two units and moved across the block to face Kellogg Avenue. The front portion of this house still stands in the center of the block on Kellogg's east side.

Prof. J. L. Budd's home on the northeast corner of Kellogg Avenue and Eighth Street as it appeared in the late 1890s. ID No.92.494.3

---

[1] *Ames Intelligencer,* September 1, 1892, p.3, report of the invitation to the Budd home of "last Friday evening."
[2] Note the use of the second letter "s" on Douglass. That was the original or correct spelling until new street signs in 1920 dropped the second "s".

George G. Tilden home located on the west side of Douglass Avenue in the 900 block. Photo taken in 1892. ID No.15.72.1

A July 1883, issue of the Ames Intelligen*cer* described a happy occasion at the Tilden home: "A very large company assembled at the George G. Tilden residence Thursday evening to commemorate the good time present. The house was crowded to its capacity by the good people of Ames who seemed to take pleasure in developing the bump of solid enjoyment to the largest extent. $76 was raised in behalf of the Congregational Society."[3]

Captain Wallace M. Greeley's home on the northeast corner of Fifth Street and Douglass avenue had a well maintained picket fence. This is the Adams Funeral Home today. Greeley's barn stood to the rear of his lot where his horse and cow were kept. Greeley would have had a fine driving horse and conveyence in that barn.

Captain Wallace Greeley's home in 1897. It was located on the northeast corner of Douglass Avenue and Fifth Street; today, it is the Adams Funeral Home. ID No.43.217.1

The Martha Jones home on the northeast corner of Douglass Avenue and Seventh Street. Photo taken June 16, 1898. ID No. 189.1074.3-5

---

[3] *Ames Intelligencer,* July 14, 1892, announced meeting on Thursday evening at the Tilden home.

The Greeley home was the scene of many social events with Mrs. Greeley the hostess. Such an occasion was on February 6, 1912, when Mary Greeley's P. E. O. sisters presented a musicale in the Greeley home. The program included two pianola selections by Mrs. Greeley.

P. E. O. Musicale

Tuesday, February 6, 1912

Mrs. Greeley, Hostess

Kammenoi-Ostrow	*A. Rubenstein*
	Pianola—Mrs, Greeley
Blossomland	*Percy Elliott*
	Mrs. Frank L. Meeker
1. Warum	
2. Nachtstucke No. 4 }	*Schumann*
	Mrs. Clyde Williams
(a) Tis Morn	*Ellen Cowdell*
(b) The Nightingale hath a lyre of gold	*B. Whepley*
	Mrs. Meeker
(a) To a Wild Rose	
(b) From an Indian Lodge	*Edward McDowell*
(c) By a Meadow Brook	
	Miss Lydia Brown
Flowers Awake	*Waldo Warner*
	Mrs. Meeker
Polonaisen Op. 40 No. 1	*Chopin*
	Mrs. Willlams
Grand Polka de Concert	*Wallac*
	Pianola—Mrs. Greely

P.E.O. Musicale, Tuesday February 6, 1912. ID No.144.792.1-4

Munn's advertisement in the Intelligencer of June 14, 1900.

The Jones home was located on the northeast corner of Douglass Avenue and Seventh Street. Martha Jones, the homeowner when this picture was taken on June 16, 1898, is the fifth from the left in this gathering of relatives and friends   The home stands today with a more modern look and minus the porch and the board fence.   Again, note the boardwalk. Lumberyards advertised ready cut boards for fences, and for boardwalks. This fence offered an attractive design that appealed to this homeowner.

23 January 1998

Appendix A

A Brief History
... OF THE ...
First Norwegian Settlement
— OF —
Story and Polk Counties in Iowa
1855 TO 1945

Compiled By
Hon. Oley Nelson of Slater, Iowa. In 1905
in Norwegian, and Translated into English
By Oley Nelson in 1930.

Re-compiled, corrected and added to by Anfin Apland,
935 Third Street,
Des Moines, Iowa.
1945

DEDICATION

This booklet is dedicated to the memory of our pioneer fathers and mothers that came to Story and Polk Counties in 1855, and their descendants. It is easy to obliterate the footprints in the sands of time; but the footprints that blazed the pioneer trail should be remembered and handed to the coming generations.

ANFIN APLAND, Compiler.

Proposed in December 1860, the first Palestine Lutheran Church was begun that year, but because of the Civil War was not completed and dedicated until August 1866. Located southeast of Huxley, it was struck by lightning and burned in 1957. It was replaced by the present church at the same location in 1959. Photo courtesy of Huxley Public Library.

A short history of the first Norwegian Settlement in Story and Polk Counties, Iowa, including the Palestine Congregation, and the soldiers enlisted in the Civil War.

In 1848 to 1854 there was a large emigration to America from the three parishes in Norway known as Etne Skaanevik and Fjelberg parishes that settled around Lisbon, Illinois. The emigrants came from Norway to seek and acquire a home for themselves and families, and they expected to find government land at government price on which to make their permanent home in this new world. They had bid goodbye to relatives and friends in Norway and had prepared for a long voyage in their sailing vessels to America, with provisions for their families that would last them from seven to fourteen weeks on their slow sailing vessels.

DISAPPOINTED

When they came to Lisbon, Illinois, it was a great disappointment to them to find that there was no government land to be had. This disappointment was especially great to the mothers, and many of them shed silent tears and said, "How can we with our families acquire a permanent home here in America?" These mothers could not sing when they were plying their shuttles in the looms, nor when they were treading their spinning wheels, or when they were rocking their babies in their cradles, thinking of the future.

Here was a new language to learn, climatic conditions were much different from those to which they had been accustomed, and this flat prairie land looked so different from the steep hills, bluffs, mountains, and rocks that they had been looking at. And where could they think of getting a permanent home when there was not government land to be had at $1.25 an acre.

COMMITTEE TO SELECT LAND

In early fall of 1854, a man by the name of Nils Olsen Naes, who was employed by a Bible Society, traveled over different parts of Iowa and Southern Minnesota selling Bibles printed in the English and the Scandinavian languages. He came to Lisbon, Illinois, and told them that in Iowa there was government land with timber along the streams; a large area of land. This made quite a stir among the emigrants at Lisbon. They called a meeting and selected a committee to go to Iowa to investigate the land which was nearly three hundred miles west of Lisbon.

They selected four men: Osmond Sheldahl, Olie Fatland, Osmond Johnson and Olie Apland, as a delegation to go to Iowa and investigate this land, and if it was found to be as described by Nils Olsen Naes, they should secure enough for the colony. These four men left Lisbon, Illinois the 25th of September 1854. They rode in a two seated spring wagon drawn by a span of horses. These men were selected because they could speak the English language fairly well. They came back in thirty days and reported that they had secured land for the colony and found it very good. Osmond (Hagefos) Johnson was one of the four delegates that came to Iowa in 1854 to select the land. But he did not come with the colony in 1855, because he had some land and livestock to look after in Illinois. He came the next year. He was the father of John O. Johnson and Mrs. Carrie Larson.

REJOICE OVER FINDING LAND

This brought cheer to all, especially to the mothers. They considered that this delegation had done a very heroic act and it was like a magnetic inspiration to the whole colony. They commenced to prepare to emigrate to Story and Polk Counties, Iowa (they had all winter to prepare in) three hundred miles away. What a change. Sadness gave way to joy, and the mothers sang songs of cheer while playing their shuttles in the looms or while at their spinning wheels, and the winter months were miraculously shortened with the thought of going to new homes in Iowa.

THE WESTWARD MARCH TO IOWA

The men made ready the covered wagons in which the journey would be made, and when the 16th day of May 1855 arrived, word went forth that all those who wished to emigrate from Lisbon to Iowa should congregate at Holdeman's Prairie a short distance west of Lisbon. And so on the 17th of May, they proceeded westward to Iowa, their future homes. They selected the 17th of May to start because that is Norway's day of liberty. These emigrants were all Lutherans and had taken with them from Norway their parishes, a heritage. They were God fearing and respected the teachings of God's word. They would not undertake the immigration to Iowa as a colony without it being a churchly colony. They had already organized a congregation and called it the Palestine Congregation. They named it Palestine Congregation in keeping with the description of the land they were to possess on coming to Iowa.

They elected Olie Anfinson as their pastor; Erick Sheldahl, chorister; Knute Bauge as teacher. They would not undertake the emigration to Iowa as a colony without it being a churchly colony, so this was a whole congregation on wheels. Every soul belonged to it. They had services every Sunday on their journey. This scene can better be imagined by us at this day as to what this tentative organization meant to this colony. We who are present and are now celebrating the ninetieth anniversary of the event, have the blessings that have come to us, their descendants, during the last ninety years.

Let us picture this scene. The order came to start one hundred and eleven souls. Twenty-one families, three widows, and five young men, were transported by twenty-five covered wagons. Eighteen were drawn by oxen, six by horse teams, and one spring wagon drawn by one horse owned by Lars Thompson. The names of the emigrants are as follows:

Rev. Olie Anfinson and wife Ingerie, and daughter Carine . . . Osmond and Anna Sheldahl and children Caroline, Erick, Halvor, Henry and Randy . . . Erick and Margaret Sheldahl and children Betsy, Randy, Erick and Martha . . . Olie and Carrie Fatland and children John, Elie, Britt, and Henry . . . Knute and Carrie Ersland and children Hactor, Madts, Anna, Anfin, Martha, Elias, Carrie, Engeborg and Amos.

Knute and Carrie Boug . . . Ivor and Malinde Tweet and daughter Martha . . . Barney and Sarah Hill, and daughter Betsy . . . Peter Christian and Serina Heggem . . . Lars and Martha Tesdahl . . . Wier and Martha Weeks and children Anfin, Halvor, Torres, Wier, Engeborg, Martha, and Hans.

Severt and Allis Gravdahl and children, Julia and Andrew . . . Askel and Golla Larson and children, Lars, Thomas and Charls . . . Orga and Ragna Hauge and children, Severt, Sarah, Lars, and Anna.

Torbjorn and Madela Houge and children Sarah

and Guste . . . Olie and Valbor Hauge and son John . . . John and Bertha Severson and children, Mary, John, and Severt . . . Salemon and Sarrah Heggen and children, Andrew, Nels, and Olie.

Olie and Anna Heggen . . . Engebrit and Sarah Heggen and daughter Susana . . . Torger and Gertrud Olson and children, Cecelia, Olie, George and Martha . . . Mrs. Julia Shaw and children, Betsy, Thomas, and Erick . . . Mrs. Torres Olson and children, Hellen and Rasmus . . . Mrs. Ragna Larson and step-daughter, Anna Wee . . . Five young men: Lars Thompson, Olie Apland, Olie Tesdahl, Erick Johnson, Eiven Olson.

These emigrants followed what was called the California trail — the same trail that the four delegates had followed. They were lucky; they had good weather on the whole journey. The worst difficulty they had was in crossing the streams. One time one wagon got in a little too deep and they needed help. Another time, the cattle went down the stream and they had quite a time to round them up. But all these men were raised right along the ocean in Norway and could swim like fish.

THEY PREPARE FOR THE JOURNEY

Before they left Holdemann's Prairie the 17th day of May, the women folk had prepared an abundance of food to eat on the way such as lepsa, flatbroe, kavring, krengla, fatost, gammelost, sotort, dravele, primeost, and they had their camp stoves so they could make raspe komla hagleta and mossmor and paatete kaka. They had prepared enough food so that nearly one half of it was left when they reached their destination, and that came in very handy. Do not think for a minute that these women could not prepare it. They had a bunch of cattle with them, some milk cows, so they had milk for the children. The journey ended on June 7th. They came to the land that was selected by the four men. They stopped on the quarter section that Osmond Sheldahl had filed for, himself, one mile east of where Huxley is now.

They formed a circle with all their wagons, removed all their camp utensils, and commenced to prepare the food for the first meal; and thanked God for the safe journey and his righteous blessings. On the following Sunday, June 10th, in this enclosure, they held their first service and thanked God for bringing them safely through their journey into this new land, and asked God's righteous blessing on the new colony.

The first Sabbath day service under the roof was held on Olie Fatland's land under the shelter of a hay shed. Under this same hay shed the first confirmation class was organized. The members were as follows: Torres Weeks, Wier Weeks, Engeborg Weeks, Anfin Ersland, Anna Wee, and Betsy Shaw. These were confirmed in the spring of 1856 in Rev. Anfinson's home.

LATER ARRIVALS TO THE COLONY

On September 30th, 1855 the colony was increased by thirty souls from Lisbon, Illinois, five families, and one young man. They came in five covered wagons drawn by four ox teams and one horse team. The first colony had good weather all the way and covered the three hundred miles without a mishap. But these last ones had cold and rainy weather all the way and it took them six weeks to make the trip. Gunder Madskaar got sick and died when they got to Iowa Center September 29th, and was buried at that place. They had almost reached their destination as they only had eleven more miles to go.

The following are the names of the members of this colony:

Benjamin and Engerie Thompson and children, Thomas, Knuts, Cecieliafi and Sarah . . . Mrs. Carrie Madskaar and children Engeborg, and Erick . . . Wier and Carrie Johnson and children, John, Olie, Sarah, Julie, Anna, Elie, and Simon . . . Nels and Carrie Christofison and children, John and Emelia . . . Erick and Barbero Tesdahl and children, Anna, Seveart, Aamon, Sarah and Bertha . . . And Thomas Berhow.

This colony was ready to start on May 17th with the rest but could not start that day on account of having to wait for Simen Johnson, who was born a few weeks after. So they started August 25th. These thirty added to the one hundred and eleven made one hundred and forty-one and three were already born, but two women and one child had died, so that left the same number to face the winter on the prairie. Lars Tesdahl, Knute Ersland, and John Severson were the first to erect their own homes.

FIRST BIRTHS AND MARRIAGES AND DEATHS

The first three children born to the colony were Anna, daughter of Solemon and Sarah Higgen, July 4th, 1855; Olie, son of Olie and Anna Heggin, August 14th; Halver, son of Lars and Martha Tesdahl, September 15th. The first couple to get married in the colony was Olie Apland and Anna Ersland. They were married in Olie Fatland's house by Rev. Anfinson. Olie Apland was the fifteenth man to apply for a marriage license in Story County, and this was the first Norwegian couple to get married in the

State of Iowa.

The first deaths were, a baby of Engebrith and Sarah Heggen, the wife of Knuts Ersland, and the wife of Erick Tesdahl. Look at the picture: one hundred and forty-one souls, fifteen horses, forty-four oxen, and another bunch of cattle on the raw prairie, and too late to plant anything that year. How could they live until they reaped their harvest the next year, facing a long cold winter? Some of them had a little money, but there was not much that you could buy with money. They had a little groceries and some foodstuff at the little store at Cambridge, also at the store at Swede's Point and at the few stores at Des Moines (but that was far to go). They got some grain from the settlers around Swede Point and probably a little at Ballard Grove, an maybe they had to go to Des Moines for some. But sometimes they got down so low that they had to grind corn on the coffee mills to get corn meal to make corn bread and corn mush. And if they had plenty milk, they would keep them from starving for a while. But the children had to have their milk first.

PLENTY WILD FOOD AND GAME

But they were like people are in all new colonics, friendly and helpful, and divided the best they could. If one had food, they all had food. There was an abundance of good upland wild hay, but the stock could not live on hay alone. They had to have a little grain with it. There were lots of wild grapes, plums, and berries; all kinds of nuts in the timber, and strawberries to the glory of all on the prairie. All kinds of game: reindeer, wolves, coyotes, ground-hogs, skunks, rabbits, squirrels, mink, and what not. There was also an abundance of wild geese, ducks, prairie chickens, and quail; lots of fish in the streams. No one ever heard of a hunter's license.

From Big Creek Grove west of Sheldahl, till you got to Skunk River, there was no timber, just the open prairie. And from Huxley south, until you got past Alleman, there was no timber. Just a little northeast of Huxley is Ballard Grove, and a little north of that is Walnut Grove. Southwest of Slater and Sheldahl is timber. About seven miles southeast of Huxley is White Oak Grove, and there were lots of timber along Skunk River on the east.

CHURCH AND SCHOOL

In the summer of 1857, they erected their fist School House. It was built by private subscription and was built just across the road from where the Palestine Church stands now. It was also used for church. They had been having church services in the homes before that. On December 28th, 1860 a very stormy winter day, it was proposed to subscribe for the erection of a church in the colony. The work was started, but on account of the great national disaster, the CIVIL WAR, and as service of the Union from this colony alone, the church was not finished and dedicated until in August 1866. It was dedicated by Rev. Haselquist. The church still stands on the same spot in the southeast corner of what was Erick Sheldahl's quarter section, just south of Osmond Sheldahl's land. But it has been remodeled several times since.

THOSE WHO WENT TO WAR

Following are the names of the young men in the colony that enlisted in the service: Olie Anfinson, Ivor Twidt, Thor Lande, Torres Scott, Halver Weeks, Torres Weeks, Wier W. Weeks, Anfin Ersland, Elias Ersland, Erick Egland, Henry Egland, John O. Severeid, Severt Tesdahl, Thomes Shaw, Sorren Olson, Lars Olson, John O. Johnson. Thor Helland, Holder Johnson, J. W. Johnson, Andrew Nelson (better known as Salemon Andrew), Andrew Gravdahl, Helge Hanson. Helge Hanson enlisted and had on a uniform inside of three weeks after he arrived in this country from Norway. He was nineteen years old, and he did not know a word of English.

Following are the names of nine young Norwegian boys that served in the Civil War that came here from other states and settled in this colony right after the war: Andrew Nelson, Oley Nelson, Anfin Anfinson, A. W. Thompson, H. O. Hendrickson, Cyres Highland, Nels Gord, Lars Boug, John Anderson (better known as "Candy John").

Following are the names of seven of the twenty-three that enlisted from here that did not come back: Halver Weeks, Elias Ersland, Lars Olson, Torres Scott, Holder Johnson, Henry Egland, Thor Helland.

When they came in 1855 there were quite a few families in Des Moines, a flour mill, a few stores, a blacksmith shop, and some sawmills. A store and a sawmill at Swedes Point (now Madrid) a small store at Cambridge, and when you started north from Des Moines and got about four miles north of where the State House stands now, there was not a house or a building of any description until you got to Ballard Grove. And when you started east from Swedes Point, got east four miles, there was not a house or a stick of any kind until you got to way past Skunk River.

PRIMITIVE TOOLS ALL WE HAD

When these settlers first came, they cut all the hay with a scythe; and the small grain with a cradle;

planted the corn by hand, plowed it with a one shovel plow and one horse. They drew the water out of the wells with a hook or a rope and bucket. (All buckets were wooden those days).

They lighted the houses with candles, and some had what they called Kaala, made by the blacksmith, of iron, rounded pointed in one end for the wick to stick up, and a handle on the opposite side so you could hang it on the wall. Or it could stand on the table. It was about one inch deep, and they filled it up with lard, and put a wick or rage in it. It gave more light than a candle. The first lanterns were lit by candles. All their clothing was made by hand. They bought their hats and leather shoes. Quite a few wore wooden shoes that were home made. They went out riding with oxen in their lumber wagons, and those that had horses used horses.

They did not have the luxuries we have now, but they were happy. They did not know of anything else. They were jolly and did lots of visiting. The nearest Railroad was at Davenport, but in a few years, the Northwestern came to State Center, and on July 4th, 1864, the first train came to Nevada. In 1874 the Northwestern built a narrow gage road from Ames to Des Moines, and they put in five stations. Kelley, Sheldahl, Crocker, Polk City and Ankeny; (Crocker is no more). In 1882 the main line of the Milwaukee Road came through Cambridge. Then Huxley started, and they put in a depot where they crossed the Northwestern, and called it Sheldahl Crossing, one and a half miles north of Sheldahl. A few years later a majority of the business men in Sheldahl moved up to Sheldahl Crossing and changed the name to Slater.

THEY GREW AND GREW AND GREW!

This Norwegian settlement spread out and grew especially after the Civil War. All around Cambridge and west to Kelley and north and west of Kelley, north and west of Slater around Sheldahl, from there to Alleman, and on to White Oak Grove, and from there to Cambridge. Huxley is about in the center of it.

There was one time that there were six school districts where every child that came to school was a Norwegian, and nine school districts in which from forty to eighty percent of the children were Norwegians. These Norwegians were very patriotic. Every child went to public school. There were always some emigrants who came from Norway every year, and they generally took out their Citizenship Papers as soon as they arrived. They had their Parochial Schools in between the Norwegian language.

The people in this whole settlement talked Norwegian nearly all together. That was natural, since it was the language they knew so well, and many of them could not talk English at all. This was especially true among the older ones, and then too, people kept coming from Norway all the time. But the children learned English in school; especially in the districts where they were mixed. They learned it right away, and the men that had to do the business and trading picked it up. They used Norwegian language altogether in the churches for a long time, but along in the nineties they commenced to use a little English, and gradually a little more. Now they do not use a word of Norwegian in any of the churches.

At first they very seldom married outside of their race; they stuck pretty well together. But now they are not particular. They marry anyone they fall in love with, whatever nationality they belong to. Quite a few of the children that grow up now can not talk Norwegian at all. It would have been nice if they had kept it up and taught them the Norwegian language, since they are Norwegian descendants. Of course, they should learn the language of the land thoroughly first. It is nice to know as many languages as possible. This is a land of languages, and I think the Norwegian language is as good as any of the other languages. It is the Danish language. We got it from the Danes, and it is so near like the Swedish that we can understand them. It is similar in many ways to the English and the German. There is so much good literature and so very much good poetry in the Norwegian language. There are so many dialects it is fun to listen to them. It is interesting too, to listen to the Swedes and Danes. While it is the Danish language, they pronounce the words a little differently, and they have so many dialects too. The Norwegian language as used today is taught at the State University of Iowa at Iowa City, Iowa. The old Norwegian language is now used by the Icelanders.

The people in this settlement did not only send their children to the public schools, but as soon as they were able, they sent off to Colleges and Universities. There used to be quite a bunch of boys and girls going away to College every fall. Some took one course, and some another. I don't think there is a course taught but what some of them took it up. There are professional men and women all over this land that were raised in this settlement, and many of them are teaching at the Colleges.

THREE-COUNTY TOWN, A REAL LIVE TOWN

When Sheldahl started it was one of the liveliest towns far and near. They had an immense territory. There was no Madrid, no Slater or Huxley, no Railroad at Cambridge, just a grain elevator and a little store in Crocker. Livestock and grain came from west of Swedes Point, now Madrid and from around Cambridge. Alleman was not dreamt of. There were so many buggies and wagons in town sometimes that they had to almost out in the country to find a place to tie their horses. The merchants did a big business. There were four saloons, and they also did a tremendous business. But there never were any women that ever stepped inside of any of these saloons.

Sheldahl is in three different counties, Story, Polk, and Boone. I should probably mention a few of the leading members of these old settlers: Rev. Olie Anfinson was a man of sturdy character, well posted, and well read, very religious, and was well thought of by the whole colony. They put him in as their first pastor. Rev. Osmond Sheldahl was another man of great character; well posted, well read, very religious, knew the English language very well, and well posted on legal matters. That made him a leader. They all went to him with their legal papers and documents. He was put in as their second pastor. Erick Sheldahl was another man of exceptionally good character; strictly honest and square in all his dealings, he was good hearted, very friendly, and had lots of friends, and I don't think he had any enemies at all. He was put in as Chorister of their church before they left Illinois, and served in that capacity until he died in about 1915. He was also very religious.

Probably I should not say anything about Olie Apland, being he was my father, but I will mention a few things. He had many friends, and a few enemies. He was of strong personality, friendly, and very jolly. He was plain outspoken, and if he did not like a person, he would tell them right to their face. That was why some did not like him. He could not stand to see anyone abuse any domestic animals. If they did, he surely would call them down. That was one of the reasons some did not like him. And if there was something that had to be done that no one liked to do, he had to do it. He was the goat. He run a big farm, and fed lots of livestock. He did lots of business, was very lenient to people that were honest and did not lie to him. He had about as many friends in Story County when he did as any man had. He died in 1879, so he did not live to more than 66 years old.

A STALWART CHARACTER OF GREAT STRENGTH

Thor Landry was another old settler of great sturdy character, and very deeply religious. He did not come with the colony in 1855, but came about two years later. If there ever lived a man that a true, honest, upright, converted Christian, he was one. He lived and practiced it in his every day life and in all his dealings. It did not make any difference how busy he was on his farm. If it was right in harvest time, he would take his time and read a chapter in the Bible at the breakfast table, and pray and sing. He would joke and tell stories, and laugh at times. He was very pleasant and friendly, but you would not talk to him very long until he would cone in on some religious matter. He was very heavenly minded. He was six feet five inches, raw boned, straight as a dye, looked very much like Abraham Lincoln, and almost as tall. He wore his beard like Lincoln, and his face was shaped a good deal like "Old Abes." One time he and seven of his neighbors took a load each of hogs to Des Moines and when they got a ways down, one hog climbed over the other hogs in the wagon and jumped out. So the other men wondered how they could get him up into the wagon again. Thor did not say a word, but grabbed the hog and put him in the wagon alone, pushed him up over the top box, which must have been at least six feet from the ground. Elick Wood of White Oak Grove was one of the gang. He had that hog weighed separately, and he weighed 400 pounds.

One time when Mr. Landy was in the army, two of the other soldiers tried to pick a quarrel with him. They insulted him and tried to get him mad, to get a fight with him. They finally got his temper roused up. He grabbed them by the nape of their necks, and held one in each hand and clinched their foreheads together until he thought they had all they could stand. They did not bother him any more.

AN UNUSUAL HAPPENING

Mr. and Mrs. Severt Helland were among the early settlers. They were very nice people and loved by everyone. Mr. Helland was a hard working man. Once when he was helping a man that lived a distance away with some work, he did not go home every evening. Mrs. Helland stayed alone with their two little boys, one 4 and one 2 years old. She put them to bed one evening. (It was in the summer time.) She was pregnant and felt that something was going to happen. It was dark. Her father and mother lived across the road, so she started to go over there. Helland's house was up from the road a ways and there was a big pond between the house and road, and a track or trail along the side of the pond. There was tall slue grass and weeds all around this pond, and she got off the trail and could not get first, until they got a school house, and later they built back on again. She was entirely lost.

It was pitch dark. She wandered around in the

weeks probably around the pond several times. So finally she got so tired she had to sit down, and then the baby came. She wrapped it up in her apron and probably a part of her dress, the best she could, and had to spend the rest of the night there until daylight came. Then she went to the house. She woke up the 4 year old boy and sent in over to her parents' house with the message. The baby was all right, grew to womanhood, and married Henry Fatland, a member of the 141 emigrants and lived a long time. She was a sister of the late Banker M. S. (Uncle Mike) Helland of Slater, Iowa. This happened in the year of 1856 or 1857.

Hon. Oley Nelson was a very honorable and outstanding man in this settlement. He and his mother came here from Wisconsin right after the Civil War. He worked in Des Moines, clerked in stores a while, married Engeborg Ersland, a daughter of Knute Ersland, who was also working in Des Moines. After they got married he started a hotel, and called it the Farmers Home. He ran that until 1874, when the Northwestern came through Sheldahl. Olie Apland, his brother-in-law wanted to help him and start him in business, so Apland built a store building (the first building erected in Sheldahl after the depot was built) and went in partnership with him, and put in a stock of general merchandise. That was the first store in Sheldahl. The firm was "Apland and Nelson." The store had living quarters upstairs, which the Nelsons moved into. Carrie, their third child, was the first child born in Sheldahl.

Apland did not work in the store. He always lived on his farm near Cambridge. He just wanted to get Nelson started. Amos K. Ersland clerked there from the start, and in a short time he bought Apland out. Then the name of the firm was "Nelson and Ersland." They had a large stock of good, and also bought grain. After a while Nelson bought Ersland out. And when so many of the business men moved to Sheldahl Crossing, Nelson also moved the store, grain elevator, and his dwelling. Oley Nelson was a very bright man, well educated, well read, and well posted on all topics. He had a clear voice and could speak on any subject. He had a strong personality, lots of friends, and was a natural leader. He was good hearted and always wanted to help the needy; too good hearted for his own good. He was also quite a surveyor and had a regular surveying outfit.

He was elected State Representative from Story County, and served in the 21st and 22nd General Assemblies. He was National Commander in Chief of the Grand Army of the Republic in 1936. He was Sergeant at Arms in the House Chamber at the State House 16 or 17 years up until he died in 1939. He was 93 years old when he died.

Oley Nelson's father joined the Eagle Regiment of Wisconsin when the war broke out and had served nearly one year when he was killed in action. Oley was the only child, and he wanted to take his father's place; so he enlisted in 1862. He was 18 years old at that time; he served until the end of the war. That left his mother entirely alone. She was a brave and very active woman. She never remarried and always stayed with her won. She lived to be real old.

Andrew Nelson, another outstanding figure in this settlement, was a brother-in-law of Oley Nelson. He married Martha Ersland, a daughter of Knute Ersland, was a veteran of the Civil War, settled in Polk County just south of the Story County line southwest of Cambridge. He had a big farm, fed lots of cattle and hogs, and accumulated quite a bit of wealth. He was one of the best auctioneers in central Iowa. He had such a loud and clear voice, and a good judgment of the value of things. He had a very strong personal character, was jovial and humorous, told stories and jokes, he was an excellent salesman, and people would nod to him quicker than to anyone else. He was a very busy man.

AN INTERESTING CHARACTER

A history of this settlement would not be complete without saying something about Ranart Nagelson, the big Dane that roamed over this settlement for a long time. Nagelson was raised a printer. His father printed a newspaper in Denmark, and he wrote a piece in this paper about the King of Denmark. He was found guilty and was sentenced for life. So a friend helped him out, put him in a casket as a dead man, and put him on board of a ship just ready to sail for America. So he kept wandering and worked his way west till he got to this Norwegian settlement. He like the people here and everybody liked him and treated him nice. He was a tall man over 6 feet, and gained in flesh right along till he got to weight over 300 pounds. He peddled medicine for a living. He got his meals wherever he stopped, and no one very charged him anything.

He would go up to the Norwegian settlements around Story City, Roland, and Mickallsburg. He got all his medicine from Druggist Gandrup in Story City. He knew 12 different languages. He was a great fellow to read, and kept posted. He would look over all the newspapers there were in the house. He gathered all the news and he could tell all the news that had happened. He laughed very heartily. He had a great memory; he could speak the first name of every child wherever he stopped. He was very friendly and could tell lots of stories. He was a hearty eater. After a big meal in the summer time, he would go out on the ground and lay down and stretch. He never married, had no home, only where he took off his hat.

He was a happy go lucky fellow with a big smile. He came here sometime in the sixties and died in the late eighties.

ANOTHER VERY INTERESTING CHARACTER

I should make a few remarks about Ames K. Ersland before I quite. He was a son of Knute Ersland, and was three years old when he came with the emigrants in 1855. He was a rather quiet man, read a lot, and was hungry for learning. He was self educated; a very great mathematician, excellent penman, and a good bookkeeper. He was of very clean habits, used no tobacco, was a total abstainer, very neat and clean about his person. Whatever he worked at had to be just so. He was quite an inventor. He invented quite a few things, and got patents on some of them. So many times someone else was just ahead of him. He had a perfect typewriter, but someone was just ahead of him on some parts.

He invented a screw nut that would not come off or get loose on freight cars, but some man was just ahead of him again. He invented a scale and a combination tool; he had a machine that sharpened and set a saw that worked perfect; he had a shop full of tools and machines that cost him several thousand dollars. He had these just for a hobby, as he did not try to make a dollar out of them. He had quite a bit of money invested in investment companies from which he got yearly dividends, on which he lived during his last years. But two of them went up with the smoke, so he did not have much when he died. He never married. He was rather shy of women; he always advised young boys not to use liquor; he was honest as the day is long, and his word was as good as if his name was written to an iron clad contract. He was a charter member of Slater Lodge I.O.O.F. No. 384 and belonged to the Lutheran church. He died when he was 82 years old.

ALMOST EVERYBODY LOVED THE HILLS

Last but not least, I want to say a few words about Oliver Hill. He came with his parents from Illinois just before the Civil War, and settled down just west of Cambridge. He lived on the farm with his parents until they died, then he became the owner of the farm, and lived there until he died. He raised two boys and two girls. He was well educated man, well posted on all topics; could get up and make a speech on any subject. He taught school for many years, both in and around Cambridge, and he was also in the mercantile business in Cambridge at one time. He belonged to the Lutheran Church at Cambridge, and was Superintendent of the Sunday School for many years. He did not use tobacco in any form, and was a very strong temperance man. He was strictly honest, and everything had to be just so. He had a lovely home which he called Hillhurst that was kept up in fine shape. Mr. and Mrs. Hill were lovely people and loved by everybody. They are both dead now.

There are many more men that I would like to mention but space doesn't permit. There were many real good outstanding women in this settlement also that should be mentioned, who surely did their part. But if I would mention one, I would have to mention so many that it would take up too much space. The next person that writes a larger history of these old settlers will have to mention those that I have left out, and correct all my mistakes.

PASTORS OF THE CHURCH

The Palestine congregation was organized in Illinois before they started. They had services in houses at the church. Their first pastor was Olie Anfinson from 1855 to 1859; followed by Osmond Sheldahl from 1859 to 1876; J. H. Myre from 1876 to 1880; H. C. Holm from 1881 to 1893; N. B. Thvedt from 1894 to 1897; A. L. Huus from 1897 to 1902; Axel Sheveland from 1903 to 1912; Peder Buland from 1913 to 1930. H. E. Jacobson took Buland's place in 1939, and is still serving. Peder Buland served 26 years, the longest of any of them. Rev. Buland is a very able man, and he knew just how to handle everyone; he has a very strong personality and knows how to handle people. Besides, he is a very sincere and upright man. He and his wife came to Cambridge about 59 years ago and they are still living in Cambridge. They have many friends and are loved by everyone.

I should probably mention the children of the first settlers that are alive and are living in this settlement. There are two in and around Cambridge whose both parents belonged to the 141 original settlers, Mrs. O. L. Severeid and Mr. O. J. Johnson and those that had one parent are as follows: A. M. Mason, C. M. Mason, K. E. Nelson, M. J. Nelson, W. J. Birkestrand, A. J. Birkestrand, O. J. Johnson, Carl Fatland, Kiser Fatland, Henry Anfinson, Elmer Severson, William Fatland, Mrs. Maggie Anderson, Miss Carrie Lewis, Mrs. Peter Holderson and Mrs. Martha Lee.

Those that live in and around Huxley that had

two parents belonging to the original group are: Osmond Larson, Oscar Larson, Andrew Larson, Lewis Larson, Henry Larson, M. L. Tesdell, John Tesdell, Mrs. Olie Chelesvig and Mrs. Charles Rinertson; and those that had one parent in the group are as follows: H. J. Birkestrand, Mrs. Tom Berhow, Mrs. O. J. Kalsem, Mrs. Sadie Travas, Mrs. Olie Legvold, Mr. and Mrs. Nels T. Sydness, Wier Sydness, O. S. Swandahl, T. H. Mason, Olie Dobbe, John Dobbe, Mrs. S. T. Larson, Mrs. Lars Wee, Joseph Olson, Yetta Olson, Mrs. H. H. Larson, Mrs. Tom Olson, Carl Tesdell, Senferd Heggen, Mrs. Andrew A. Wenos, Rose Heggen, Ellen Heggen, Mrs. Terenious Larson, Mrs. Andrew Tesdell, Lars Ritland, Wier T. Weeks, Andrew Ritland. (Olem Tesdell and Mrs. Carl Tesdell came very near being in this list, but their father was not born quite soon enough. He was the third child born in the settlement in 1855. Their mother belonged to this list; she was a daughter of Betsy Shaw, who belonged to the First confirmation class).

There are only three in and around Slater who had both parents in the original settlers. They are: George Houge and Peter Apland and Mrs. Belle Ryen; (and the late Joseph Houge). Those who had one parent are as follows: Mrs. Charls Skortman, Mrs. A. L. Peterson, Mrs. C. E. Larson, Miss Nellie Thompson, Mrs. Sack Sydness, Mrs. William Cassel, Mrs. Bessie Skola, George Christianson, Tom T. Wicks, (and the late Tom A. Wicks), and Dr. George J. Severson, M. S. Heggen, Mrs. John Simonson, Mrs. Oley Storing, Mrs. Nellie Iley, Mrs. Nels Ersland, Mrs. Maggie Tweedt, Mrs. Andrew Estrem, Sanford Tesdell, Andrew Sheldahl, and Mrs. Bertha Nerveg, J. C. and Harald Ersland came very near belonging to this list, but their mother was not born soon enough. Julia Severson, a daughter of John Severson. There are three at Ames who had two parents who were members of the original emigrants: Mrs. Carrie Nelson, Mrs. Mattie Rayness, and Erick Tesdell. Those at Ames with one parent are: H. R. Sheldahl, Mrs. Anna Grove, Mrs. Carrie Apland, Mrs. Carrie Rayness, and Mrs. Lena Bates, Mrs. Chester Persons, Severt Severson and Milford Severson. There are six in Sheldahl who had one parent that belonged to the 141: Martin Sheldahl, Anna Sheldahl, and Caroline Anderson, Mrs. Ernest Nelson, Carrie (Berhow) Anderson and Arnie Christofer and the children of Aamond Tesdahl, if there are any of them in that neighborhood. Also H. S. Heggen and Mrs. Gene Barnes, of Alleman and Mrs. Belle Richardson and Eddie Oakland of Kelley.

O. J. Johnson and Mrs. Ernest Nelson would have been in the two parent list, but their grandfather, Osmond Johnson (who was one of the delegates who came out here in 1854) did not come with the colony in 1855, but came in 1856. That also kept Amos T. Larson and Charles T. Larson from being in the one parent list.

There might be some that I have missed, and if I have, it is unintentional. There are quite a few more of the second generation scattered all over the land. There are a large number of the third, fourth, and fifth generations all over this country from coast to coast; a large number in all branches of the Armed Services; and there are also quite a few of the second, third, fourth, and fifth generations in Des Moines, Iowa.

REUNION PICNICS

IN 1905 THEY had their first reunion picnic at Huxley, and celebrated their FIFTIETH ANNIVERSARY. It was a nice day and there was a tremendous big crowd. Andrew Nelson was Chairman of the day, and the speakers were Hon. Oley Nelson, Rev. Olie Anfinson, Rev. Osmond Sheldahl, Rev. K. L. Gotteboe, Rev. H. C. Holm, Erick Sheldahl, Severt Hilland, and others.

THEY DECIDED to have the meetings every five years. The next one was at Cambridge in 1910; and the next at Slater and so on. They have met every five years since 1905.

This year, 1945, we are meeting at Huxley. When they met in Huxley the first time, there were 70 still living out of the 141, and 71 dead. And when they met at Slater in 1940, all of the 141 were dead.

WHAT SHALL WE DO ABOUT WAR AND WHISKEY?

I have some LEAFLETS on how to make a just, perfect and lasting PEACE. Shows how to wipe WARS entirely off the face of the earth. Also one about the LIQUOR laws; how to remedy the intoxicating drinks habit.

You may not agree with me on most of what I say, but I'm sure quite a few will agree with me on some of the things I say. We don't all see things alike. This is simply my idea and opinion as to how to make this a better world. A real fit place to live in; a place where we can live in peace, enjoy life and be happy.

Things are pretty bad now and apparently are getting worse every day. Crimes are increasing very few have any respect for law. No justice in the courts. A majority of humans have booze on their brains; women as well as men. And there is everything but righteousness in politics.

Some years from now when things get so bad

that something effective just must be done more people will likely agree with me and say I was right.

Appendix B

INTRODUCTION TO "IN THE NEWS" INDEX:

This index is not offered as a detailed accounting of all of the significant or interesting subjects that have been covered in the news reports found in the newspapers published in Ames, Iowa. It is, however, a record of items that I have run across in my numerous searches for information in the microfilms of the several papers that have been published in Ames. When a news item appeared on the microfilm screen that might be of future interest, I placed it in my notes to eventually be entered in this data base.

It is suggested that this index might make it possible to locate certain historical information as it was recorded in original news accounts. Items found in this index will not provide complete information on subjects covered, but the index will provide clues as to when events occurred. With information found here as a starting point, one should expect to pursue further research.

A limited amount of cross-indexing is provided. It may be necessary to try more than one "keyword" in the process of finding a subject.

Some day a more sophisticated index will be developed. However, this index may be of assistance for some and *just fun for others.*

Under the heading "Event" the item subject is described. Quotation marks indicate the title or headline for the item. The heading "Clip Page" provides the page number reference in my original note books which can be found in the Ames Public Library's "Iowa Room."

One final point: this index reflects my personal idiosyncrasies. Perhaps they can be overlooked. It just grew like topsy, since I did not originally plan it to be as extensive as it has turned out to be.

I suggest checking the footnotes with the stories that are found in my two books for further references.

A number of obituaries are listed in this index. An alphabetical list is provided to assist in locating names, since the number is limited.

Obituaries or death announcements for the following people will be found in the "News Index". They will be found in alphabetical order unless otherwise indicated:

Adams, J. W.; Beach, Spencer; Beardshear, Mrs. W. M.; Beardshear, William M.; Bigelow, D. A.; Bradley, Dr. Edgar; Bradley, Dr. James; Budd, Mrs. Sarah; Coover, Prof. W. F.; Curtiss, Mrs. C. F.; Dehart, Pearle; Diehl, Katharina; Duckworth, Raymond; Duncan, John; Duncan, Harriet; Fitch, C. L; Fowler, Frank; Fox, Rodney; Gaessler, Mrs. Myrtle; Gaessler, William G. (Bill); Gamrath, Lewis; Geddes, James L.; Gerbrach, Joe; Graves, Andrew; Grove, Walter; Harding, Warren G.; Harriman, Dr. W. E.; Hayden, Ada; Hoggatt, Mrs. L.Q.; Kaynor, E.; Knapp, Dr. Seaman A.; Lee, Judge C. G.; Lincoln, Mrs. James Rush; Lincoln, James Rush; Long, Sam, (See: Fire Department); Loughran, Edmund; Luke, Judge J. Y.;

Marston, Dean Anson; Maxwell, George Henry; May, Henry; McCarthy, Dan; McCarthy, Henry; McCoy, Arthur (Art); McGriff, Sheriff; McLain, Howard; McLain, Willis; Munn, H.L.; Nelson, John I.; Ney, Christopher; Nichols, George (Fatty); Noble, Prof. A. B.; Nosbeck, Henry; Noyes, LaVerne; O'Neil, Clem; O'Neil, P. H.; Quade, Mrs. C. R.; Read, Benedict; Rice, Dr. Tom; Richmond, Dr. Albert; Ricketts, Bill; Ruth, Chelsea; Sheldon, Mrs Parley; Sheldon, Parley; Sloss, Margaret; Smith, M. K.; Smith, Laura West (Mrs. M. K.); Stalker, Dr. Millikan; Star, Rose (See: "Octagon House"); Stevens, Mrs. Rowena; Tilden, Dr. Julius F.; Tilden, Frederick C.; Tilden, George G.; Trice, Jack; Welch, Mary B.; Welch, Adonijah S.; West, William; Wilkins, Eleanor M.; Wilson, "Tama Jim"; Wilson, Henry; Woolfries, Andy; Wynne, Prof. W. H.; Young, Ben (See: "Pop Corn Wagon").

APPENDIX B

Date	Date2	Who	Event	Clip Page	Where Found
1892	9/29	A & C Motor Line.	Time Card	1309	Times
1989	4/12	Abortion	Letter/Editor	781	Tribune
1989	4/ 8	Abortion	Right to kill babies	1989	DMReg
1989	4/29	Abortion Opinion	Rights of Unborn	744	DMReg.
1909	3/25	Acacia Fraternity	First in State here	1758	Time p.7
		Accident	See:Arm Torn	1365	Trib. p.1
1908	8/ 8	Accident	Car Hits Buggy	1858	Times p.1
1909	11/ 8	Accident	Student Hit by train	1836	Times p.8
1914	11/12	Accident	Buggy / Car on Main Street	662	Tribune
1919	5/ 5	Accident	R.R.Grand Ave. Funeral story	293	Times
1919	7/ 5	Accident	Dayton Park / Fireworks	1365	Trib p.1
1923	7/ 2	Accident	Car / Buggy on Duff Ave.	503	Tribune
1925	7/ 7	Accident	Girl dies of burns in bus accident		Tribune.p.1
1925	12/19	Accident	"Award $3,095 in bus accident"	237	Tribune
1931	6/30	Accident	Deans Beyer & Marston inj ured	2368	Trib. p.1
1920	10/25	Accident -	See: Horse / Train	412	
1920	10/13	Accidental electrocution	Iowa State student killed	190	Tribune
1994	12/ 1	ACLU	Need Cold Shower?	1874	Tampa Trib.
1924	1/26	Adams Furniture Store	Interest sold to Henderson	159	Tribune
1924	1/28	Adams Furniture Store	Sold	441	Tribune
1911	6/29	Adams, M.J.	Barn on fire.	1	Times p.6
1913	12/ 1	Adams,Clinton	Lost is found	229	Times
1946	3/26	Adams,Clinton	Elected Mayor	162	Tribune
1911	11/27	Adams,Elmer	Breaks arm and hip	211	Times
1913	9/17	Adams,Howard	Opens Confectionary Store	1173	Times
1919	6/7	Adams,J.W.	Death Account	301	Times
1911	12/ 7	Adams,J.W.Grocery	Sold to Bates & Keigley	1215	Times p.1
1904	7/28	Addition to Ames	Adv. for Harriman's Addition	1358	Times p.54
1876	1/26	Advertisement	Village Lots	1364	Intell.
1876	1/26	Advertisement	Tilden&McLain	1364	Intell.
1876	1/26	Advertisement	Livestock/IAC	1365	Intell.
1876	1/26	Advertisement	Lucas, Banker	1364	Intell.
1877	8/ 4	Advertisement	Bigelow Huntington & Tilden		Intell
1877	8/10	Advertisement	Various	320	Intelligencer
1877	9/28	Advertisement	Various		Intelligencer
1896	9/10	Advertisement	Medical Clinic	1887	Times p.1
1898	9/25	Advertisement	Tilden Store ad	1318	Intell. p.1
1898	9/15	Advertisement	3rd Anniverary of Fair Store	1318	Intell. p.4
1898	9/15	Advertisement	For:Millinery	1318	Intell. p.1
1911	8/17	Advertisement	"Dudgeon,C.W."	1852	Times
1911	8/17	Advertisement	Lockwood Grain Co.	1847	Times p.1
1911	8/17	Advertisement	Cramblit's Music House	1847	Times p.1
1911	8/17	Advertisement	Ames Auto Co.	1852	Times
1911	8/17	Advertisement	Loughran & Bauer	1852	Times
1911	8/17	Advertisement	Duckworth Undertaker	1847	Times p.1
1911	8/17	Advertisement	Bosworth Drug	1847	Times p.1
1918	11/ 2	Advertisement	Sheldon-Munn Menue	1321	Times p.2
1939	9/26	Advertisement	Collegiate Mfg Co.	1374	Trib.p.12
1919	7/23	Aeroplane	"Harriman,Walter"	1220	Times
1916	5/11	Ag.Carnival	Parade	1942	Times
		Airplane	See:Banning,Herman		
1913	6/30	Airplane	See: Weeks,Elling	235	Times
1928	7/27	Airplane	Gerbraght Fl.to W.Coast	416	Tribune
1928	11/14	Airplane	Big Plane here	314	Tribune
1926	7/2	Airport	Opens	285	Tribune
1931	10/13	Airport	Committees named	396	Tribune
1939	9/26	Airport	Ad:Marion Wearth	1374	Trib.p/15
1947	1/11	Airport	U.S.Funds for	165	Tribune
1991	10/17	Airport, Ames	Article about	1302	Trib.p.B5
1929	10/12	Airport,Gerbracht	passengers to W.Coast	1365	Trib.p.5
1993	4/10	Alcogas,Ethanol	Lauren Soth	1890	DMReg.
		Alcohol	Also see: Liquor		
		Alcohol	See: Booze		
1868	4/ 7	Alcohol	State Law adopted	856	Allen Hist.p.238
1919	1/15	Alcohol	Iowa app.18th Am.	863	Tribune
1986	10/29	Alcohol	Hangover or not - has effect	2288	Trib. p.15
1987	12/30	Alcohol	Lttr.to Editor	575	DM Reg.
1988	1/ 3	Alcohol	Lttr.to Editor	575	DM Reg.
1989	6/14	Alcohol	Fight T V Adds	800	Dm.Register
1989	4/ 8	Alcohol	Editorial comment re: non use	778	DMReg.
1989	3/26	Alcohol	No.1 Threat in Iowa		DMReg
1989	9/21	Alcohol	Fatal Accident		DMReg.
1989	10/17	Alcohol	Letter/Editor	859	Tribune
1989	9/20	Alcohol	Bible reference	854	Tribune
1989	4/ 9	Alcohol	Coachs mission (Article)		DMRegister
1989	10/24	Alcohol	Letter/Editor	860	Tribune
1989	5/ 4	Alcohol	Non users seek new society	784	DMReg
1989	9/ 5	Alcohol	Wine-Lousy Med.	857	Tribune
1992	12/24	Alcohol	more than fools	1780	D.M.Reg p.6A
1995	3/1	Alcohol	Frat Ban: May be 1st in State	1937	DMReg. p.1A
1997	April	Alcohol	U. of Wisc. Study: Gr.Juice/Wine	2335	Amer. Issue p.3
1997	6/1	Alcohol	Oxymoron of Drinking	2213	DMReg. p.6C
1997	10/3	Alcohol	What Alcohol Does	2363	Trib.(Boston Gl.)
1991	7/10	Alcohol Ads	Letter/Editor	1245	Tribune
1997	6/15	Alcohol Free	Fraternities	2381	DMReg. p.6C
1989	4/12	Alcohol Pressure	Letter/Editor	781	Tribune
1987	7/17/19	Alcohol Rate Off	Article about	780	USAToday
1989	12/24	Alcohol-Drinkers	Gallup Poll	913	Parade Magazine
1989	3/ 9	Alcohol-Drunks	Tolerance Down		USAToday
1989	5/22	Alcohol-Letter	To Editor	785	Tribune
1913	11/ 3	Alexander Mfg.Co.	Garden plows	231	Times
1915	3/15	Alexander Mfg.Co.	Plows made in Ames		Times
1918	4/10	Alexander Mfg.Co.	Mayor Graves Talks about	418	Times?
1918	4/ 1	Alexander Mfg.Co.	Invited to Marshalltown	561	Tribune
1918	4/24	Alexander Mfg.Co.	May stay in Ames	418	Times?

1919	5/14	Alexander Mfg.Co.	Sells plows	55	Times
1919	4/19	Alexander Mfg.Co.	3rd Largest in US	383	Times
1919	6/12	Alexander Plows	Carr Hwd. ad	110	Times
1911	7/13	Alexander,J.G.	Invents rake	52	Times
1987	9/15	Alumni Hall	Remodeling	585	Tribune
1989	1/18	Alumni Hall	Offices Move to	741	ISDaily
1989	1/19/20	Alumni Hall	Remodled		ISDaily
1906	9/20	Alumni Hall YMCA	Architects for	905	Times p.8
1917	7/19	American Boy Magazine	Ames Boy now editor	379	Times
1919	5/13	American Legion	Ames may have Post	259	Times
		Ames	See: Milestones / Ames		
1893	1/ 5	Ames	Story about growth	1254	Intelligencer
1893	1/ 5	Ames	Improvements (1892)	1311	Times
1893	1/ 5	Ames	Special report	1306	Times p.1
1893	1/ 5	Ames	A .& C. R.R. helped Ames grow	1253	Intelligencer
1909	9/30	Ames	Makes Gains	1236	Intelligencer
1909		Ames	Semi-Centennial	363	Tribune
1939	9/26	Ames	Celebrates 75th Ann.	1374	Trib. p.1
1913	2/24	Ames	City & College -Get together+	1277	Times p.1
1939	9/20	Ames	Celebration - 75th Birthday	1423	Trib . p.1
1911	8/17	Ames Auto Co.	Advertisement	1852	Times
1915	6/19	Ames Bldg./Loan	First Loan made	728	Intelligencer?
1919	5/16	Ames Bottling Co.	Advertisement for	277	Times
1894	6/14	Ames Celebration	4th of July quiet	245	Times
1909	7/ 8	Ames Celebration	Founding of College	659	Times
1964	Jul 6	Ames Centenial	Parade Committee	280	Tribune
1911	3/ 9	Ames City	Postpones paving again	209	Times
1911	4/ 6	Ames City	Ball & Chain Hoboes	209	Times
1923	5/19	Ames City	Council accepts 9th St.Ext.	395	Tribune
1957	319	Ames City	New Commission	365	Tribune
1916	10/ 2	Ames City of	Municipal Court approved	317	Tribune
1989	4/17	Ames City Ord.	Re: Underage in Bars	774	Tribune(Letter)
1870	Census	Ames Clergy	Names of	417	USCensus
1903		Issue for Year	Ames Directory	List of Businesses	
1002		Iowa Gazetteer			
1903		Issue for Year	Ames Directory	Ames Businesses	
1003		Iowa Gazetteer			
1903		Issue for year	Ames Directory	Names Businesses	
1001		Iowa Gazetteer			
1911	11/23	Ames Gun Club	Hold Turkey Shoot	209	Intelligencer
1980	11/17	Ames Heritage Assoc.	Art. of Incorporation	2321	Bk.21 p.163
1984	12/15	Ames Heritage Assoc.	Henry May's Stone	358	Tribune
1894	6/14	Ames High School	Graduation 1894	246	Times
1981	8/22	Ames High School	1912 Building Torn down	306	Tribune p.B7
1918	4/ 8	Ames History	"Looking Back"	1366	Trib.p.5
1986	8/27	Ames History	Milestones	460	Advertiser
1988	11/21	Ames History	F.Brown Talk at Rotary	789	ARC Bulletin
1915	9/1	Ames Hotel	Cupps buys from Clark	362	Times
1924	7/16	Ames Hotel	One More Chance	1874	Trib. p.1
1982	12/7	Ames Hotel	Torn down (5th & Douglas)	324	Tribune
1917	2/ 8	Ames Improvement Asc.	Meet in Nevada	250	Tribune
1914	2/ 9	Ames Improvement Co.	Stock selling	231	Times
		Ames In RHYME		2385	
1914	10/14	Ames Jail	Called Ricketts Hotel	39	Times
1870	Census	Ames Lawyers	Named	417	USCensus
1992	9/22	Ames Monument	Mrs.Chalmer Roy	1413	(with snap shots)
1913	10/13	Ames National Bank	in new Building	83	Times
1913	6/13	Ames National Bank	About new Building	85	Times
1913	1/31	Ames National Bank	Contract new building	81	Times
1915	2/22	Ames National Bank	H.W.Stafford elected Pres	235	Times
1870	Census	Ames Physicians	Named	417	USCensus
1912	2/ 8	Ames Savings Bank	Changes hands		Times
1918	5/13	Ames Seed Company	Organized	59	Tribune
1924	1/25	Ames Slogan	Ames Advertises America	159	Tribune
1939	9/26	Ames 75th Celebration	Ames Ready to Celebrate 75th	2436	Trib. p. 1
1911	10/ 5	Ames, City"	History Sketch	52	Times
1909	9/30	Ames, Gains"	Improvments	1383	Intell. p.1
1876	7/ 4	Ames, History of	"Turner,C.E.writes"	518	Intelligencer
1928		Ames, Oakes	Bell given to Church	735	Tribune
1989	12/15	Ames, Oakes	Texters Column	866	867
1989	12/27	Ames, Oakes	Letter to Editor	868	Tribune
1993	9/ 4	Ames, Oakes	Gerlach's Story	1776	Tribune
1991	4/15	Ames, Oakes III	Story About		Tribune
1994	3/ 0	Ames, Oakes III	Teaching in Conn.	1780	Conn.Col.Mag.
1989	8/18	Ames, Old Town	Great Houses	848	Tribune
1915	9/13	Ames, Opinion	Student opinion	1189	Times/college pg.
1877	5/25	Ames,City	Water from C&NW RR	544	Intelligencer
1909	1/1	Ames,City	Plan to pave Main Sreet	269	Intelligencer
1910	8/11	Ames,City	Pave Main St.	411	Times
1911	7/27	Ames,City	Case settled	74	Tribune
1911	7/ 6	Ames,City	Defends Suit	74	Tribune
1911	7/20	Ames,City	Hearing at Ft.Dodge	74	Tribune
1913	7/1	Ames,City	Propose City Hall- Hotel Compl.	92	Times
1913	7/11	Ames,City	Population 5000	82	Times
1913	2/8	Ames,City	Final Bids	73	Times
1913	4/ 9	Ames,City	Vote Squaw Creek location	86	Times
1913	1/ 8	Ames,City	vote on light plant		Times
1913	8/6	Ames,City	Council: no on light plant		Times
1913	Sep 3	Ames,City	Atty.warns of litigation	97	Times
1913	Feb10	Ames,City	Public meeting at Armory	86	Times
1914	Mar26	Ames,City	City Election	227	Times
1914	Oct22	Ames,City	West Ames threatens	79	Tribune
1914	Apr 1	Ames,City	Sheldon 425/Scott 354	227	Times
1914	Sep25	Ames,City	50 year of City Devel.	234	Times
1915	Jun 3	Ames,City	"Pop. now 5,000"	78	Times
1915	Apr 9	Ames,City	City Hall bids	75	Tribune
1915	Sep23	Ames,City	Sewer/street contracts	98	Times
1915	Dec30	Ames,City	Will pave 6 miles	98	Times

1915	9/15	Bryan, Wm.Jennings	Visits Campus	314	Times
1915	4/10	Bryan, Wm.Jennings	Speaks @ St.City (Jingoes)	2393	Times p.1
1916	9/21	Bryan, Wm.Jennings	Speaks at Ames High	493	Times
1916	5/13	Bryan, Wm.Jennings	Here today	350	Times
1916	5/18	Bryan, Wm.Jennings	Speaks at State Gym	932	TribubeF.Pg.
1892	5/19	Budd, Etta	Reads Paper	508	Intelligencer
1918	12/23	Budd, Etta	Bro.at Shellsburg,Ia	563	Times
1915	2/11	Budd, Mrs Sarah	dies	78	Times
1892	9/ 1	Budd, Prof. J.L.	"Boquet Party"	480	Intelligencer
1902	7/3	Budd, Prof. J.L.	Tribute to him	1928	Times p.1
1940	12/ 0	Budge, Dr.Ben	Birthday Party for		Tribune
1914	5/28	Building & Loan	Cert. of Authority	1204	Times p.1
1916	12/19	Building / Ames	Listing of new construction	1759	Times p.1
1916	12/10	Building Remod.	List for 1916	1268	Times p.1
1893	1/ 5	Building(Agr.Hall (1892)	Cut Photo of		Times
1893	1/ 5	Building(Bank,Union Nat.	Cut Photo of		Times
1892	9/29	Building(CreameryISC)	Cut photo of Bldg.	1310	Times
1893	1/ 5	Building(Opera Ho)	Cut Photo of		Times
1893	1/ 5	Building(Perkins/O'brien)	Cut of New Bldg.		Times
1893	1/ 5	Building(Tilden Store)	Cut of new Bldg.		Times
1919	7/11	Building, (Linebaugh)	Remodeling	2352	Trib. p.1
1916	6/16	Building, Masonic	Contract let	1356	Times p.1
		Building,New	See: Rice		
1883		Building,New	Tilden Block	1319	
1893	10/12	Building,New	K.W.Brown at 223 Main Street	1998	Times
1898	12/26	Building,New	Brick Block (Main Street)	1768	Times p.2
1902	1/8	Building,New	Times 400 Bl. on Diouglass	1482	Times
1908	10/ 7	Building,New	Champlin (In Campustown)	284	Times
1909	3/11	Building,New	1908 listing		Times p.7
1912	12/12	Building,New	Kooser builds Garage	1366	Intell. p.1
1912	May 2	Building,New	Ames National Bank	340	Trbune?
1913	6/13	Building,New	Ames Sav.;Goble;Little Bldg.	1639	Times p.1
1913	6/ 2	Building,New	Goble Building	1276	Times p.1
1913	6/ 2	Building,New	Roberson Garage	1276	Times p;1
1915	12/23	Building,New	Bank,Union Nat.	520	Tribune
1915	9/29	Building,New	Bates' Bakery	1190	Times
1916	12/19	Building,New	During 1916		Times p.1
1916	12/15	Building,New	Dragoun Transfer	1269	Times p.1
1917	7/5	Building,New	Lee builds on Main & Burnett	1971	Trib. p.1
1919	Feb21	Building,New	Commercial Sav.Bank	353	Times
1924		Building,New	Rice builds at 323 Main St.	1761	City Record
1925	10/9	Building,New	Pantorium Building-410 Doug.	2425	Trib. p.1
1926	11/4	Building,New	Tilden Mfg. Co. on 5th St.	1467	Tribune p.1
1928	9/26	Building,New	Max Duitch at 327/329 Main St.	1761	City Record
1893	1/ 5	Building,New(1890)	Union National Bank		Times
1893	1/ 5	Building,New(1890)	Tilden Store	1319	Times
1893	1/ 5	Building,New(1891)	Story County Bank		Times
1893	1/ 5	Building,New(1891)	Opera House Block		Times
1893	1/ 5	Building,New(1892)	Perkins & O'Brien Block		Times
1916	4/7	Buildings	3 to be remodeled (Bosworth)	2176	Times p.1
1898/1930		Buildings,Campus	Map of Pete Day's Book		
1913	3/31	Bullock Hardware	Advertisement	1700	Intell. p.1
1949	2/11	Bus Depot / Cafe	Opens (Main & Clark)	1779	Tribune p.1
1928	9/21	Bus Service	Ft.D.Dm&So.add bus service	1674	Tribune p.1
1916	12/26	Bush, Dr.Earl	Home from Border	466	Times
1917	4/ 5	Bush, Dr.Earl	Medical Corp.Unit	108	Tribune
1917	6/21	Bush, Dr.Earl	Medical Unit ready	379	Times
1919	1/21	Bush, Dr.Earl	Banquet honors Med. Corp.	1454	Times p.1
1940	12/28	Bush, Dr.Earl	Miltary Service again	888	Tribune p.1
1919	1/21/22	Bush, Dr.Earl	Med.Unit honored	352	Times
1917	6/ 1	Business / Professional	Roster of	462	Times
1905	5/11	Business Men of Ames	Biographical sketches	247	Intelligencer
1897	Sv.Ed	Business men of Ames	37 Biographical skethces	247	Intelligencer
1893	1/26	Business Mens Assoc.	Organized: J.L.Budd, Pres.	1472	Times p.3
1917/8		VariousBusiness Men-List	Cartoon Likeness	916	Times
1936	7/22	Business Places	Mgt.by Employees	651	Tribune
1920	6/12	Buster Brown (Adv.)	At Bauge Shoe St.	2016	Times
1910	9/16	Buster Brown Shoes	In Town	924	Intell. p.6
1923	8/29	Butter Tub Factory	At Story City	503	Tribune
1926	12/18	C.& N.W. Underpass	Up To Railroad	2228	Conference
1926	8/28	C.& N.W. Underpass	Condemnation for	2224	Trib. p.1
1928	3/29	C.& N.W. Underpass	Case Aired	2192	Trib. p.1
1937	8/19	C.& N.W. Underpass.	Bids being received	263	Tribune
1900	6/14	C.& N.W.Depot	Chas W.Gindela Contractor	354	Intelligencer
1900	6/14	C.& N.W.Depot	Start on new depot	1985	Times
1900	6/14	C.& N.W.Depot	Start work on	330	Intelligencer
1900	9/ 6	C.& N.W.Depot	New Depot	569	Times
1906	9/ 7	C.& N.W.Depot	Flower Gardens	905	Times p.7
1907	2/21	C.& N.W.Depot	Man rescued by Thompson	1896	Times p.1
1909	6/ 6	C.& N.W.Depot	Wants Sioux City to copy	712	Intelligencer
1911	6/15	C.& N.W.Depot	Agent does good turn	904	Times
1912		C.& N.W.Depot	Ad for Cafe in Depot	1666	ISC Directory
1915	3/24	C.& N.W.Depot	Jerry Sexton, Gardener	235	Times
1916	10/ 5	C.& N.W.Depot	Dry Speakers here	669	Times
1917	12/ 8	C.& N.W.Depot	Train Caller	914	Times p.3
1917	8/30	C.& N.W.Depot	Arrest Pickpockets	1406	Trib.
1917	8/ 9	C.& N.W.Depot	Foot subway	1402	"Trib,"
1917	12/ 6	C.& N.W.Depot	Pickpockets	1268	Trib. p.1
1923	8/ 2	C.& N.W.Depot	Redecorate		Trib.
1924	6/ 2	C.& N.W.Depot	Pigeons Turned Loose	1881	Times p.1
1926	11/15	C.& N.W.Depot	Subway Accident	424	Tribune
1946	3/ 7	C.& N.W.Depot	Remodel plans		Tribune p.1
1950	10/ 7	C.& N.W.Depot	"New Depot" $100 Thousand"	1801	Tribune p.1
1987	8/ 3	C.& N.W.Depot	Student Proposals		Tribune
1990	11/13	C.& N.W.Depot	Re:Restoration etc.	982	Tribune p.1
1905	(Dir.)	C.& N.W.Depot	Ad for cafe (Lunch Room)	463	ISCDir.
1916	9/17	C.& N.W.Depot	Meet Trains (Visitors)		Times
1916	9/19	C.& N.W.Depot	Gal Steals Roll (Pickpocket)	1374	Times p.1
1908	10/29	C.& N.W.Foot Bridge	Built over Squaw Creek	712	Intelligencer
1960	3/12	C.& N.W.Pass.Trains	Service ends	1407	Trib. p.1
1885	6/20	C.& N.W.R.R	Time Tables	1302	Intell.p.3
1896	1/ 9	C.& N.W.R.R	Time Tables	1301	Times p.8
1981	4/27	C.& N.W.R.R	Train Wreck	875	Register
		C.& N.W.R.R.	See: Underpass		
1877	5/18	C.& N.W.R.R.	Train Wreck	884	Intelligencer
1888	3/1	C.& N.W.R.R.	Ad Stone Ballasted steel	2354	Intell.
1893	10/5	C.& N.W.R.R.	Round Trip to Chicago: $7.85	1999	Times p.3
1900	4/12	C.& N.W.R.R.	About high bridge	378	Times p.6

1901		C.& N.W.R.R.	Lunchroom Advertisement	1974	ISC Directory
1902	10/12	C.& N.W.R.R.	I.S.C.grant ROW	400	Times(p.2)
1905	12/19	C.& N.W.R.R.	Girl rescued at crossing	1358	Times p.1
1905	(Stud.Dir)	C.& N.W.R.R.	Lunch Room Ad		Directory ISC
1908	10/29	C.& N.W.R.R.	Build Footbridge (See Clip710)	234	Intelligencer
1911	6/1	C.& N.W.R.R.	Crushed Rock Ballast Installed	2251	Times p.1
1911	8/3	C.& N.W.R.R.	Time Table	1378	Intell. p.1
1912	9/25	C.& N.W.R.R.	Special Train: Foreign Chemists	1944	Times p.1
1913	3/28	C.& N.W.R.R.	Overland Limited (Ad)	1700	Intell.p.4
1914	9/26	C.& N.W.R.R.	Some History of	1331	Times
1914	6/ 1	C.& N.W.R.R.	Special Student Train	1857	Times.p.7
1914	5/25	C.& N.W.R.R.	Schedule	1368	Times p.5
1915	3/24	C.& N.W.R.R.	Park Noticed	632	Times
1915	3/17	C.& N.W.R.R.	Park Noticed	266	
1915	6/18	C.& N.W.R.R.	Special Trains	881	Times
1917	11/20	C.& N.W.R.R.	Special Train to Iowa City	1269	Times p.1
1918	5/ 7	C.& N.W.R.R.	Carroll Ave.viaduct propopsed	351	Times
1918	12/18	C.& N.W.R.R.	City wants overhead	415	Tribune
1919	3/10	C.& N.W.R.R.	Train wreck at Ontario	1816	Times p.1
1919	10/14	C.& N.W.R.R.	Rogers retires	1270	Trib . p.1
1924	2/16	C.& N.W.R.R.	Keep Julia Laughlin on job	252	Tribune
1926	12/18	C.& N.W.R.R.	Subway Talk	456	Tribune
1926	11/27	C.& N.W.R.R.	Crossing Accident	421	Tribune
1928	2/29	C.& N.W.R.R.	Objects to Subway	1201	Tribune
1929	7/17	C.& N.W.R.R.	Nix Clark Ave. R.R.crossing	1269	Times p.1
1929	7/ 8	C.& N.W.R.R.	Depot painting	1270	Times p.2
1929	8/18	C.& N.W.R.R.	Corn King stops here	1270	Trib. p.2
1929	7/ 8	C.& N.W.R.R.	Depot painting	1270	Times p.2
1930	7/1	C.& N.W.R.R.	Ad: 3 day Excursion	1434	TRIB. P.5
1930	8/12	C.& N.W.R.R.	$14.04 - round trip to Chicago	2294	Trib. p.5
1935	7/7	C.& N.W.R.R.	$5.50 - round trip to Chicago	2321	Trib. p.8
1941	10/16	C.& N.W.R.R.	275 Eng.Students to Chicago	1817	ISC Student p.6
1946	3/ 7	C.& N.W.R.R.	Remodel Depot	164	Tribune
1954	1/25	C.& N.W.R.R.	Last Pass.Train Gilbert	266	Tribune
1959	7/15	C.& N.W.R.R.	Beedle Dies/Yd.MasterAst.	633	Tribune
1960	3/12	C.& N.W.R.R.	Passsenger train service ends	571	Tribune
1981	4/27	C.& N.W.R.R.	Train Wreck	872	Tribune
1990	1/23	C.& N.W.R.R.	Train Caller (In History)	876	Tribune
1906	9/ 6	C.& N.W.R.R.	Article about Park	933	Times p.7
1915	3/24	C.& N.W.R.R.	Finest found	1403	Times
1915	6/17	C.& N.W.R.R.	Tourist Comments about park	1402	Trib.
1919	10/14	C.& N.W.R.R.	Rogers, G.W. retires (Agent)		Tribune
		C.& N.W.R.R.	See: Time Table this index		
1916	5/ 9	Cafeteria, Virginia	Kurtz's new restaurant	239	Times
1908	10/15	Cairns, Bob	Saw Chicago Fire	1383	Intell.p.2
1916	5/ 1	Cakoulis,Frank	Buys Grove Building	279	Times
1916	8/25	Caldwell, A.F.	Enters business	1355	Times
1916	5/ 9	Caldwell, A.F.	to better teaching job	240	Times
1914	6/ 8	Caldwell,A.F.	Supt. of Schools	325	Board Minutes
1916	5/ 6	Caldwell,A.F.	Resigns	325	Board Minutes
1995	6/8	Cambridge,Iowa	Jubilee scheduled	2070	Trib. p.1
1913	7/30	Camp Anamosa	Road Work	1333	Times
1913	9/29	Camp Anamosa	"Is Still Popular" (See:2385b)	2385	Times p.1
1899	12/21	Campanile	Bells installed on ISC Campus	1906	Times p.3
1899	10/26	Campanile	Stanton Memorial	400	Times
1899	10/19	Campanile	Bells arrive	401	Times
1899	11/ 2	Campanile	Story About chimes	405	Times
1900	2/20	Campanile	Concert	406	ISCStudent
1900	2/23	Campanile	Re:Dedication of chimes	401	Times
1929	7/5	Campanile	Being remodeled	2310	Trib. p.2
1926	8/7	Campfire G irls	Cabin north of City (Canwita)	1482	Trib. p.1
1910	1985	Campfire Girls	History - By:Sue Peters	1373	Document
1914	6/25	Campfire Girls	Campus/Conference	1673	Tribune p.1
1914	6/24	Campfire Girls	Seton / Girls (Indian Council)	1367	Times p.1
1923	8/22	Campfire Girls	Official visits Ames	2383	"Trib, p.1"
1923	1/23	Campfire Girls	Guests of Chamber of Com.	2198	Trib. p.1
1924	5/13	Campfire Girls	Council Meet - 29 ranked	2341	Trib. p.2
1926	10/9	Campfire Girls	Open House	2227	Trib . p.1
1929	9/27	Campfire Girls	"Unusual Dress"	2241	Trib. p.1
1930	1/18	Campfire Girls	"Campfire News"	2240	Trib. p.8
1935	7/16	Campfire Girls	Camp Canwitta Still Booming	2205	Trib.
1951	10/15	Campfire Girls	Leaders entertained	2147	Trib. p.1
1912		Campus Buildings	Map showing	1655	ISC Directory
1913	8/15	Campus Roads	Prison Labor Here to work on	1172	Times p.1
1913	4/16	Campus Rules	List of	1658	Card.Guild
1911	11/29	Canadian Land Sale	Ad in Times	37	Times
1909	9/ 9	Canady,Walter	Ames Hotel enlarged	38	Intelligencer
1919	7/14	Canning factories	Ames headquarters for	121	Times
1918	4/24	Canning Factory	Ground Broken For -	2386	Trib. p.1
1918	1/17	Canning Factory	Favored for Ames	989	Tribune p.1
1918	4/26	Canning Factory	Belching Smoke	505	Tribune
1918	8/26	Canning Factory	Opens	406	Times
1918	9/ 4	Canning Factory	140 Cans a minute	352	Times
1918	9/23	Canning Factory	Women Offer Services	1873	Times p.1
1918	4/26	Canning Factory	Story about	410	
1918	4/ 1	Canning Factory	New Officers	414	Tribune
1918	4/24	Canning Factory	Ground Broken for	504	Tribune
1922	8/28	Canning Factory	Operating full time 125 workers	2307	Trib. p.1
1924	4/24	Canning Factory	Building starts	380	Times
1930	11/ 5	Canning Factory	Cans potatoes	1892	Trib.p.9
1931	8/31	Canning Factory	F.1918-Advertisement for		Tribune
1939	9/26	Canning Factory	Big Ad - names brands canned	2074	Trib. p.17
1968	6/10	Canning Factory	Burns Firms Inventory-Coll. Mfg.	2364	Trib .p.1
1949	1/18	Cannning Factory	Sold by Mrs.Chavis	1779	Trib. p.1
1923	6/23	Carnival	Sherriff Raids	504	Tribune
1928	7/18	Carnival	Sponsored by Am.Legion	2346	Trib. p.1
1917	2/20	Carr Hardware	Improvements		Times
1917	2/16	Carr Hardware	Improvements	417	Tribune
1944	2/24	Carr Hardware	Ad: Hoover Service	1871	Milepost
1964	Sv.Ed	Carr Hardware	Store started	281	Tribune
1929	6/28	Carr's Pool	Ad for	891	Tribune
1930	7/ 2	Carr's Pool	Ad for	898	Tribune p.10
1930	6/27	Carr's Riverside Park	Ad for	898	Tribune p.10
1929	1/ 4	Cars, Collegiate	Flivvers a nuiscance: Hughes		DM Reg
1921	6/11	Carver,George	Pammel visits	115	Tribune
1991	Feb.	Carver,George	Legacy Remembered	1497	Ia.Stater 7 pgs.
1929	6/12	Catt, Carrie Chapman	"World Peace Near"	2225	Trib. p.1
1930	6/8	Catt, Carrie Chapman	Will Address Senior Class	2377	DMReg. p.L3

1887	4/20	Church,Christian	Founded-12 members	361	Notation
1887	5/19	Church,Christian	Purchase Methodist Bldg.	244	Intelligence
1894		Church,Christian	About Bell/Officers	309	Notation only
1897	Sv.Ed	Church,Christian	Historical sketch	245	Intelligencer
1908	11/19	Church,Christian	Rev.Williams leaves Ames	84	Times
1908	10/15	Church,Christian	Novel Idea	30	Times
1915	7/ 5	Church,Christian	Rev.Harris to C.E.Convention	244	Times
1915	7/ 4	Church,Christian	Patriotic Service	178	Times
1915	12/23	Church,Christian	Surprise Party	520	Tribune
1919	8/11	Church,Christian	Sell parsonage	385	Times
1919	10/19	Church,Christian	Houser reception	171	Times
1919	10/ 4	Church,Christian	Revival Meetings	370	Tribune
1927	9/29	Church,Christian	Dedication new Church	2292	Trib. p.1
1908	10/15	Church,Christian	Novel Plan	34	Times
1926	6/ 1	Church,Col.Methodist	Dedicate ColllegiateChurch	6	Tribune p.1
1926	6/ 6	Church,Col.Methodist	Dedicated See:Bk#15		Tribune
1926	6/ 4	Church,Col.Methodist	Dedicate tonight	1326	Trib. p.1
1877	6/ 8	Church,Congregational	State Meeting	555	Intelligencer
1883	6/2	Church,Congregational	Elequent Sermon	1950	Intell. p.1
1883	7/18?	Church,Congregational	Meet at Tilden Home	864	Inyelligencer
1885	3/24	Church,Congregational	Choir / One of City's best	883	Intelligencer
1885	7/23	Church,Congregational	Rev.Moulton encounters flood	247	Intelligencer
1885	7/30	Church,Congregational	Ladies Sewing Society	251	Intelligencer
1890	4/24	Church,Congregational	Carrie Lane Chapman Speaks	899	Intelligencer
1890	5/ 8	Church,Congregational	Rev.Brown preaches(bro:KWB)	900	Intelligencer
1890	5/ 8	Church,Congregational	Association Meet at Ogden	900	Intelligencer
1890	5/ 1	Church,Congregational	About Carrie Lane Chapman talk	899	Inyelligencer
1890	5/ 1	Church,Congregational	Prs.Chamberlain Speaks	899	Intelligencer
1892	7/21	Church,Congregational	Give Social	446	Intelligencer
1892	8/18	Church,Congregational	Picnic at Watkins'Well	446	Intelligencer
1892	8/18	Church,Congregational	Women's Miission Soc.	446	Intelligencer
1892	5/19	Church,Congregational	Rev.Douglas at Meeting	508	Intelligencer
1892	7/14	Church,Congregational	Guest Speaker	446	Intelligencer
1892	9/ 8	Church,Congregational	Former Pastor Talks	480	Intelligencer
1897	2/25	Church,Congregational	Sermon: -Street vs Home+	2397	Times p.4
1897	Sv.Ed	Church,Congregational	Historical sketch	245	Intelligencer
1898	3/17	Church,Congregational	Sermon - Rev.Douglas		Intelligencer
1898	5/ 8	Church,Congregational	"Old Truths in New Light"	901	Intelligencer
1898	3/17	Church,Congregational	Ladies have market	556	Intelligencer
1899	12/21	Church,Congregational	Hold Ladies Market Day	1905	Times p.3
1899	12/21	Church,Congregational	Old bldg.to Dr.Templeton	1906	Times p.3
1899	4/20	Church,Congregational	New Church Bldg.Begun	1976	Times p.1
1900	3/18	Church,Congregational	Dedication		Intelligencer
1900	10/ 5	Church,Congregational	Lay Cornerstone	400	Times
1900	5/31	Church,Congregational	Entertain 40 Students		Intelligencer
1900	3/22	Church,Congregational	Dedicate church	378	Times
1900	3/22	Church,Congregational	New Church Dedication	354	Intelligencer
1900	6/14	Church,Congregational	Musical Program	332	Intelligencer
1900	10/ 4	Church,Congregational	Sermon subject	1399	Intell.
1900	11/29	Church,Congregational	Dinner held	472	Times
1901	5/30	Church,Congregational	Council Trial	1854	Intell p.1
1902	2/20‘	Church,Congregational	Rev.Secombes Sermon	2246	Intell. p.7
1902	1/30	Church,Congregational	The School of Christ	2462	Intell. Local Items
1909	10/21	Church,Congregational	Sermon Topic- Minchin	984	Intell.
1909	4/ 1	Church,Congregational	Minchin remains here	1760	Times p.1
1910	6/16	Church,Congregational	New Church Pride of Gilbert	2315	p.4
1910	6/16	Church,Congregational	Gilbert,new church	1357	Times p.4
1911	11/22	Church,Congregational	Pagent opens	207	Intelligencer
1912	10/19	Church,Congregational	Sunday School Class	832	InTelligencer
1913	1/17	Church,Congregational	Annual Meeting	825	Times
1913	1/16	Church,Congregational	In Good Shape	1919	Intelligencer
1914	7/15	Church,Congregational	Dedicate Park	570	Times
1914	9/21	Church,Congregational	Rev Dunn,Campus Minister	234	Times
1914	7/15	Church,Congregational	Men's Br,hood dedicate park	232	Times
1914	9/21	Church,Congregational	Rev.Dunn Arrives	975	Times p.1
1914	10/ 5	Church,Congregational	Pray for peace	234	Times
1914	9/ 4	Church,Congregational	Rev. Minchin's bad fall	234	Times
1915	1/21	Church,Congregational	Rev.Moulton's death	873	Tribune
1915	5/17	Church,Congregational	Call Rev.Hawley	76	Times p.1
1915	1/ 6	Church,Congregational	Minchin to Mason City	233	Times
1915	9/24	Church,Congregational	Sermons Hawleys	970	Times
1915	11/ 3	Church,Congregational	50th Yr.Celebration	487	Times
1915	11/ 4	Church,Congregational	Golden Jubilee	445	Tribune
1915	6/29	Church,Congregational	Hawley arrives July 5th	244	Times p.1
1916	12/11	Church,Congregational	Hiking Club	7830	Times p.1
1916	5/21	Church,Congregational	Hawleys Sermon on Blue Laws	1505	Times p.1
1916	11/26	Church,Congregational	Sunday Among Churches	1174	Times/p.3
1916	3/6	Church,Congregational	Sermon Hawleys	2183	Times p.1
1916	12/ 6	Church,Congregational	Men's Hiking Club	1200	Times p.1
1916	3/27	Church,Congregational	Sermom - Hawley on Citizenship	1356	Times p.1
1916	1/ 5	Church,Congregational	Frisbie House named	319	Times
1917	2/19	Church,Congregational	Frisbie House Opens	448	Times
1917	5/21	Church,Congregational	Rev.Hawley on Blue Laws	1006	Times p.1
1917	5/14	Church,Congregational	Mother's Day Sermon	1006	Times p.1
1917	6/ 6	Church,Congregational	Dedicate Frisbie House	417	TTimes p.1
1918	8/ 7	Church,Congregational	Asks City pay for walk	443	Tribune
1918	8/ 7	Church,Congregational	City's no on retaining wall	406	Times
1919	4/ 1	Church,Congregational	Sermon - Hawley	380	Times
1919	8/ 2	Church,Congregational	Student Pastor	734	Intelligencer
1923	1/24	Church,Congregational	Brotherhood/Talks	984	Times
1924	7/13	Church,Congregational	Hold annual picnic	391	Tribune
1924	1/17	Church,Congregational	Remodeling voted	159	Tribune
1924	7/13	Church,Congregational	Picnic on Campus	3	Tribune p.1
1926	10/ 8	Church,Congregational	Bosworth Speaks	438	Tribune
1928		Church,Congregational	Bell from Oakes Ames	735	Tribune
1929	1/19	Church,Congregational	Hawley Resigns	1897	Trib. p.1
1930	9/13	Church,Congregational	Stud.Pastor(new)	1892	Trib. p.5
1930	1/18	Church,Congregational	Plan New Building	2232	Tribune p.1
1930	1/8	Church,Congregational	$14,000 Add.in 29	2233	Trib. p.1
1930	9/ 5	Church,Congregational	New Bldg.Ready	1892	Trib. p.1
1935	7/ 1	Church,Congregational	Hawley elected Emeritus	319	Tribune
1935	12/14	Church,Congregational	Denmark Ch.History	862	Tribune
1940	11/ 8	Church,Congregational	Celebrate 75th Year	975	Tribune p.1
1949	2/ 7	Church,Congregational	Merger report by F.Brown	1779	Tribune/F.p.c7
1958	1/21	Church,Congregational	Bldg.Permit$75000	2233	City File
1986	11/21	Church,Congregational	Harvest Home Dinner	361	Tribune
1987	2/20	Church,Congregational	Conference Minister Speaks	360	Tribune
1990	7/ 3	Church,Congregational	Jesse Jackson Speaks		Tribune
1990	11/ 2	Church,Congregational	125th Anniverary	980	Tribune
1990	11/ 2	Church,Congregational	Restore Cemetery Stones	981	Tribune(Rel.)
1899	12/28	Church,Episcopal	Reg.Services	1804	Times(Local Miscl)
1899	12/21	Church,Episcopal	1st Service in church	1804	Times(Local Miscl)
1899	12/ 7	Church,Episcopal	Social in New Church	1804	Times(Local Miscl)
1899	12/21	Church,Episcopal	1st Service next Sun.		Times p.3
1899	12/14	Church,Episcopal	Ladies Guild	1804	Times(Local Miscl)
1915	5/21	Church,Episcopal	Improve Church	442	Times
1919	7/ 1	Church,Episcopal	Let Contract	670	Tribune
1919	7/11	Church,Episcopal	Buy 4th Ward site	118	Times
1919	9/26	Church,Episcopal	Student Pastor	388	Tribune
1927	2/ 4	Church,Episcopal	Bishop here	1767	Tribune
1930	5/6	Church,Episcopal	Dedicate new church	2331	Trib. p.6
1880	10/ 8	Church,Episcopal	Reunion of	886	Intelligencer
1976	10/15	Church,L.D.S.		566	Tribune
1925	1/31	Church,Lutheran	Ded. new church 7th&Kellogg	2274	Trib.p.1
1928	9/22	Church,Lutheran	Ded.new church	1674	Tribune p.1
1880	8/27	Church,Methodist	Hold Concert	889	Intelligencer
1890	5/ 1	Church,Methodist	sell lots to Judge Stevens	900	Intelligencer
1892	7/30	Church,Methodist	Bloomington Ch.Constitution	1953	File source
1897	Sv.Ed	Church,Methodist	Historical sketch	247	Intelligencer
1900	6/14	Church,Methodist	Sermon subjects	332	Intelligencer
1908	10/29	Church,Methodist	Dedication	1238	Intelligencer
1908	10/22	Church,Methodist	New Building dedicated	1382	Intell. p.1
1908	10/22	Church,Methodist	Dedicate new Church	230	Times
1908	7/ 2	Church,Methodist	Building Going up	922	Times
1909	3/11	Church,Methodist	Install costly organ	2331	TIMES P.4
1910	12/11	Church,Methodist	Down Town Lecture Series	924	Intell. p.1
1910	2/24	Church,Methodist	Gift:Organ / Carnegie	1838	Trinb. p.1
1914	10/ 7	Church,Methodist	Build near campus	233	Tribune
1917	9/27	Church,Methodist	Women feed 2500 Soldiers	250	Tribune
1917	2/22	Church,Methodist	Student center plans	108	Tribune
1917	2/16	Church,Methodist	Talk new Church (4th Ward)	495	Times
1918	2/14	Church,Methodist	Center near Campus	1267	Trib. p.1
1918	2/21	Church,Methodist	Feed troop trains	109	Tribune
1921	1/20	Church,Methodist	Ded. Collegiaste Center Ded.	1839	Tribune p.1
1922	11/22	Church,Methodist	District Meeting	489	Tribune
1923	6/21	Church,Methodist	Build Wesley Hall	504	Tribune
1950	8/25	Church,Methodist	1895 Class Reunion	576	Tribune
1993	1/12	Church,Methodist	Long history in Ames	1754	Trib. p.N6
1911	2/23	Church,Presbyterian	Organize church	72	Times
1911	2/23	Church,Presbyterian	Organize at College	1964	Times p.1
1912	4/11	Church,Presbyterian	$500.from Billy Sunday	217	Times
1913	12/15	Church,Presbyterian	$2,000 bequest	231	Times
1914	11/ 9	Church,Presbyterian	Billy Sunday gives $5M	233	Tribine p.1
1915	6/18	Church,Presbyterian	Start New Church	1884	Times.p.8
1915	4/12	Church,Presbyterian	Construction starts soon	235	Times
1915	9/13	Church,Presbyterian	Cornerstone laid	315	Times
1915	5/24	Church,Presbyterian	Room for All - Minister	361	Times
1916	12/19	Church,Presbyterian	$75,000 Building	494	Times
1917	12/ 7	Church,Presbyterian	Dedication	914	Times p.5
1919	9/13	Church,Presbyterian	Twin Churches at W.Gate		Tribune
1920	12/17	Church,Presbyterian	Tama Jim Memorial Organ	294	Times
1920	12/17	Church,Presbyterian	"Organ dedic. to Tama Wilson	2265	ISC Student p.1
1922	2/17	Church,Presbyterian	Pageant	817	Tribune?
1922	12/28	Church,Presbyterian	$10,000 for Pipe Organ	296	Tribune
1923	4/14	Church,Presbyterian	Presbytry meets/Organ recital	296	Tribune
1923	3/20	Church,Presbyterian	New organ installed	192	Tribune
1923	4/12	Church,Presbyterian	To dedicate $10,500 organ.	2391	ISC Student p.2
1988	4/29	Church,Reformed Ministry	New Minister	602	Tribune
1894	4/24	Church,United Brethern	Ice Cream Social	1929	Times p.5
1897	Sv.Ed	Church,United Brethern	Historical sketch	245	Intelligencer
1899	12/21	Church,United Brethern	Christmas Service	1905	Times p.3
1924	7/ 2	Church,United Brethern	Dedicate new Church	1417	Tribune p.1
1963	8/23	Church,United Brethern	Historical Sketch	1490	Anniversary
		Church/State	See: Prayer in schools		
1979	11/15	Church/State	Discussion regarding schools		Sp.Report
1981	12/ 8	Church/State	Can't bar religion	720	DMTrib
1983	7/ 0	Church/State	Trueblood writes		S.E.Post
1984	8/14	Church/State	Editorial	716	DMReg
1984	10/ 3	Church/State	Father Hesburg		"Rutland, Vt.Herald"
1984	8/24	Church/State	Liberty not stopped at door	771	DMRegister
1984	11/ 7	Church/State	Articles	711	Minn.Paper
1985	6/ 5	Church/State	Editorial	715	USA Today
1985	9/ 1	Church/State	Editorial	725	DMReg.
1985	6/29	Church/State	Editorial	713	DMReg.
1985	7/14	Church/State	Letters to Ed.	707	DMReg.
1985	5/23	Church/State	Court O.K.'s Prayer	712	Tribune
1985	6/ 4	Church/State	Court Upholds	726	Tribune
1987	3/22	Church/State	Survey/Educators	1770	D.M.Reg. p.1B
1988	12/ 1	Church/State	Invocations		DMRegister
1990	6/ 5	Church/State	Religion/Schools	892	U.S.News
1990	2/ 3	Church/State	Letters to Ed.		DMRegister
1990	6/10	Church/State	Supreme Court Rulling	921	DMReg.
1993	6/8	Church/State	S.Court: They can mix	1560	DMReg
1994	5/28	Church/State	Court approves rental	1782	D.M.Reg.
1994	3/28	Church/State	Editorial		Trib./p/A6
1877	5/18	Churches	Union Meeting of	884	Intelligencer
1908	6/18	Churches	Union Serices	922	Times
1913	5/14	Churches	Sunday School Baseball	85	Times
1913	5/14	Churches	First baseball game	82	Times
1923	6/ 8	Churches	Three Bible Schools	504	Tribune
1924	2/21	Churches	Sunday School Tourniment	278	Times
1916	9/14	Cinder Path	New path being built	1739	ISC Student
1907	10/10	Cinder Path	To College Discussed	923	Intell. p.1
1872	9/5	Circus	Coopers Circus Ad (Nevada)	2359	Nev.Rep.p.10
1885	6/20	Circus	Show Coming to Ames	1301	Intell.p.3
1885	6/20	Circus	Ringlng Bros. here.	2263	Intell. p.3
1898	7/28	Circus	Ringling Bros. at Nevada	1978	Intell. p.2
1905	9/14	Circus	Gentry Bros. here.	2262	Times p.3
1910	8/18	Circus	Fisk Circus to Ames	902	Times
1910	8/26	Circus	The Great DODE FISK Shows	2445	Intell. p,7

169

1920	12/11	Farm Bureau	Nat. Office leaves Ames	2434	Trib. p.1
1923	8/29	Farm Bureau	Special Farm Bureau Edition	2354	Trib. Vol.LVII
1923	8/29	Farm Bureau	Special Edition	503	Tribune
1988	4/30	Farm House	Open house	607	Tribune
1997	4/18	Farm House	Needs Fixing	2313	Trib. p.1 M
1918	9/23	Farmer's Market	Assured	1873	Times p.1
1918	9/10	Farmer's Market	Plans for	1873	Times p.2
		Fat Man, Ames	See: Nichols,George (Fatty)		
1916	9/28	Fat Man, Ames	Has own show	1208	Times p.1
1992	5/28	Fatherless Kids	in poverty	1398	DM Reg.Edito.
1916	9/28	Fatty Nichols	See: Fat Man	1208	Times p.1
1917	9/27	Feeding Troops	2500 @ Meth Church	250	Tribune
1993	9/26	Feminist ms.take	By Cal Thomas	1668	DMReg.
1991	8/ 4	Feminists	Editorial	1202	DM Reg
1991	11/ 7	Feminists/Ms-Represent	Editorial	1245	Wall St.Journal
1904	8/11	Fence Wire Factory	Comming to Ames	2319	Intell. p.3
1905	6/29	Festival	Midsummer Festival	2071	Times p.2
1924	10/ 7	Festival	Thousands in Ames for	2	Trib. p.1
1928	1/31	Field House	Dedicated	895	Tribune p.1
1928	2/14	Field House	800 attend Dedication	895	Tribune
1964	9/ 5	Field House	Sold	1787	Tribune/p.6
1915	8/26	Fifth Street	Part Improved	520	Tribune
1920	5/10	Find Greek+s Body	Squaw Creek	2018	Trib. p.1
1885	1/21	Fire	Holocaust on Main St.		Intelligencer
1886	1/21	Fire	Halocaust on Main Street	1218	Intelligencer
1886	1/28	Fire	K.W.Brown's Bldg.		Intelligencer
1887	10/ 6	Fire	Another Major Fire	1217	Intelligencer
1900	12/13	Fire	Old Main In Ruins	1894	Times p.1
1901	10/31	Fire	Experiment barn	1892	Times p/3
1902	9/14	Fire	Old Main again	1893	Times p.1 & 2
1911	7/27	Fire	Report on West Ames fire.	1215	Times
1912	1/11	Fire	Music Hall burns	1215	Times
1913	3/26	Fire	Chem Bldg/Campus	1891	Times p.1
1917	12/13	Fire	Odd Fellows Bldg.	1274	Trib p.1
1922	10/7	Fire	Experiment Station (ISC)	193	Trib.
1922	12/18	Fire	Armory (College) Burns	193	Trib.
1925	7/15	Fire	Ontario Elevator(Ames Reliable)	2350	Trib.p.1
1935	8/17	Fire	Dairy Barn burns	284	Tribune
1938	4/ 9	Fire	Margaret Hall burns		Tribune
1938	4/11	Fire	Margaret Hall Burns	19	Tribune
1941		Fire	Agr.Engineering B ldg.		
1943	1/30	Fire	Iowa Sanitarium Burns	1376	Trib. p.1
1957	6/	Fire	Ontario Chapel (Burned)	2447	Trib.
1957	1/16	Fire	Cook's Paint Store		Tribune p.1
1968	6/10	Fire	Collegiate Mfg. Co. big fire	2364	Trib. p.1
1982	6/16	Fire	Octagon House / Fire Training	2414	Trib. p.1
1987	11/23	Fire	Ames Stationers	1466	Tribune p.1
1916	9/28	Fire Department	New (1st Motor) Truck	1223	Times
1916	5/30	Fire Chief Morris	Injured/Runaway	932	Tribune p.1
1892	1/21	Fire Department	Ames buy s hose cart	1242	Council Minutes
1911	8/ 3	Fire Department	"Morris, Chief Lynn"	1272	Times p.1
1917	1/25	Fire Department	Five N members	495	Times
1922	2/18	Fire Department	Gets new truck	817	Tribune?
1928	6/12	Fire Department	Organized 33 years ago.	2168	Trib. p.1
1956	5/23	Fire Department	Sam Long Dies (Obit)	2076	Trib..p.1
1958	10/ 3	Fire Department	Has Grown	1335	Trib.p.12
1976	3/24	Fire Department	Story about Ames department		Tribune
1976	1/17	Fire Department	Photo / Story		Tribune
1978	10/25	Fire Department	Story about		Tribune
1900		Fire Map (Sanborn)	Business District of Ames	2276	
1926		Fire Map (Sanborn)	Key Protection facilities	2278	
		Fire Maps	See:Sanborn Map		
1916	9/23	Fire Truck	First motor truck for Ames		Times
1922	2/18	Fire Truck	Second Motor Truck	817	Tribune
1918	7/ 1	Fire Wagon	Kept in Champlins barn. C.Twn.	1177	Times p.1
1903		Fire, Grain Elevator	See dates for	6	(Bob Deppe)
1911	2/16	Firemen	Hear Rev . Minchin talk	195	Times
1914	7/24	Firemen	Ames men attend tournament	929	TimesF.Pg.
1915	5/ 3	Firemen	say need new truck	232	Times
1918	4/ 5	Firemen	New Officers	415	Tribune
1929	6/28	Fireworks	At Spring Lake on July 4th		
		Fireworks(Dayton Park)	See:Arm Torn		
1962	2/3	Fitch, C.L.	Dearh of. Veg. G rowers Head	2438	Trib. p.1
1877	5/11	Fitchpatrick,J.A.	Add for Abstractor	507	Intelligencer
1908	4/6	Flag Pole	46 Star Flag - Gen.Lincoln speak	2436	ISCStudnet
1908	3/3	Flag Pole	Flag Will Be formally Raised	2435	ISCStudent
1929	1/ 4	Flivvers(Fords)	See: Cars/Collegiate		DM Reg.
1881	7/23	Flood	Story/Boone Co.Kate Shelley)	1636	DMReg.
1891	5/19	Flood	Stop A.& C. R.R	1274	Intell.
1908	6/ 4	Flood	Too Much Rain!	924	Intell. p.1.
1915	9/29	Flood	Rains/High Waters	1190	Times
1915	7/21	Flood	Noyes+ commentary of 1870	2368	Times p.1
1915	5/26	Flood	Rains: creek into rivers	1758	Times/p1
1918	6/ 4	Flood	Story about	335	Times
1944	5/19	Flood	In Ames	1321	Trib. p.1
1944	5/22	Flood	College Creek rampage	1321	Trib p.1
1944	5/20	Flood	Worst in History		Tribune
1944	5/20	Flood	Ames 'Phones cut off'	515	Tribune
1944	5/20	Flood	Ames'Cut Off'	513	Tribune
1948	12/ 7	Flood	4th Ward Control Plan	1779	Tribune p.1
1993	7/13	Flood	James Flansburgs Editorial	1945	D.MReg.p/18A
1993	7/23	Flood	Predicted Hilton to flood	1569	DMReg. 15A
1909	7/ 1	Flood	Heavens Unloaded	1829	Intell. p.1
1916	2/22	Flood	Squaw Creek Overflow	2175	Times p.1
1918	6/ 4	Flood	Property damage	1210	Times p.1
1915	7/21	Flood on Squaw Creek	LaVerne Noyes letter about	2368	Times p.1
1818	11/11	Flu Epidemic	Phone Mgr.Dies	475	Tribune
1918	12/17	Flu Epidemic	6 New cases	482	Times?
1918	9/ 5	Flu Epidemic	Quarantine	407	Times
1918	12/ 7	Flu Epidemic	Boone Lid On	477	Times?
1918	12/ 7	Flu Epidemic	Quarantine again	477	Times?
1918	10/11	Flu Epidemic	Quarantine hits campus	1803	ISC Student p.1
1918	12/ 9	Flu Epidemic	Nevada improves	477	Times?
1918	12/20	Flu Epidemic	Quarantine Lifted	478	Times?
1919	4/15	Flu Epidemic	I.S.C.receives Gov't Thanks	117	Times
1919	1/ 8	Flu Epidemic	Favoritism Question	482	Times?
1986	2/23	Flu Epidemic	Story About	481	DmRegister
1919	10/1	Follies Review	Twin Star	1929	Trib.p.2

1908	3/26	Foot Bridge (Sq. C reek)	Big Crowd Is Walking	2456	Times p.8
1908	2/6	Footb all Game	Camp says: It was our game!	2416	Times p.1
1908	10/28	Footbridge	C.& N.W.Builds	1235	Intelligencer
1908	10/29	Footbridge	C&NW Builds Sq.Cr.Bridge	1382	Intell. p.1
1927	10/11	Footbridge	Squaw Creek	1277	Tribune
1916	2/11	Fort Dodge Line	Large adv. for	2268	Times p. 3
1924	12/ 8	"Fosdick,Harry Emerson"	Speakes at Ames	1878	Trib. p.1
1916	10/31	Fourth Ward Committee	List needs for fourth ward	1209	Tomes p.1
		Fourth Ward	See:West Ames		
1902	10/16	Fourth Ward	Extend electric service to	1862	Intell.
1916	9/13	Fourth Ward	New Homes there	1355	Times p.1
1919	3/28	Fourth Ward	Improves road	1360	Trib. p.1
1921	6/ 6	Fowler, Frank	Dies	157	Times
1919	12/31	Fox B.K.	Sells farm		Trib. p.1
1936	10/29	Fox, Rodney	Joins Staff (ISC)	515	Tribune
1978	5/31	Fox, Rodney	Retires	323	Tribune
1991	12/31	Fox, Rodney	Obituary	1298	Tribune
1991	12/31	Fox, Rodney	Memory of	1296	Tribune p.A3
1992	3/ 6	Fox, Rodney	ISU Gift	1905	Trib.
1992	1/ 4	Fox, Rodney	Bequest to I S U	1297	DMReg.p.5M
1917	2/22	Franchise	People want	1212	Trib. p.1
		Fraternities (List)	In Downtown Ames	1375	Compiled
1995	3/1	Fraternity (Alcohol Free)	First In State?	1937	DM Reg.p/A1
1995	3/16	Fraternity (Alcohol Free)	Refreshing Change	1939	Trib.p.A8
1928	6/25	Fraternity (SAE)	New House	674	Tribune
1949	9/30	Fraternity, History	By:Walter Miller (on Sale)	1816	ISC Studnet p.1
1916	Bomb	Fraternity,Beta Phi	SW Cor.-9th&Douglas	1336	Bomb (1916) p.221
1913	4/14	Frats & Clubs	Moving Day	1176	Times p.1
1919	5/6	Frats (High School)	Get Blow today	2233	Times p.1
1988	7/14	Free Speech	ACLU Attitude		DMRegister
1919	9/26	Frosh Caps	Same Size	740	ISCStudent
1939	10/10	"Frost,Robert"	Talks here	975	Tribune/ p.1
1931	6/4	"Fuhrer, Lynn"	Services Held	2378	ISC Student p.1
1959	4/ 3	G.A.R	Plan to Move monument	1335	Trib.
1915	5/31	G.A.R.	Veterans honored	227	Times
1918	8/24	G.A.R.	40th meeting	1295	Times p.1
1965	7/8	Gaessler, Mrs.Myrtle B.	Death account	2404	Trib.
1965	7/8	Gaessler, Mrs.Myrtle B.	Services set for Mrs. Gaessler	2405	Trib.
1985	3/26	Gaessler, William G. (Bill)	Death reported	2406	Trib.
1985	4/6	Gaessler,William G. (Bill)	Tribute to Bill Gaessler	2404	Trib. p.C5
1989	4/30	Gambling	Cartoon	775	DMReg
1989	7/14	Gambling	Gambling-Bad Call (Editorial)	849	Tribune
1994		Gambling	"Fools Editorial"	1768	D.M.Reg.
1994	3/21	Gambling	Editorial	1754	Trib. p.A8
1996	5/6	Gambling	Study by Iowa State U.	2348	Trib. p.A6
1924	2/18	Gamrath, Lewis	Death account	160	Tribune
1994	5/ 0	Gandhi Quote(Truth)	Ann Landers Col.	1794	DMReg. 2T
1916	12/ 6	Garage, John Allan"	On Douglas(n.of Bank)	1200	Times p.1
1915	9/27	Garden Club	Children's day	334	Times
1915	9/27	Garden Club	Award prizes	315	Times
1915	3/29	Garden Club	103 Children join	41	Times
1915	9/27	Garden Club	awards prizes	106	Times
1917	3/19	Garden Club	Plan meeting	1210	Times p.1
1917	4/21	Garden Club	Meets	497	Times
1918	2/24	Garden Club	Discuss organizing	1985	Trib.
1918	2/21	Garden Club	Organizes	109	Tribune
1918	2/20	Garden Club	noon lunch	1212	Times p.1
1918	2/20	Garden Club	Outline plans	1210	Times p.1
1926	10/18	Garden Club	Dinner	475	Tribune
1928	10/26	Garden Club	New Officers	415	Tribune
1928	5/24	Garden Club	Meet at Formal Gardens	896	Tribune p.3
1929	3/20	Garden Club	5 Meetings	1898	Trib. p.1
1929	7/26	Garden Club	3rd Glad Show held	316	Tribune
1931	7/31	Garden Club	Sponsor Glad Show Aug. 8th	2317	Trib. p.2
1928	9/11	Garden Club,Junior	Zinnia Show	1674	Tribune p.1
1911	4/ 6	Garfield,James R.	Talks at Ag Hall	211	Times
1910	10/27	Garland,Hamlin	Speaks on Campus	370	Tribune
1915	9/24	Garretson & Smith	Large ad	105	Times
1913	3/19	Gas Company	sued	1426	Times p.1
1915	10/22	Gas Company	Lawsuit	334	Times p.1
1919	1/21	Gas Company	Ask city to buy	352	Times
1910	2/9	Gas Company	REORGANIZED	2175	Times p.1
1910		Gas office	At 206 Main St.	902	Times
1909	12/23	Gas Plant	Started Up Here	1946	Intell. p.1
1916	7/29	Gas Plant	New Plant/new Management	257	Times
1916	8/22	Gas Plant	New Start on	474	Times
1933	10/24	Gasahol (Blended Fuel)	Corn product	1392	Trib. p.8
1990	11/28	Gasahol (Ethanol)	Bright Future	979	Tribune
1933	10/24	Gasahol/Alcogas	Blended Fuel	1392	Blended Fuel..Product
1931	6/25	Gearhart,Russell	Rescues 5 from DM River	396	Tribune
1887	2/24	Geddes,James L.	Report of death		Intelligencer
1964	5/26	Gerbrach,Joe	Death of (Note changed spell.)	1193	Tribune
1918	1/17	Gerbrach,Joe	Charges filed/Soper's Court	989	Tribune p.1
1918	1/24	Gerbrach,Joe	To Grand Jury / Assault	988	Tribune p.1
1918	1/17	Gerbrach,Joe	Takes Poke at Man	987	Tribune p.1
1928	4/ 9	Gerbraght ,Wilford	Open new air-port	79	Tribune
1913	4/16	Gerbraght,Fred	Buys Scenic Theater	81	Times
1928	Ju;y 27	Gerbraght,Wilford	1st Pass.Flt.to W.Coast	416	Tribune
1918	10/24	German farmer	Harassed WW I (Kissed the flag)	1321	Times p.1
1917	11/29	German Student	"Hazed" during WW 1	2444	Trib. p. 1
1902	2/6	Ghrist,Drs.D.M.&Jennie	Ad: Office in Budd building	1605	Intell. p.2
1924	6/4	Ghrist,Drs.D.M.&Jennie	Sell practice to Richardson etc.	2284	Trib. p.1
1985	6/24	Gideon's	Editorial	706	DMReg
1904	5/6	Gilbert	Gilbert Station Incorporated	2405	Nevada Watchman
1904	5/6	Gilbert S tation	Incororated by 2 to 1 vote	2413	Nev.Watchman
1917	8/14	Gilbert School	Court Action	404	Times
1917	3/ 6	Gilbert School	Vote Apr.5 on Consolidation		Times
1917	7/ 5	Gilbert School	In Court	633	Tribune
1917	2/ 6	Gilbert School	Consolidation Voted	404	Times
1917	7/ 7	Gilbert School	Court Case	631	Times
1918	9/ 2	Gilbert School	Contract for building	407	Times
1926	3/ 2	Gilbert School	IIn volved in lawsuit	1397	Trib. p.1
1990	4/ 0/34	Gilbert School	In History Photo of Buses	880	Tribune
1986	11/10	Gilman, Henry Prof.	Obit	1796	Tribune
1913	4/14	Girl Athletes	Miss Tilden stages exhibition	2264	Times p.1

1929 6/25/28	Lions Club	Officers/Program	673	Tribune
1989 6/23	Lions Club	New Officers	833	Tribune
1910 3/19	Liquor	Girl & Boy drunk. Boy Expelled	2397	Intelligencer
1988 10/19	Liquor Ads	Ban Them (Letter)	794	Tribune
1928	Liquor banned	within 2 miles of Ames	735	Tribune
1915 8/4	Liquor Foes	Are in town on tour	400	Times
1926 3/22	Liquor Poll	Drys in Ames-Wets State	379	Tribune
1926 3/12	Liquor Poll	Drys ahead	371	Tribune
1913 1/21	Little Brothers	Build new Building	85	Times
1877 5/11	Livery Stable	Ad for	507	Intelligencer
1909 7/29	Livery Stable	Bootleggers	450	Intelligencer
1990 1/9	Livery Stable	Photo of (In History)		Tribune
1912	Livery,Morris,F.E.	Ad for	1667	ISC Directory
1912	Livery,Morris,L	Ad for	1665	ISC Directory
1887 1/26	Livery,Nichol&Maxwell	Add for Horses etc	885	Intelligencer
1876 1/26	Livestock (I.A.C.)	Advertisement	1365	Intell.
1911 8/17	Loclwood Grain Co.	Advertisement	1847	Times p.1
1912 7/10	Log House,Craig	In use now	753	Intelligencer
1905 11/2	London,Jack	Speaks Here	1946	Intell.
1916 9/14	Loop,Street Car	Opens Oct.1	1739	ISCStudent
1918 4/8	Lost Boys	Take Refuge in Empty House	2027	Trib.p.1
1918 4/8	Lost Boys	Gale & Glen Clem locked in ho.	2065	Times p.1
1877 1/26	Lots for Sale	Near Depot'(Blacks Addn.)	2236	Intell. p.2
1989 4/28	Lottery Iowa	Editorial Regarding	755	Triune
1986 2/19	Loud,George	Store next to recent fire	243	Nevada Watchman
1911 8/17	Loughran & Bauer	Advertisement	1852	Times
1914 2/14	Loughran Drug Store	Ad vertisement for	890	Tribune
1898 7/7	Loughran Machine Float	Pic: ID #5.22.3-4	1952	Times p.3
1886 1/21	Loughran,Edmund	Comes to Ames	1218	Intelligencer
1923 11/15	Loughran,Edmund	Pioneer dies	412	VR
1923 4/26	Loughran,Stephen L.	Death account	192	Tribune
1917 10/11	Loughran.Tom	Sells Drug St.to Lowrey	250	Tribune
1885	LoughranFamily	Enumeration	698	Ia.Census
1915 9/6	Lowrey,Joe	Buys Theis Drug Store	314	Times
1925 5/19	Lowrie & Theis Drug	217 Main-Add for	893	Tribune
1928 6/8	Lowrie,The Tailor	Add for	1324	Trib.p.6
1876 1/26	Lucas, Private Banker	Advertisement	1364	Intell.
1949 10/15	Luke,Judge J.Y.	Death account	264	Tribune
1915 12/6	Lumber Co.(Dragoun)	Re:Transfer Co.	1179	Times p.1
1917 2/15	Lumber Company	Spahn & Rose buys yard.	670	Tribune
1991 11/18	Lumber Yard	Schoeneman Closes		Tribune p.C11
1912	Lumber, Citizen's	Advertisement for	1663	ISC Directory
1991 11/18	Lumber, Schoeneman	quit business	1291	Trib.Bus.Times
1924 3/27	MacDonald, G.B.	Slaps back	158	Tribune
1934 12/22	MacDonald, Tom	H onored	2379	Trib. p.1-2
1976	MacDonald, Tom	U.S.D.O.T. (Tom MacDonald)	1599	D.O.T. Pub.
1919 7/7	MacDonald, Tom	with U.S.Roads	2234	Tribune p.1
1928 12/6	Macy,Ted	Death account	414	Tribune
1915 7/28	Madison,Walter G.	Writes re.Uncle Tom's Cabin	176	Times p.5
1917 8/30	Madison,Walter G.	30 Negroe Soldiers Dined	935	Tribune p.1
1917 6/1	Madison,Walter G.	Add for		Times
1918 12/23	Madison,Walter G.	Visits Texas	563	Times
1922 2/24	Madison,Walter G.	sues restaurnt	238	Tribune
1923 4/5	Madison,Walter G.	Street Sewer contract	270	Tribune
1923 1/19	Madison,Walter G.	Court award $100.	238	Court records
1928 9/21	Mail Delivery	In Early Day	1674	Tribune p.1
1910 10/13	Main Street	New Lights on Main Street	904	Times
1930 2/15	Main Street	Bosworth sold to Dixon Drug	1324	Trib. p.1
1924 10/6	Main Street	Will close for Festival Parade	2	Tribune p.1
1919 2/5	Maniufacturing	Company Makes silos	59	Tribune
1946 3/19	Manning,Hollis	ends term as Mayor	162	Tribune
	Manufacture	See: Tilden Mfg.		
	Manufacture	See:Barbed Wire		
	Manufacture	See Bottling Company		
	Manufacture	See: Silo		
	Manufacture	See: Allexander		
	Manufacture	See: Ice Cream		
	Manufacture	See Tilden Mfg Co.		
	Manufacture	See: Pop		
	Manufacture	See: Collegiate		
1919 9/26	Manufacture	Olson's Drawing Instrument	388	Tribune
	Manufacturie	See Canning Factory		
1963 1/14	Margerine Fight	Begins	863	Tribune
1898 6/16	Marston Water Tower	Marston Describes h is w .tower	2460	Times p.1
1988 3/0	Marston Water Tower	Restored	466	Iowa Stater
1932 6/3	Marston, Dean Anson	Retires	396	Tribune
1949 10/22	Marston, Dean Anson	Killed in Accident	1816	ISC Student p.1
1919 4/14	Martin, A.J.	Comes to Ames Bank	59	Tribune
1949 1/19	Martin, Fred	Student Body President	1779	Tribune/Web p.
1912 12/18	Martin, Gus	Starts store	1900	Intell. p.1
1913 2/5	Martin, Gus	opens new store	85	Times
1913 2/8	Martin, Gus	New Store ad	86	Times
1926 10/7	Martin, Gus	Bankruptcy	438	Tribune
1926 10/27	Martin, Gus	Bankruptcy	438	Tribune
1919 4/4	Martin, Henry	Cashier of Bank	383	Times
1915 12/9	Mary Greeley Hospital	Bids to be received	78	Times
1915 12/20	Mary Greeley Hospital	Bids Opened	1743	Times p.1
1915 7/23	Mary Greeley Hospital	Plan announced	76	Tribune
1916 9/26	Mary Greeley Hospital	K.Diehl Hires	701	Times
1916 12/28	Mary Greeley Hospital	Now Open	670	Tribune
1916 9/26	Mary Greeley Hospital	Miss Diehl arrives	662	Times
1964 9/5	Mary Greeley Hospital	Story about	280	Tribune (Cen.Ed.)
1915 12/19	Masonic Building	$75M Cost	494	Times
1916 4/6	Masonic Building	To Be Errected This Summer	2180	Times p.1
1916 7/16	Masonic Building	Contract to build	279	Times
1897	Masonic Lodge	Early History of	1337	Intell.Souvenir
1913 10/12	Masonic Lodge	purchase Brooks House	83	Times
1915 4/29	Masonic Lodge	Announce new building	78	Times
1915 4/28	Masonic Lodge	About new Lodge Bldg.	45	Times
1915 6/18	Masonic Lodge	Building plans	235	Times
1915 7/21	Masonic Lodge	Plan Big Event	2237	Times p.1
1915 7/23	Masonic Lodge	Clears Lot for Bldg	376	Times
1915 6/18	Masonic Lodge	Discuss Bldg. Plans	244	Times
1917 4/19	Masonic Lodge	Meet/ New quarters	2237	Times p.1
1917 3/7	Masonic Lodge	Meetin new quarters		Times
1917 4/17	Masonic Lodge	Ded.new quarters	497	Times

1924 6/12	Masonic Lodge	DeMolay Meet here	2199	Trib.p.1
1924 5/31	Masonic Lodge	De Molays Chartered here	2355	Trib.p.1
1915 8/2	Maxwell Car	Ad for	505	Tribune
1931 8/31	Maxwell, A.B.	Keeps City Records	2297	Trib. p.1
1924 7/29	Maxwell, Geo.Henry	his birthday	3	Tribune p.1.
1924 12/8	Maxwell, Geo.Henry	"Death: Dec.4,1924"	985	Tribune p.1
1908 10/8	May,Henry	First Teacher	1383	Intell. p.1
1916 10/14	May,Henry	recalls Ames History	1005	Times p.7
1908 4/30	May,Henry	Golden Wedding	923	Intelligencer
1908 10/8	May,Henry	79th Birthday	924	Intell. p.1
1908 4/30	May,Henry	Golden Wedding	924	Intell p.4
1916 10/14	May,Henry	Recalls Ames History	1005	Tomes p.7
1919 5/16	May,Henry	Obituary	58	Tribune
1919 5/16	May,Henry	1st Teacher dies	384	Times
1984 12/15	May,Henry	Cemetary Stone	358	Tribune
1966 12/5	Mayor Newbrough	Visits Ecuadore (sister city)	2362	Trib. p.1
1916 3/30	Mayor Baker	Elected over Sheldon	932	Tribunne p.1.
1898 3/31	Mayor Cramer	Elected	450	Intelligencer
	Mayor List		398	
1916 12/14	Mayor, Ames' 1st	visits here	1387	
1916 12/12	Mayor, First	Visits here	1196	Times p.1
1923 5/29	Mayser Controversary	Mayor Rice quoted	167	Register
1923 5/29	Mayser Controversary	Mayor backs Mayser	167	Register
1923 5/26	Mayser Controversary	Pearson calls for change	167	Register
1923 5/28	Mayser controversary	Special Edition	177	Iowa State Student
1923 6/6	Mayser controversary	Mayser resigns	168	Iowa State Student
1923 6/1	Mayser Controversy	'A'Club Report	177	Iowa State Student
1923 5/30	Mayser Controversy	Majority Report	177	Iowa State Student
1923 5/28	Mayser Controversy	Protest to Pearson	510	Dm.Register
1923 6/5	Mayser Resigns	Athletic Director @ ISC	1418	Tribune.p.1
1908 4/30	McCarthy, Dan	Golden Wedding	923	Intelligencer
1921 9/28	McCarthy, Dan	Death records	247	Court Records
1923 12/17	McCarthy,Hank	Death account	250	Tribune
1877 3/11	McCarthy,Stevens&Underwood	Add for Atty.s	506	Intlligencer
1898 3/17	McClain, F.T.	buys farm	1324	Intell.
1916 1/5	McCoy, Arthur (Art)	Son is abroad	565	Times
1916 8/2	McCoy, Arthur (Art)	Flushes Water Main	474	Times
1938 1/21	McCoy, Arthur (Art)	Vol.Fireman dies	262	Tribune
1924 5/27	McFadden, Alfred	Editor of the Intelligencer	2341	Trib.p.4
1962 1/31	McFarland Clinic	Start building at 12th & Douglas	2442	Trib. p.1
1941 10/31	McGriff, Sheriff	Slain	1273	DesM.Trib
1919 2/18	Mclain, Howard	dies	353	Times
1923 12/11	McLain,Willis	Death account	409	Tribune
	McNally, Mary	Article about	1653	Tribune
1912	Meat Market, Gamrath	Ad for	1667	ISC Directory
1918 12/23	Medical Assoc.	Meet at Hospital	564	Times
1896 9/10	Medical Clinic	Ad:Ames Visit	1887	Times p.1
1896 9/10	Medical Clinic	Advertisement	1887	Times p.1
1896 9/10	Medical Clinic	At Davis House	1887	Times p.1
1915 9/6	Medicine Man	Patent Medicine Show here	2413	Times p.3
1909 2/18	Meeker Case	Settled	1932	Times p.1
1909 2/19	Meeker, Mrs. Carol	Divorce granted	659	Times
1909 2/18	Meeker, Mrs. Carol	Awarded Alimony	486	Times
1913 5/21	Memorial Day	Program set	1384	Times p.1
1919 5/15	Memorial Day	Observed in Ames	267	Times
1981 5/23	Memorial Day	Program	557	Tribune
1915 7/2	Memorial Elm Tree	"old Abe near Cath.Church"	244	Times
1911 11/9	Men & Religion	92 members meet	1380	Intell. p.1
1911 11/9	Men & Religion	Commitee of 100	1362	Intell. p.1
1902 3/13	Men's Reformatory	To be at Animosa, Iowa	1978	Intell. p.1
1911 11/9	Men's Movement	Church Plans	1380	Intell. p.1
1908 12/10	Men's Revival Meeting	Sunday afternoon large crowd	1549	Intell.
1877 5/11	Meredith,G.A. (M.D.)	Ad for Doctor	506	Intelligencer
1935 6/12	Miles,Dr.W.B.	Visits here	1366	Trib.p.2
1986 8/27	Milestones / Ames	History Sketch	460	Advertiser
1898 9/25	Miliinery Shop	Advertisement	1318	Intell. p.1
1924 7/9	Milk	for School Children	1874	Trib. p.1
1928 9/29	Mill,Hannum's	Article about	224	Times
1912	Mill,Lanning's	Ad for	1664	ISC Directory
1898 8/11	Millinery Shop	Cups buys stock	1772	Intell. p.4
1912	Millinery, Pikes	Ad for	1664	ISC Dirfectory
	Mine	See: COAL MINE DISASTER		
1921 3/9	Mine	Coal SW of Gilbert	408	Times
1920 9/27	Minert,H,L.	Purchase Plane	77	Times
1959	Minerva (Statue)	Ends up at SAE Fraternity	2437	Trib.
1989 4/24	Minors in Bars	Protest group	778	Tribune
1989 4/13	Minors in Bars	Letter objecting	779	Tribune
1989 4/5	Minors in Bars	Letters/Editor	782	Tribune
1989 4/13	Minors in bars	Student Advocate	779	Tribune
1899 12/14	Minstral Show	Sheperd's Famous Show	1907	Times p.4
1897 2/11	Minstrel Show	Minstrels are coming (Tent)	2395	Times p.2
1916 6/2	Minstrel Show	Busby's Colored Minstrel Show	2457	Times p.2
1924 1/4	Minstrel Show	Ames High Prepares	1514	Tribn. p.1
1927 2/4	Minstrel Show	Engineering Profs. put on	2293	Trib. p.4
1905 5/18	Minstrel show	at Opera House	1275	Times/ pers.Paragraphs
1919 9/26	Moberly,Della	Tribute to teacher	388	Tribune
1909 1/6	Mono Clan	4th Anniversary	710	Intelligencer
1911 8/17	Mono Clan	Chautauqua Hop	1855	Times
1913 2/12	Mono Clan	Have guest nite	73	Times
1916 4/15	Mono Clan	Annual Banquet	2169	Times p.1
1919 2/10	Mono Clan	Newly-weds entertained	410	Tribune
	Moore Dairy	New Bldg.	1320	
1925 8/1	Moose Lodge	Speakers in Churches	1417	Tribune p.1
1890 8/7	Morrill Hall	Under construction	543	Intelligencer
1890 8/7	Morrill Hall	Built new	2178	
1996 2/7	Morrill Hall	Uncertain future	2186	IS Daily p.1
1913 2/10	Morrill,Justin S.	1890 Letters to Stanton	87	Times
1908 5/28	Morris Livery	Bus & Baggage Line	907	Times
1916 4/4	Morris Livery	Lynn M. Plans New Bldg.	932	Tribune p.1.
1908 5/21	Mosher, M.L.	To Mexico	907	Times
1919 7/31	Motor Convoy	(with Eisenhour)	660	Boone Paper
1922 5/26	Movie star	Fatty Arbuckle is censored	1899	Trib. p.1
1915 9/22	Movie Actress	Visits Ames	487	Times

1910 3/17	Paving Main Street	Cost figure	1700	Times p.1
1911 6/29	Paving (a new tack)	Attorney investigates	213	Times
1916 11/21	Paving (Ames)	Stops for Winter	1209	Times p.1
1913 11/10	Paving / Campus	Completed ($1.06 per yd.)	1206	Times p.1
1910 8/18	Paving / Main Street	Wood blocks arrive	1672	Intell. p.1
1911 2/16	Paving controversy	Articles about		Times
1911 3/ 9	Paving Grand Ave	Council postpones	209	Times
1911 6/15	Paving Grand Ave	Block Paving selected	213	Times
1916 1/21	Paving Project	Begins May 1, 1916	557	Times
1916 2/17	Paving Project	Controversy		Tribune
1916 1/ 5	Paving Project	Lincoln way plan	565	Times
1911 10/26	Paving Qiuestion	Amended Law	300	Times
1915 12/29	Paving Streets	Big Project	1181	Times p.1
1923 6/16	Paving-Block	Big Problems	504	Tribune
1924 3/ 3	Peabody	For State Senate	1909	Trib p.1
1926 12/12	Pearson's succcessor	selected soon	393	Tribune
1913 2/24	Pearson,Pres.R.M.	Invites Bus.Men	1277	Times p.1
1926 11/13	Pearson,Pres.R.M.	Final Report	1422	Trib. p.1
1923 5/28	Pearson,Pres.R.M.	Students Defy	510	Dm.Register
1926 8/ 5	Pearson,Pres.R.M.	Article about	394	Tribune
1911 2/23	Penfield,E.J.	Wrecks Kelley Bank	1960	Intell. p.1
1911 2/23	Penfield,E.J.	Skips bank	66	Times
1911 2/23	Penfield,E.J.	Kelly Bank loss	64	Tribune
1912 5/27	Penitentiary for Ames	Committee proposed	1900	Intell. p.1
1929 5/29	Penney, J.C. Store	Moves	1928	Milepost p.14
1912	Photographer,Quade	Ad for	1667	ISC Directory
1987 8/29	Photographs(FTB)	To Library	478	Tribune
1870	Physicians	Census List of	417	USCensus
1909 7/ 8	Pickpockets	on street cars	659	Times
1917 9/ 6	Pickpockets	released	1406	Trib.
1917 9/ 6	Pickpockets, circus	Get Hoyer's purse	1406	Trib.
1931 8/15	Picnic, Huxley	Piicnic to be Aug 19th	2316	Trub. p.1
1898 7/7	Picnic Party in woods	Pic: ID#174.972.3	1952	Times p.3
1928 9/ 4	Picnic, Gilbert	700 at Hutchison's Pond	1901	Trib.p.4
1929 8/22	Picnic, Huxley	200 attend	2299	Trib.p.1
1928 9/10	Picnic, Zenorsville	300 there	1902	Trib.p.4
1928 9/29	Pioneers/Trails	Jubilee Story	1674	Tribune p.1
	Pipe Organ	See: Church, Presbyterian		
	Pipe Organ	See: Church, Methodist		
1936 107	Pipe Organ	Given to M.Union	2242	Trib. p.1 + 16
1925 6/26	Playground Program	Tournament Events	893	Tribune
1925 6/ 6	Playground Program	Winners Announced	920	TribunePg.6
1930 5/28	Playground program	C.S .Roberts	1435	Trib.
1996 5/15	Police Department	Celebrate 100 year mark	2346	Trib. p.A3
1919 10/1	Police Chief	Knocks Janitor out of chair!	2177	Trib. p.1
1919 4/ 7	Police Chief	Fired	1360	Trib. p.1
1916 5/ 3	Police Department	Willey new Chief	225	Times
1955 11/19	Police Dept.	Remodel basement for	1273	Trib.
1919 4/ 9	Pool Hall	Knocked Out	1360	Trib. p.1
1919 2/10	Pool Hall	Petition denied	1359	Trib p.1
1919 4/ 8	Pool Hall	Council says 'no'	782	Times
1919 4/ 8	Pool Hall Question	1300 Oppose.	380	Times
1919 3/25	Pool Hall Question	K.W.Brown / G.B.MacDonald	380	Times
1919 3/25	Pool Hall Question	Letters about	536	Times
1915 8/ 5	Pop Corn Man	Weather Hurts	176	Times
1958 8/12	Pop Corn Wagon	Ben Young Dies	892	Tribune
1908 8/27	Pop Factory	Tipton Plant to Ames	381	Intelligencer
1908 8/27	Pop plant	Installed here	32	
1916 11/11	Popcorn Wagon	G.H.Carlton robbed	1209	Times p.1
1938 10/18	Popcorn Wagon	City Council Bans from streets.	901	Tribune
1877 8/17	Pope, Prof.	New House -Bartlett, Architect	2241	Intell.p.3
Various	Population	1870 thru 1930	496	
1877 6/29	Post Office	Dead Letter Rule	557	Intelligencer
1911 5/18	Post Office	Work starts soon on new bldg.	213	Times
1911 10/ 5	Post Office	Lay cornerstone	52	Times
1910 12/10	Post office	now for new hotel!	230	Times
1908 12/10	Post Office(Fed.Bldg.)	Site selected	1267	Intell. p.1
1939 9/26	Pottery/Ames	Ad for	1374	Trib..p.4
1916 9/27	Practice House	(1203 Kellogg)	661	Times
1908 3/12	Prairie Fire	A Prairie F ire In An Early Day	2416	Intell p.1
1898 8/11	Prank (College Boys)	freight cars down grade	1772	Intell. p.4
1949 11/30	Prank - Dead Horse	"Horse Still Dead"	2373	ISC Daily p.1
1986 3/25	Prayer in schools	Article about	706	Tribune
1988 3/ 4	Preservation Ordinance	Ordiinance (new)	588	Tribune
1988 3/ 4	Preservation Ordinance	Debate about	589	Tribune
1988 2/26	Preservation Ordinance	Opposition	586	Tribune
1988 3/ 9	Preservation Ordinance.	Passes		Tribune
	President	See Clinton,Pres. Bill		
	President	See name of U.S. President.		
1981 3/ 0	President Reagan	here in 1958	373	Iowa Stater
1981 3/ 0	President Eisenhower	Here in 1952	373	Iowa Stater
1981 3/ 0	President Ford	Here in 1976	373	Iowa Stater
1923 8/ 6	President Harding	Funeral Train here		Tribune
1913 4/5	President Hoover	Speaks in Ames	270	Tribune
1981 3/ 0	President J.Carter	here in 1975	373	Iowa Stater
1924 2/4	President of U.S.	His Uncle Founder I.S.C..	2341	Trib. p.1
1981 3/ 0	President Truman	Veishea Torch 1950	373	Iowa Stater
Various	Presidents	See:Taft-Roosevelt-McKinley		
1911 11/ 9	Princes Theater	Near completion.	35	Times
1913 8/15	Prison Labor	Campus Road Work	1172	Times p.1
1913 11/19	Prison Labor	Parolees camp here	230	Times
1900 9/ 6	Prohibition	Temperance Day	354	Times
1906 9/20	Prohibition	State Meet at Ames	1427	Intell.
1909 4/ 1	Prohibition	Cambridge lid on.	36	Times
1914 12/25	Prohibition	Carpenters endorse	975	Times p.1
1914 8/12	Prohibition	State Camp DRY	1203	Times p.1
1915 2/19/15	Prohibition	Clarson Bill/Ia dry Jan 1st	235	Times
1915 8/4	Prohibition	Liquor Foes stop here.	2399	Timea
1916 1/10	Prohibition	No Booze in Ames	557	Times
1916 1/10	Prohibition	No Booze in Ames	1274	Times p.1
1916 6/16	Prohibition	High Cost to drink	1356	Times p.1
1916 7/13	Prohibition	Ia. Democrats declare in favor	2409	Times p.1
1916 8/24	Prohibition	Attitude of Politicians	1005	Times p.1.
1917 10/ 4	Prohibition	"Vote Dry Oct 15th"	380	Times
1917 10/ 9	Prohibition	A War Issue	919	Times p.2
1917 2/26	Prohibition	Ames nearly dry	1355	Times p.1
1918 9/ 7	Prohibition	War Measure	1872	Times p.1
1919 5/15	Prohibition	Starts July 1 - History	267	

1919 1/16	Prohibition	Nebr. ratifies 18th Amendment	352	Times
1923 3/ 6	Prohibition	Liver deaths down 12%	192	Tribune
1926 3/22	Prohibition	Poll Closes	512	Tribune
1930 6/27	Prohibition	Forces realigned	897	Tribune
1930 1/23	Prohibition	Women support	252	Tribune
1932 6/ 9	Prohibition	Mott/Rockerfeller/McAdoo	396	Tribune
1937 1/ 9	Prohibition	Gov.Turner Upholds	1224	Tribune
1919 1/15	Prohibition In Iowa	42 to 7 In Senate	782	Times
1928 10/ 6	Prohibition Law	Hoover's Talk about	817	Tribune
1926 3/ 8	Prohibition Poll	700 Papers involved	299	Tribune
1906 9/20	Prohibitionists	Met in Ames	1427	Intelligencer
1924 12/ 8	Prowler / Gunshot	At Tilden Home	1877	Tribune p.1
1921 6/17	Puritan Restaurant	Ad for	115	Tribune
1926 10/26	Puritan Restaurant	Pulos to Smith	438	Tribune
1909 9/16	Push Ball	First Look At	925	Times
1917 9/22	Push Ball	Man Injured	918	Times p.1
1916 6/29	Quade Music Store	Opens in Sheldon-Munn	932	Tribune
1905 (Dir.)	Quade,C.R.	Ad for	457	ISCDirectory
1908 10/ 8	Quade,C.R.	Quits Counter	34	Times
1916 10/14	Quade,C.R.	Ad for Edison Shop	1191	Times p/7
1925 8/12	Quade,C.R.	Add for Edison	525	Tribune
1928 12/12	Quade,Mrs C.R.	Death account	414	Tribune
1910 12/ 8	Quick,Herbert	Speaks at ISC	462	Times
1881ca	Quotation,Famous	"what we learn from history"	1221	Phil of Hist.
1994 1/24	Quotation,Famous	That "good men do nothing"	1221	DesM.Reg.
1926 11/27	R.R.Accident	Crossing Injuries	421	Tribune
1936 9/23	R.R.Crossing Job	carried over 1937	2242	Trib . p.1
1911 8/ 3	R.R.Time Card	Ames vs DesMoines	1378	Intell. p.1
1915 12/ 6	Race across Iowa	Car Trouble	1179	Times p.1
1915 12/10	Racers	Fail to hit mark	1753	Times p.1.
1914 7/6	Racers, Sioux City	Pass through Ames	2434	Times p.1
1923 2/21	Rachmaninoff,Sergei	Appears here	2151	Trib. p.1
1938 11/15	Rachmaninoff,Sergei	3,500 hear him plan (State Gym)	1591	Trib.p.2
1938 11/12	Rachmaninoff,Sergei	Appears here Monday 11/14)	1574	Trib. p.1
1915 12/ 6	Racing Car	Behind time	1359	Times p.1
	Radio	SEE: Wireless		
1930 1/18	Radio (Amateur Stations)	Operate Here	2232	Trib.
1922 5/18	Radio Station WOI	Begins broadcasting	190	Tribune
1917 4/20	Radio Stations	Closed by USGov't	497	Times
1905 6/23	Railroad	Time Cards	1757	Intell . p.4
1908 12/24	Railroad	Fight on Train	1267	Intell. p.1
1877 7/13	Railroad (Narrow Gauge)	Extend to North of Ames	544	Intelligencer
1877 7/27	Railroad (Narrow Gauge)	Extend N. of Ames	2244	Intell. p.3
1911 8/3	Railroad Time Card	Study- Ames Rec.	1378	Intell.
1916 8/23	Railroad Train	Special: Lousiana to Iowa State	2258	Times
1877 7/27	Railroad(Narrow Gauge)	Begin Survey	558	Intelligencer
1877 1/26	Railroad, Narrow Gauge	DesMoines & Minnesota	2247	Intell. p.4
1988 3/ 2	Railroads in Iowa	Geo.Mills Story	791	DMReg
1877 5/11	Rainbolt & Barnes	Ad for Atty.s	506	Intelligencer
1921 8/13	Ray School Picnic	Reorganize - have picnic	2282	Trib. p.3
1927 6/ 0	Ray School Picnic	News items about		Tribune
1924 7/30	Read's Barn	Being Torn Down	391	Tribune
1908 11/ 5	Read,Benedict	Obituary		Intelligencer
1908 10/29	Read,Benedict	Death Occurs	862	?
1958 5/16	Reagan, Ronald	Speaker at Veisheathon	2432	Trib. p.1
1981 3/ 0	Reagan, Ronald	On Campus / Ames	373	IowaStater
1911 11/ 9	Rebekah Lodge	To Webster City Meet	1381	Intell. p.1
1925 6/26	Recreation,Summer	See:Playground Program		Trib. p.1
1924 7/30	Reed's Barn	Torn down	1417	Tribune p.1
	Referendum	See: Underpass (Gr.Ave.)		
	Referendum	See: School Bond Issue.		
1869 12/18	Referendum	Vote to Incorporate Ames		P.Record
1893 12/31	Referendum	Viote to Annex Campus etc.		P.Record
1913 2/12	Referendum	Vote to relocate light plant		P.Record
1915 4/28	Referendum	Vote new City Hall		P.Record
1920 3/11	Referendum	Vote L.Way bridge bonds		P.Record
1926 3/30	Referendum	Vote -no+ on Swimming pool.		P.Record
1930 3/11	Referendum	School Bonds Approved	1324	Trib . p.1
1936 11/3	Referendum	Transfer funds for Underpass		P.Record
1937 3/8	Referendum	Yes H.School 5th & Clark		P.Record
1937 3/8	Referendum	No H.School @ 13th & Grand		P.Record
1951 8/28	Referendum	Nix Gunder Golf Course.	1274	Tribune p.1
1967 11/7	Referendum	Vote $207 M for Golf Course		P.Record
	Referendum	See: Lincoln Way Bridge.		
1987 7/ 4	Religion	and Politics		DmReg.
1995 7/27	Religion	Returns	2007	Dick.N.D .Press
1911 9/28	Religion and Men	Movement Starts	1941	Times p.1
1958 1/18	Religion in Life	Week on Campus	1697	ISStudent
1905 12/19	Rescue, Crossing	Girl rescued at crossing	1358	Times p.1
1907 2/21	Rescue, Depot	By Bill Thompson	1896	Times p.1
1931 6/ 2	Rescue, DMRiver	See:Gearhart,Russell	396	Trib.
1925 6/ 2	Rescue/Sand Pit	See:Darner,Edward	284	Trib.
1918 4/ 1	Restaurant	Rogers Opens	414	1918 Apr 5
1988 12/17	Restaurants-Ames	List/Ratings	793	Tribune
	Reunion	See: Zenorsville		
	Reunion	See: School Name		
1919 6/ 7	Reynolds,Dorothy	fell from window	384	Times
1926 10/11	Rhodes,Billy	Hurt by Car	438	Tribune
1924	Rice Bldg./Younkers	Built 1924	1761	City Rec.
1933 10/30	Rice, Dr.Earl	Death occurs	1372	Trib. p.1
1920 3/30	Rice, Tom	Elected over Sheldon	394	Tribune
1921 7/19	Rice, Tom	Row at Knoll	147	Tribune
1922 3/28	Rice, Tom	Reelected Mayor	146	Tribune
1941 11/18	Rice, Tom	Gets load of oats in front yard!	1511	Tribune p.1
1947 6/ 6	Rice, Tom	Former Mayor dies	157	Tribune
1941 12/18	Rice, Tom	Oats upset on yard	1837	Tribune p.1
1950 10/16	Richardson,Geo.	Death report	1803	Tribune
1913 3/19	Richmond,Dr.Albert	Death of	207	Times
1913 3/26	Richmond,Dr.Albert	Obituary	73	Times
1914 10/14	Ricketts'Hotel	Full to capacity	39	Times
1910 9/15	Ricketts,Bill	Carries suit case for chorus girl	902	Times p.1
1915 2/ 4	Ricketts,Bill	Gus Martins charges Marshall	78	Times
1922 9/16	Ricketts,Bill	Sheriff dies at Nevada	238	Tribune
1923 6/ 9	Ridgewood 2nd Add.	Plat	1337	Co.Record
1916 9/30	Ridgewood Addition	Many signers	1208	Times p.4
1916 10/17	Ridgewood Addition	Sold out now	1208	Times p.1
1992 5/ 5	Riot	Veishea/Alcohol	1401	ISUDaily
1909 10/ 9	Riot, Students	Excursion Day Excitement	1835	Times p.8

1993	12/20	Skudder's Store	Money-Trolley		DMReg.
1919	7/24	Skunk River Project	Dredging Plans	633	Tribune
1921	5/10	Skunk River Bridge	Replaced	382	Tribune
1893	10/ 5	Skunk River Ditch	Letting Notice	2000	Cambridge Press
1919	6/ 4	Skunk River Project	Drain Dust.#4 (Straightening)	782	County Record
1919	7/24	Skunk River Project	Hearing (straightening project)	734	Intelligencer
1919	2/24	Skunk River Project	Drainage District	782	County Record
1924	1/25	Slogan	"Ames Advertises Ames"		Tribune
1979	12/13	Sloss, Margaret	Obituary		Trib. p.16
1908	2/6	Small Towns	Death of Small Towns	2421	Times p.4
1994	1/ 3	Smedal,Olav	Memory of	1693	Tribune
		Smith,M.K.	Laura West his widow	862	Cem.Rec.
1915	5/17	Smith,M.K.	Death Occurs	862	Cem.Rec.
1925	5/31	Smith,M.K.	Obituary	76	Tribune
1892	4/28	Smith,Mrs.Laura (M.K.)	her death(Dau. of 1st Mayor)	1654	Intell.
1913	4/19	Smoking on Campus	Ban Voted		ISC Student
1913	4/16	Smoking on Campus	Student Poll	1657	Card.Guild Notice
1913	4/24	Smoking on Campus	Students against weed	1700	Intell. p.1
1913	4/12	Smoking on Campus	set referendum date	1757	ISCStudent p.4
1913	4/15	Smoking on Campus	Beckman Quoted	1791	ISCStudent p.1
1913	4/15	Smoking on Campus	Dean Stanton Talks	1791	ISCStudent p.1
1916	4/18	Smoking on Campus	Pearson's Notice bannimg	1656	Card Notice
1921	1/20	Smoking on Campus	Free Cigarette wrong	1839	Tribune p.1
1992	3/13	Smoking on Campus	To Hook Young	1327	DMReg.
1995	3/16	Smoking Sickness	Editorial	1943	Trib.Ed.p.
1931	2/23	Smoking Women	Criticised:Pres Hughes	1757	Trib.
1913	4/14	Smoking,Students Vote	Will hold ISC Vote	1176	Times p.1
1917	12/ 6	Snook, Neta	Join Curtiss Club	1268	Trib. p.1
1919	3/ 3	Snook, Neta	Gov't Priviledge	1360	Trib. p.1
1919	9/18	Snook, Neta	Mmember Aero Club of Ia.	2021	Trib. p.1
1919	8/29	Snook, Neta	Accident at Manson,Ia.	132	Tribune
1920	6/ 7	Snook, Neta	Ad in ISC Daily	2026	ISCDaily p.2
1920	5/15	Snook, Neta	Smashes Plane	2018	Trib. p.1
1920	6/3	Snook, Neta	Bombs Campus	2209	ISC Student p.1
1922	5/18	Snook, Neta	Marries Wm.Southern	190	Tribune
1990	3/ 6	Snook, Neta	With Plane(IN History)	880	Tribune
1920	5/5	Snook, Neta	Not afraid	2018	Trib. p.1
1942	1/ 2	Snow Storm	Ames Digs Out	1795	Tribune
1908	8/6	Social Life	Schedule for	1932	Times p.6
		Social Life (See:Tango)	Also See: Shimmy		
1917	2/24	Soldiers W W I	Fed by Ames ladies	1985	Trib.
1917	9/27	Soldiers W W I	Women enjoy feeding	1985	Trib.
1906	7/12	Soper's Mill	Remembering Old Soper+s Mill	2071	Times p.6
1920	9/27	Sousa's Band	To Appear on Artist Series Here	2252	ISC Student
1929	6/28	Spring Lake Park	Fire Works - 4th of July	891	Tribune
1995	1/20	Squaw Creek	Letter about	1958	Letter
1908	4/23	Squaw Creek Bridge	Cement Bridge Over Squaw	2415	Times p.1
1908	12/31	Squaw Creek Bridge	Fine Structure Now Completed	2415	Times p.1
1918	7/ 1	Squaw Creek Bridge	Collapsed	79	Tribune
1918	6/29	Squaw Creek Bridge	Question up	51	Times
1920	4/15	Squaw Creek Bridge	up to Board now	148	
1920	3/ 6	Squaw Creek Bridge	Bond Issue Editorial	148	
1920	3/10	Squaw Creek Bridge	Editorial about	148	
1920	4/20	Squaw Creek Bridge	Car in Creek	1741	ISCStudent
1920	3/11	Squaw Creek Bridge	Bond Issue Carries	148	
1920	4/ 2	Squaw Creek Bridge	Car off Bridge 1 dead	148	
1920	3/ 4	Squaw Creek Bridge	Editorial/Bd. of Control	148	
1920	1/19	Squaw Creek Bridge	City / Club helps promote vote	1382	Times p.1
1921	5/ 7	Squaw Creek Bridge	Now Open	382	Tribune
1958	4/ 4	Squaw Creek Bridge	Widening	1335	Trib. p.1
1910	3/17	St Patrick's Day	On Campus	1700	Timesd p.3
1911	3/16	St.Patrick's Day	Parade		Intelligencer
1915	2/22	Stafford, H.W.	Elected President of Bank	41	Times
1941	8/16	Stage Coach Road	Named by Boy Scouts	2068	Tribune p.1
1914	1/23	Stage Driver	Recalls Ames History	977	Times p.1
1914	1/21	Stage Driver	Recalls Ames History	977	Times p.1
1909	6/17	Stalker, Dr. Millikan	Obituary (Vet College Pioneer)	48	Times
1898	1/13	Stanley,George	Wants pardon Murder E.of Ames		Intelligencer
1899	11/ 2	Stanton Memorial	Dedication	400	Times
1911	9/ 7	Stanton,Dean Edgar	Advises stay out of Boone	1372	Intell. p.1
1982	2/20	Stanton,Dean Edgar	Feature	63	Tribune
1017	10/6	Star, Rose	Death reported		Times
1920	4/23	State Park	Club seeks state park here	1322	Trib. p.1
1920	4/22	State Park	Ames Can Have	1322	Trib. p.1
1920	4/22	State Park	Proposed at Sunset Rock	394	Tribune
1913	7/26	State Prison Camp	Inmates work College roads	229	Times
1916	6/16	Steffey A.J.	Prin.Ames High	325	Board Minutes
1918	4/15	Stevens, Rowena	Death of	2012	Trib. p.1
1925	6/15	Stevens,Judge	In court over Oil Station	237	Tribune
1877	9/28	Stickney & Taylor	Ad: Better Goods, Better Prices	313	Intelligencer
1893	3/ 9	Store,Bigelow & Smith	Ad for	1200	Times p.2
1912		Store,Briley's	Ad for	1662	ISC Directory
1912		Store,Champlin's	Ad for	1666	ISC Directory
1916	12/ 7	Store,Woolworth	Opens here	1196	Times p.1
1933	10/24	Stores	Adopt 48 hour week	1392	Trib.p.8
1944	5/19	Storm	Damages	1313	Trib.
1909	3/ 0	Storm, Big	Wake of	1758	Times p.1.
1919	5/ 5	Storms,Dr.A.B.	Talks in Ames	293	Times
		Story City	History of		S.C.Herald
1917	4/ 4	Story City	Misses Chinese Laundryman	399	Times
1923	8/29	Story City	Butter Tub Factory	503	Tribune
1929	8/17	Story City	See:Tenor	1270	Trib p.1
1928	9/29	Story County	History / Jubilee (Clip p.1694 &	1696	Tribune p.1
1940		Story County	History of	375	Ia Press Assoc
1877	7/27	Story County	Described	2244	Intell.p.3
1893	1/ 5	Story County Bank	Picture of	1254	Intelligencer
1917	6/ 7	Story County Bank	Sheldon reorganizes	379	Times
1905	5/18	Street Car Company	Electric Cars maybe?	1275	Times
1911	12/ 2	Street Car Company	Build Station House	213	Intelligencer
1915	6/25	Street Car Company	Loop planned	288	Times
1929	7/ 2	Street Car Company	Discontinue Running	786	Tribune
1913	11/ 7	Street Car Loop	Run to Knapp St.	1205	Times p.1
1916	10/19	Street Car Loop	First car around	176	Tribune
1916	10/19	Street Car Loop	Opens	494	Times
1914	7/17	Street Car Loop	Work Progresses	928	Times p.1
1914	10/21	Street Car Service	Declare War on	975	Times p.1
1914	10/21	Street Car Service	Complaints about	39	Times

1917	2/15	Street Car Service	Run every 15 Min.	495	Times
1921	2/17	Street Car Service	conductors fired!	185	Tribune
1908	3/5	Street Cars	Conductors all get fired	2416	Times p.3
1919	12/31	Street Marking	New Street Signs	1389	Tribune p.1
1926	1/19	Street Name	changed	1397	Trib. p.1
1917	3/20	Street Work Starts	Low Brick Walk	399	Times
1912	9/25	Student Snake Dance	Raid Down town!	1944	Times p.1
1946	10/31	Student fatality	Lincoln Way / Beech Ave.	161	Tribune
1912	9/25	Student Raid	March down town	1944	Times p.1
1898	3/22	Student wearing sweaters etc.	Chapel Attendance	1802	ISC Stundent p.1
1912		Student, ISC	Ad for Newspaper	1662	ISC Directory
1916	5/20	Students Suff.Issue	On June 5th	1803	ISC Student p.1
1916	8/23	Subway	Wanted	474	Times
1926	12/18	Subway	Requested of C&NW	456	Tribune
1917	8/9	Subway	Foot subway Connects Tracks	1402	Tribune
1920	8/18	Suffragists	"Get Vote Today"	2158	Trib. p.1
1924	6/ 6	Summit Coal Mine	Ad for	1417	Tribune. p.1
		Summit Mine	See: Coal or Zenorsville		
1917	5/ 7	Sunday Movies	Blue Laws Enforced	1005	Times p.1
1922	3/25	Sunday Movies	Opinions about	699	Tribune
1922	3/28	Sunday Movies	Vote Against	699	Tribune
1913	5/19	Sunday School League	Meth.press Congr.	1384	Times p.1
1916	12/ 6	Sunday, Howard	Laid to Rest (Corey Cemetery)	1196	Times p.1
1908	9/ 7	Sunday,Billy	Destroys Plates	1845	Times p.12
1908	9/24	Sunday,Billy	Destroys Plates	39	Times
1909	5/27	Sunday,Billy	Little Stingers	1848	Times p.8
1909	5/27	Sunday,Billy	Quotes from	46	Times
1909	5/27	Sunday,Billy	Comes Monday	1846	Times p.1
1911	8/17	Sunday,Billy	4000 hear him	1846	Times p.1
1911	8/17	Sunday,Billy	Editorial	52	Times
1911	7/20	Sunday,Billy	Speak at Chautauqua	52	Times
1911	8/17	Sunday,Billy	"Sundayisms"	1847	Times p.1
1911	8/17	Sunday,Billy	A Religious Enigma		Times
1911	8/17	Sunday,Billy	At Chautauqua	54	Times
1912	4/11	Sunday,Billy	Sends $500 to Presbyterians	1849	Times p.5
1914	11/30	Sunday,Billy	Visits in Ames	1849	Times
1914	12/ 3	Sunday,Billy	On Campus	75	Tribune
1914	11/26	Sunday,Billy	To speak in Ames	75	Tribune
1914	12/11	Sunday,Billy	Ames Day at Des Moines	39	Times
1914	12/ 2	Sunday,Billy	Plea to Friends	1850	Times p.1
1914	12/ 3	Sunday,Billy	Editorial about	74	Tribune
1914	11/30	Sunday,Billy	Here today	233	Tribune
1915	7/ 2	Sunday,Billy	Rests in Oregon	442	Intelligencer
1915	9/15	Sunday,Billy	Greets Sheldon	362	Times
1916	6/26	Sunday,Billy	morther dies	1356	Times p.1
1916	6/28	Sunday,Billy	Burried this AM	1356	Times p.4
1916	5/ 5	Sunday,Billy	His Money	350	Times p.6
1917	1/ 6	Sunday,Billy	Retire here?	448	Times
1920	8/11	Sunday,Billy"	Visit Graves here	77	Times
1920	6/30	Sunday,Billy"	Dr.Maxwell recalls	154	Times
1921	10/31	Sunday,Billy"	Speaks to Rotarians	150	Tribune
1935	11/ 8	Sunday,Billy"	Bob Murray's Editorial	153	Tribune
1970	9/27	Sunday,Billy"	Mills on Sunday	155	Register
1978	8/29	Sunday,Billy"	Religeous Diversity-Editorial	154	Register
1913	2/17	Sunday,Billy's S.Leader	Breach Promise Suit	825	Intelligencer
1916	12/ 6	Sunday,Howard"	Buried here	153	Times
1914	7/15	Sundial	Arrives for Library (D .A.R.)	2434	Times p.1
1915	6/15	Sundial for Library	By D.A.R.	881	Times
1920	4/22	Sunset Rock	State Park Proposed	394	Tribune
1919	4/24	Swimming Pool	At Dayton Park	383	Times
1920	4/ 7	Swimming Pool	'Be Square to the Children'	394	Tribune
1920	7/27	Swimming Pool	Kids want one	2015	Trib . p.1
1926	2/22	Swimming Pool	Voters asked for	285	Tribune
1926	5/28	Swimming Pool	Carr Will construct	1397	Trfib. p.1
1926	5/26	Swimming Pool	Carr Will construct	237	Tribune
1898	10/ 6	Taft, William Howard	to visit Ames	269	Intelligencer
1910	10/ 6	Taft, William Howard	coming to Ames	1259	Intelligencer
1916	3/23	Taft, William Howard	Visits Ames	890	Tribune
1917	6/ 5	Taft, William Howard	Speaks on Campus	6	Times
1917	1/20	Taft,Lorado	Speaks Here	495	Times
1913	5/28	Tallman,(Jewler)	Buys out Baker (Jewelry)	1384	"Times p,1"
1911	2/26	Tallman,L.C.	Talks paving	70	Times
1913	12/ 8	Tango Banned	by ISC Frats	1206	Times p.8
1930	1/21	Tax on Men	City Dads ($5)	1898	Trib. p.1
1916	10/11	Taxes (Ames)	How spent	1211	Times p.5
1912		Taylor Shop, Hisk's	Ad for	1666	ISDC Directory
1978	11/28	Technocrats	Story /Poem	721	Boston Herald
1878		Telephone	In Ames	832	General
1880		Telephone	Bigelow/Hunt/&Tilden	866	Tel.Co.Record
1881		Telephone	College Link	866	Tel.Co.Rec.
1910	10/6	Telephone	Mutual Telephone, removed	1983	Times p.5
1918		Telephone	1st Telephone Bldg.	866	Tel.Co.Rec.
1921		Telephone	N.W.Bell	866	Tel.Co.Rec.
1923		Telephone	Add to Bldg.		Tel.Co.Rec.
1939	9/26	Telephone	Some History	2072	Trib.p.16(Spc.)
1950		Telephone	7200 in Ames	866	Tel.C.Rec.
1975		Telephone	40000 in Ames	866	Tel.C.Rec.
Various		Telephone	History(Ames)	832	General
1955	725	Telephone Company	Dedocate Dial S ystem	2203	Tribune p.1
1917	6/ 8	Telephone Building	Work starts on it.	918	Times p.1
1915	12/29	Telephone Cables	Laid on L.Way	1181	Times p.1
1909	9/30	Telephone Company	to merge companies	1383	Intell. p.1
1910	9/ 8	Telephone Company	Unified	1383	Intell. p.1
1916	12/28	Telephone Company	Textrum vs Phone Co.	1756	Trib. p.1
1917	5/22	Telephone Company	New Building	782	Times
1917	3/ 8	Telephone Company	To build bldg.		Times
1955	7/23	Telephone Company	Go to Dial system Sunday A.M.	2206	Trib. p.1
		Telephone Service	Dial Kayo's '444'	266	Tribune
1878		Telephone.T.Can	Ames Drug/Dr.Beverly	866	Tel.Co.Record
1917	9/21	Temperance Women Meet	Institute	918	Times
1905	6/23	Templeton / Sawyer	Wedding	1757	Intell. p.4
1899	12/28	Templeton, Dr.	Has Specialist available	1936	Times p.3
1929	8/17	Tenor (Famous)	Quite life @ Story City	1270	Trib p.1
1898	8/18	Tent (Big)	For Excursion Days on Campus	1314	Intell.
1915	6/14	Tent City	News Item (Ft.DodgeTeachers)	2349	Times p.1
1926	6/29	Tent City	14 Families Inhabit Tent Colony	1410	Tribune p.1
1929	7/ 8	Tent City	7 States 17 Families on campus	316	Tribune
1908	9/11	Tent Meeting	Evangelist here	1784	Times?

1922	8/1	Tourist Camp	Many Entries: Horseback Riders	2309	Times p.1
1922	8/28	Tourist Camp	Many Tourists Stop At Local C	2307	Trib. p.1
1922	6/28	Tourist Camp	Many tourists stop at local camp	1411	Trib. p.1
1923	8/8	Tourist Camp	Crowded following heavy rain.	2382	Trib. p.1
1923	8/13	Tourist Camp	Oppose Tourist Camp Charges	1418	Trib. p.1
1924	6/12	Tourist Camp	Special For College Visitors	2362	Trib. p.6
1921	5/17	Tourist Park	O.K.'d on College Land / L.Way	2411	Trib. p.1
1921	6/11	Tourist Park	Nixed by City Attorney Luke	2411	Trib. p.1
1886	4/23	Town Hall	New town hall plans considered	281	Intelligencer
1911	8/3	Town Fathers	Don't Tie Horses on Main Street	52	Times
1916	'1/10	Town Marshall	Bill Ricketts - story about him	2173	Times p.1
1908	10/8	Town Pump	Remove Handle	925	Times p.1
1996	8/17	Train	Vintage Train S tops In Ames	2197	Trib. p. A3
1909	10/28	Train Caller	Bill Thompson	1758	Times p.1
1908	10/15	Tramps	Got ten days	84	Times
1931	8/14	Trancontinental Racer	Old Scout: Ia.Roads Are Best	2317	Trib. p.10
1911	8/3	Tranportation(Train)	Ames vs DesMoines	1362	Intell. p.1
1914	6/18	Transcontiinental Drive	Midgit Car Crosses US L.Way	2427	Trib. p.1
		Transcontinental Drive	See: Cross Country Drive		
1911	5/25	Transcontinental Route	Gets boost across Iowa	2410	Times p.1
1914	7	Transcontinetal drive	Lincon Higfh way-Packard Co.	2397	
1924	1/26	Trial-Coe vs Obrien	Perjury conviction	159	Tribune
1921	2/18	Tribune	J.L.Powers buys paper	185	Tribune
1921	2/28	Tribune	Sold:J.L.Powers	841	Tribune p.1
1929	12/30	Tribune	Now:Trib.-Times	1325	Trib. p.1
1931	8/31	Tribune	Special Edition (Anniversary)	2319	Trib. p.1
1964	9/5	Tribune	History traced	501	Tribune
1923	10/6	Trice,Jack	Killed In Minn.Game	394	Tribune
1923	10/8	Trice,Jack	Death Reported	1793	ISCStudent
1924	1/3	Trice,Jack	Fund paid to mother of J.Trice	2343	Tribune p.1
1922	8/2	Trick Cyclist	Main & Kellogg - 200 see him	2309	Times p.1
1917	9/22	Troop Train	Men Eat Here	918	Times p. A1
1925	6/6	Trueblood Shoe Store	Ad for Ladies Shoes	920	Tribune p.6
1908	9/17	Tug-O-War	Freshmen win	1	Times p.11
1908	9/10	Tug-O-War	On Campus	870	Times
1908	9/11	Tug-O-War	Frosh win it	1784	Times?
1877	5/11	Turner,Cyrus E.	Ad for Attorney	506	Intelligencer
1890	7/31	Turner,Cyrus E.	Buys Osceola Business	543	Intelligencer
1892	8/4	Turner,Cyrus E.	Came to Tilden Funeral	501	Intelligencer
1884	8/2	Turner,Mrs.C.E.	Visits here	713	Intelligencer
1915	7/26	Uncle Tom's Cabin	Tent Show	505	Tribune p.6
1924	7/22	Underpass Proposal	Riverside to Brookridge	3	Tribune p.1
1926	8/28	Underpass Proposal	Road under Tracks proposed	2227	Trib. p.1
1926	10/28	Underpass(Gr.Ave.)	Sketch of etc.	483	Tribune
1936	11/4	Underpass(Gr.Ave.)	Vote passes	484	Tribune
1936	11/2	Underpass(Gr.Ave.)	Ad 'Against'	485	Tribune
1936	11/2	Underpass(Gr.Ave.)	Letter about	479	Tribune
1883	6/30	Union Bank of Ames	Becomes Nat.Bank	868	Intelligencer
1913	1/15	Union Nat.Bank	Annual meeting	88	Times
1917	2/21	Union Nat.Bank	Siverly elected		Times
1917	4/16	Union Nat.Bank	Remodels	497	Times
1989	9/26	University Duplication	More thoughts on subject.	799	Dm.Register
1964	9/5	Utilities	Show growth	280	Tribune
1910	3/17	Valentine, E.W.	Pres.of School Bd.	450	Intelligencer
1914	12/7	Valentine, E.W.	Pres.Commercial Club	233	Tribune
1915	3/17	Valentine, E.W.	Pres.of School Board	442	Intelligencer
1918	8/15	Valentine, E.W.	Sells Home on Douglas	1301	Trib. p.1
1914	5/27	Valentine, Hannah	wins History Medal	890	Tribune p.1
1921	7/6	Valentine,E.W.	Buys Fair Store	359	Tribune
1931	10/3	Vallee, Rudy"	His wife Here	396	Tribune
1991	1/11	Vehicular Homicide	Sop Sign Violation	983	Tribune
1922	3/28	VEISHEA	Plans Underway For Celebration	2469	Trib. p. 1
1922	5/10	VEISHEA	Veishea Opens Thursday	2469	Trib. p. 1
1922	5/11	VEISHEA	Veishea Opens with May Fete	2470	Trib. p. 1
1922	5/12	VEISHEA	Veishea Parade Displays Talent	2470	Trib. p. 1
1922	5/13	VEISHEA	Veishea At Ia. St. Biggest Show	2470	Trib. p. 1
1922	5/6	VEISHEA	College Will Have Big Fete -	2469	Trib. p. 1
1940	10/3	VEISHEA	Abolished - Too Much Apathy	1707	ISC Student p. 1
1922	3/22	VEISHEA	College Celebration - New Name	699	Tribune
1922	3/29	VEISHEA	Name - Word coined	1793	ISC Student p. 1
1908	10/8	Vet.Medicine	Announce bldg.plans	283	Times
1918	5/7	Viaduct,C&NW	Nixed by Railroad	2230	Times p.1
1916	8/23	Viaduct,C&NW	Ames wants Viaduct	1005	Times p.1.
1916	8/23	Viaduct,C&NW	Agitate for it	1355	Times p.1
1916	8/23	Viaduct/Subway	Agitate for	1005	Times p.1
1907	5/2	Vice. Pres.Fairbanks	Speaks at Ames	923	Intell.
1876	1/26	Village Lots	Advertisement for	1364	Intell.
1928	12/31	Vitaphone	Adv. for audeville Show	1385	Trib.
1992	10/23	W O I - T V	Pomerantz comments	1421	Student p.12
1992	7/15	W O I - T V	Comment on by Farwell Brown	1415	Tribune p.A6
1992	5/28	W O I - TV	Sale/Politics		Trib.
1992	10/30	W.O.I. Radio	80 Yrs.old	1425	D.M.Reg. p.3M
1922	7/1	W.O.I. Radio	New Uses found	2	"Tribune p,1"
1919	5/15	Walkers	Women walk Coast to Coast	267	Times
1911	12/14	Wallace,Uncle Henry	Speaks at Religeous Mtg.	37	Times
1917	4/6	War Declared	WW I	496	Times
1928	9/29	War Veterans	Story about	1674	Tribune p.13
1916	1/5	Washington Twp.	Secedes from Ames?	335	Times
1911	3/16	Washington,Booker T.	Speaks in Ames	71	Times
1911	3/16	Washington,Booker T.	Speaks in Ames	549	Intelligencer
1877	8/25	Water Line	C.& N.W. Tank to City	544	Intell.
1924	7/28	Water Main	in 4th Ward completed	3	Tribune p.1.
1910	2/10	Water supply	Limited?	1259	Intelligencer
1891	12/7	Water Tower	To be painted red	1241	Cit Co.Min.
1891	1/21	Water Tower	To be filled up tomorrow	1545	Intell. p.3
1892	2/3	Water Tower	Chas.Graves in charge	1241	Cit.Co.Min.
1898	8/18	Water Tower	Is Cleaned	1801	Intell.p.5c3
1906	10/11	Water Tower	New Steel Tank	1485	Times p.1
1898	6/16	Water Tower (Marston)	See: Marston Water Tower		
1898	8/11	Watkins Well	Bapt./U.Breth. Picnic	1778	Intell.Local Parag.
1898	8/11	Watkins Well	Methodist picnic	1778	Intell.Loc.Parag.
1898	8/11	Watkins Well	Methodist Picnic there	1771	Intell.-p.4
1914	11/26	Watkins Well	Founder of	651	Tribune
1919	7/5	Watts,John	Early Editor near death	109	Tribune
1920	11/22	Watts,John	Death Occurs	1381	Trib. p.1
1920	11/22	Watts,John	Editor dies	150	Tribune
1920	11/22	Watts,John	Dies -age 75 (Editor of Intell.)	264	Times
1916	12/9	WCTU Meets	At Boone	1759	Times. p.1
1930	10/3	Wearth, Marion	Wins suit / Banning	1892	Trib. p.1
1964		Webster House	First house in Ames	310	Tribune
1964	9/5	Webster,Noah	First Ames home	280	Tribune
1913	8/29	Weeks,Elling	plane to C.Ia.Fair?	83	Times
1913	9/17	Weeks,Elling	Accident in Colorado	83	Times
1915	6/30	Weeks,Elling	Lands Griffiths oat field	235	Times
1915	6/30	Weeks,Elling	Lands at Ames!	185	Tribune
1915	5/7	Weeks,Elling	To be at Fair	288	Times
1915	7/1	Weeks,Elling	Lands plane in Griffith+s field	2439	Trib. p.1
1924	1/11	Weismuller,Johnny	Visits ISC	441	Tribune
1889	3/18	Welch, Adonijah S.	Date of his death	2462	Univ. Cem. Rec.
1923	1/2	Welch, Mrs. Mary B.	Date of her death	2462	Univ. Cem. Rec.
1928		Welch,A.S.(Pres)	Story about	735	Tribune?
1880	12/10	Welch,Mrs.A.S.	Wants to hirescCapable girl.	886	Intelligencer
1923	5/11	Welch,Mrs.Mary B.	Inter Ashes May 20,1923	2394	ISCStudent p.1
1923	1/13	Welch,Mrs.Mary B.	Death reported	2178	Trib. p.1
		West Ames	See: Severance		
1914	10/29	West Ames	Disclaim Seceding	666	Tribune
1914	10/22	West Ames	Threat Secede	665	Tribune
1916	10/3	West Ames	Ist Legal Step	667	Times
1917	1/25	West Ames	Court Hearing Severasnce Case	667	Tribune
1924	11/18	West Ames	Annex to Ames	191	Tribune
1892	7/21	West Hotel	New Manager	464	Intelligencer
1898	8/11	West, William	daughter visits	1771	Intell./Loc.Para.
1919	9/5	West, William	dies at Rock Rapids (1st Mayor)	1270	Trib. p.1
1920	1/8	West, William	Funeral for Ames' 1st Mayor	1800	Rock Rapids paper
1902	2/13	West, William Jr.	Not Guilty of Murder	1420	Intell. p.7
1893	6/1	West,Agatha	Married to James Ramsey	2073	Intell. p.3
1892	4/28	West,Laura	her death(See:Smith)	1654	Intell.
1916	12/14	West,William	1st Mayor visits Ames	250	Tribune
1916	12/12	West,William	Visits here(1stMayor)	494	Times
1919	12/31	West,William	Death of	1389	First Mayor of Ames
1902	2/6	West,William Jr.	Letter about	934	Intell.
1915	12/17	Western Union	Leases office	334	Times
1893	7/27	Wheelmen	Gates Brown returns fr. long trip	2354	Times p.4
1893	7/6	Wheelmen	Boys leave for Minneapolis	2356	Intell. p.3
1893	7/6	Wheelmen	Boys leave for Minneapolis	2354	Times p.13
1893	7/13	Wheelmen	Diary - ride to Minneapolis	2357	Times p.2
1893	7/11	Wheelmen	Ames Boys bike to Twin Cities	2250	Minn.Trib. p.4
1919	4/19	White,Fred R.	Succeeds McDonald at Hiway	117	Times
1919	4/18	White,Fred R.	Head Highway Comm.	383	Times
1919	4/5	Wickham,J.Q.	Fired by City Council	380	TImes
1919	4/21	Wickham,J.Q.	Resigns	383	Times
1919	4/8	Wickham,J.Q.	Flays Town Council	380	Times
1929	8/6	Wild Life School (McGregor)	Opens for 11th Yr.		Times
		Wilkins, Eleanor	See: Duncan, Martha		
1975	1/25	Wilkins, Eleanor M.	Dearth of: AKN Martha Duncan	2463	Trib. p.14
1919	5/3	Williams	Duckworth/Williams killed	384	Times
1917	10/1	Wilson Highway	Goes thu Ames	918	Times
1917	10/16	Wilson Highway	Start Marking	919	Times p.1
1919	1/22	Wilson Highway	Sheldon's Plan adopted	1178	Times p.1
1897	2/4	Wilson,-Tama Jim	To be Feted	2298	Times p.3
1897	2/11	Wilson,-Tama Jim	His visit to Ames	2395	Times p.4
1900	6/7	Wilson,-Tama Jim	Commencement Speaker	403	Times
1920	8/26	Wilson,-Tama Jim	Dies at his home	2159	Trib. p.1
1914	5/25	Wilson,-Tama Jim	Rural Life Program	1368	Timews p.5
1894	11/22	Wilson,-Tama Jim	Sues E.J.Burrage (Lawsuit)	318	Intelligencer
1913	3/12	Wilson,-Tama Jim	Wilson Day	86	Times
1913	1/29	Wilson,-Tama Jim	Accepts invitation	86	Times
1913	3/21	Wilson,-Tama Jim	Emeritus Professor	73	Times
1913	5/21	Wilson,-Tama Jim	Emeritus Professor	86	Times
1913	3/14	Wilson,-Tama Jim	Banquet on campus	86	Times
1920	8/27	Wilson,-Tama Jim	1897 Reception recalled	77	Times
1994	8/21	Wilson,-Tama Jim	Birth of Ethics	1935	DMReg. J1
1915	6/18	Wilson,Henry	Death account	244	Times
1915	6/24	Wilson,Henry	Death accont	442	Intelligencer
1915	7/18	Wilson,Henry	death account	192	Tribune
1996	9/19	Wine	What's Moderate?	2224	DMReg. p.2T
1996	9/19	Wine	Guidelines	2223	DMReg. p.2T
1893	7/27	Wire Fence Mfg.	Northwestern Fence Co. Ad.	2353	Intell.
		Wireless	SEE: Radio		
1909	7/22	Wireless	1st in Ames	1267	"Intell. p,1"
1911	1/28	Wireless Station	W O I Radio History	1371	Intell. p.1
1913	8/25	Wireless Station	Attracts attention at State Fair	2367	Times p.1
1915	12/20	Wireless Station	I.S.C. Picks Up Arlington	1742	ISCStudent
1923	3/2	Wireless Station	Make plans for studeo	2395	ISCStudent p.3
1923	5/7	Wireless Station	Many States Hear band concert	2395	ISCStudent p.1
1926	1/11	Wireless Station	on Campus	1362	Intel. p.1
1950	10/13	WOI TV	Cameras for Live TV	1803	Tribune
1950	9/30	WOI TV	Football Broadcast	1801	Tribune p.1
1950	10/5	WOI TV	UN Sessions on T V	1801	Tribune p.1
1950	9/29	WOI TV	Irish vs NC Game	1801	Tribune p.1
1953	3/26	WOI TV	Italian visits W O I Station	1412	Trib. p.1
1992	2/28	WOI TV	Commentary (Sale)		Trib. p.A7
1992	6/25	WOI TV	Sue Regents	1385	DM Reg.
1992	5/28	WOI TV	Sale of W O I Hurts Education	1393	Trib. p.A7-8
1916	11/2	Woman Butcher	Now In Huxley	393	Tribune
1965	11/10	Woman Council Member	Helen LeBaron was first.	2070	Trib. p.1
1917	2/1	Woman County Agent	Only one - She was a first.	495	Times
1947	3/12	Woman Elected	To School Board	473	Tribune
1920	12/13	Woman Juror	First womam juror in Story Co.	2434	Trib. p.1
1918	10/3	Woman Mail Carrier	17 yrs.at Zearing	1205	Times p.1
1936	6/16	Woman Postmaster	Mrs. Sh ane named postmaster	2368	Trib. p.1
1924	2/16	Woman Train Caller	Mrs Laughlin kept on job	159	Tribune
1915	3/24	Woman's Club	to be organized here	235	Times
1915	3/16	Woman's Club	Organized here	41	Times
1916	5/9	Woman's Club	Ends good year	237	Times
1918	4/10	Woman's Club	New Officers	418	Times
1919	6/12	Woman's Club	State Meeting here	259	Times
1968	10/31	Woman's Club	Bus Tour of Ames	303	Tribune
1877	5/4	Woman's Suffrage	Debated	885	Intelligencer
1908	2/6	Woman's Suffrage	Discusas Suffrage - Col.Debate	2416	Intell.p.1
1916	6/17	Woman's Suffrage	St.Louis Riot (Tom Boys)	2170	Times p.1
1916	4/15	Woman's Suffrage	Ames Women Campaign	2169	Times p.1
1920	8/23	Woman's Suffrage	Antis Fight to block women	2159	Trib. p.1

1920	8//13	Woman's Suffrage	Win battle in Tennessee	2157	Times p.1
1920	8/26	Woman's Suffrage	Now Basic Law	2159	Trib. p.1
1920	8/11	Woman's Suffrage	Win Early Struggle	2156	Trib. p.1
1920	8/19	Woman's Suffrage	B ribery Chared in Tennisee	2159	Trib. p.1
1908	3/19	Womans Suffrage	ISC Debaters Lose & Win	2416	Times p.1
1892	7/ 7	Women / Equal Rights	Meeting Held	508	Intelligencer
1916	11/16	Women Drivers	For the Jitneys	393	Tribune
1964	9/ 5	Women in News	Story about	280	Tribune
1916	3/ 5	Women Vote	School Election	632	Times
1908	Bomb	Women's Basketball	Photo of Team	1319	ISC Bomb
1914	/16	Women's Gym	New Pool in Margaret Hall	399	ISULibrary
1928	12/31	Women's Gym	"Hammill Swats Gym"	2349	Trib. p.1
1939	3/9	Women's Gym	High Hopes For	2340	ISC Student p.6
1939	4/21	Women's Gym	Coed go to Bat - get it passed!	2147	Trib. p.2
1893	10/5	Women's Suffrage Ass.	Of Ames - Story	2070	TIMES
1923	4/18	Women,League of Voter	Will Organize	1816	ISC Student p.1
1986	10/26	Woolfies, Andy	Death announced (WOI)	361	DM Reg.
1917	2/ 1	Woolworth's	Store Opens here	670	Tribune
1991	7/12	Word Censors	"Politically Correct" Editorial	1888	DMReg.
1918	4/26	World War I	1st Ames Casualty		Tribune
1919	5/21	World War I	Veterans welcomed Home	55	Times
1989	2/20	Writers & Alcohol	Editorial	783	DMReg
1992	11/10	WW I Veteran	Last in Story County	1494	Trib.
1915	8/13	Wynne, Prof. W.H.	Editorial in Tacoma,Washington	176	Times
1917	10/23	Wynne, Prof. W.H.	Dies-age 85	1993	Times p.1
1918	12/23	Y.M.C.A.	Mott Answers Critics	2407	Times p.1
1911	12/28	Year's Review (1911)	By:L.C.Tilden)	37	Times
1906	9/20	YMCA	Alumni Hall Bldg.	1427	Intelligencer
1912	10/14	YMCA	At High School	821	Intelligencer
1915	8/23	YMCA	Fred Hanson new Sec.	1753	Times p.8
1927	7/20	YMCA	Ray Cunninham's Report	502	Tribune
1928	9/ 5	YMCA	Sells Restaurant Equipment	1674	Tribune p.3
1931	8/6	YMCA	Start work on Fuhrer Lodge	2317	Trib. p.1
1911	11/ 9	YMCA	John Clyde, Sec.	1377	Intell.
1920	6/7	YMCA	Fred Hanson Writes thanks	2252	ISC Student p.3
1989	8/18	YSS	Belitsos Letter	848	Tribune
1989	9/20	YSS	Forum-Youth Problems	853	Tribune
1992	6/20	YSS	Rosedale House	1303	Brochure
1995	6/8	YSS	Project - Former City Hall	2069	Trib. p.1
		Zenorsville	See:Picnic-Zenorsville		
		Zenorsville	See: Coal or Summit		
1880		Zenorsville	Pop.of 256	1330	U.S.Census
1919	7/31	Zenorsville	Reunion At Mine Site	2022	Trib. p.1
1920	8/27	Zenorsville	Reunion	1376	Trib.p.4
1922	8/18	Zenorsville	News from	2269	Trib.p.2
1928	9/10	Zenorsville	Reunion	1934	Trib.p.4
1930	9/9	Zenorsville	Old Settler's Picnic	2390	Trib. p.2

INDEX